Bob Batchelor
Editor

Basketball in America
From the Playgrounds to Jordan's Game and Beyond

More pre-publication
REVIEWS, COMMENTARIES, EVALUATIONS . . .

"**B**asketball in America is a fascinating book that is must reading for anyone interested in the interconnection between basketball and popular culture. Taking as its premise that basketball is America's new 'national pastime,' the book includes fifteen beautifully written chapters that cogently analyze everything from Michael Jordan as icon to playground basketball and the portrayal of basketball in movies and the evolution of the WNBA. The book makes clear that since 1970 basketball has witnessed significant changes, being transformed into a sport with close ties to corporate America, an expanded world market, and a collection of talented players who have garnered unprecedented media attention and influenced clothing styles, body art, and other changes evident in a burgeoning age of celebrity.

Perhaps the most intriguing section of the book is Part One, which deals with basketball in American culture. Each of the section's four authors provides important insights into how basketball has impacted other aspects of American life. With great passion and solid interpretations, each describes how basketball has been woven into American society and establishes a connection with hip-hop, black style, and celebrity culture."

David K. Wiggins, PhD
Professor and Director,
School of Recreation,
Health, and Tourism (RHT),
George Mason University

The Haworth Press®
New York • London • Oxford

Basketball in America
From the Playgrounds to Jordan's Game and Beyond

THE HAWORTH PRESS
Contemporary Sports Issues
Frank Hoffmann, PhD, MLS
Martin Manning
Senior Editors

Minor League Baseball: Community Building Through Hometown Sports by Rebecca S. Kraus

Baseball and American Culture: Across the Diamond edited by Edward J. Rielly

Dictionary of Toys and Games in American Popular Culture by Frederick J. Augustyn Jr.

Football and American Identity by Gerhard Falk

Basketball in America: From the Playgrounds to Jordan's Game and Beyond edited by Bob Batchelor

Spectator Sports: Fans, Consumers, and Corporate Culture by Gregory J. Thompson

Basketball in America
From the Playgrounds to Jordan's Game and Beyond

Bob Batchelor
Editor

The Haworth Press®
New York • London • Oxford

For more information on this book or to order, visit
http://www.haworthpress.com/store/product.asp?sku=5287

or call 1-800-HAWORTH (800-429-6784) in the United States and Canada
or (607) 722-5857 outside the United States and Canada

or contact orders@HaworthPress.com

The Haworth Press, Inc., 10 Alice Street, Binghamton, NY 13904-1580.

Cover design by Lora Wiggins.

Library of Congress Cataloging-in-Publication Data

Basketball in America : from the playgrounds to Jordan's game and beyond / Bob Batchelor, editor.
    p. cm.
  Includes bibliographical references and index.
  ISBN-13: 978-0-7890-1612-6 (hard : alk. paper)
  ISBN-13: 978-0-7890-1613-3 (soft : alk. paper)
  ISBN-10: 0-7890-1612-5 (hard : alk. paper)
  ISBN-10: 0-7890-1613-3 (soft : alk. paper)
    1. Basketball—United States—History—20th century. 2. Basketball—Social aspects—United States. I. Batchelor, Bob.

GV883.B38 2005
796.323'0973—dc22
                                                        2004012032

To my family: Linda and Jon Bowen, Bill Coyle, and my wife, Katherine, whose love makes everything possible.

CONTENTS

ABOUT THE EDITOR

Bob Batchelor is an award-winning business writer and historian who currently serves as Public Relations Instructor in The School of Mass Communications at the University of South Florida. He is the author of *The 1900s* and co-author of *Kleenex, Kotex, and Huggies: Kimberly-Clark and the Consumer Revolution in America* (forthcoming). Batchelor has published more than 350 articles and essays in magazines, Web sites, and reference works, including *The American Prospect Online, Dictionary of American History, Inside Business,* and *Northern Ohio Live.* He has taught both history and writing at Cleveland State University and Neumann College. As a historical consultant, Batchelor has worked for numerous Fortune 500 companies, including BellSouth, International Paper, Kimberly-Clark, and Accenture.

CONTRIBUTORS

Bijan C. Bayne is the author of *Sky Kings: Black Pioneers of Professional Basketball* (Scholastic, 1998), which was added to the suggested reading list of the Kentucky Library System in 1998. In July 2002 he won the Robert Peterson Research Award for his presentation "The Struggle of the Latin American Ballplayer," given at the National Baseball Hall of Fame and Museum in Cooperstown, New York. Bayne's chapter on black baseball in North Carolina appears in the book *Baseball in the Carolinas* (McFarland, 2002). Bayne has guest lectured on the social significance of the life of Jackie Robinson each year since 1996 at The George Washington University, in classes and events such as Charter Day 1996 and Unity Week in 1999. His book reviews have been featured in *Washington Post Book World,* the *Boston Herald,* and *The Crisis.*

Michael Buchert was born in 1979 in Birmingham, Alabama. The product of a family steeped in the tradition of Friday night football, he attended the University of Florida in Gainesville, where he worked as a student manager for the men's basketball team. He was a member of two SEC Championship seasons at UF, including the miraculous run to the NCAA Final Four in 2000. He currently lives in New York City, where he is working on a master's degree in Art Therapy.

Chris Burtch is the former head boys' basketball coach and a history teacher at Slippery Rock Area High School in Slippery Rock, Pennsylvania. Burtch played college basketball and baseball at Butler County Community College, and then finished his education at Slippery Rock University, where he earned a BA in education and an MA in history. Burtch's teams are known for their tough, hard-nosed defense and their dedication to fundamentals. His teams averaged fifteen wins a year and after a twenty-one-year stretch of the school not making the play-offs, he took the Rockets to the postseason four times in five seasons as head coach.

Peter Cashwell, a native of Chapel Hill and alumnus of the University of North Carolina, is the author of *The Verb "To Bird"* and co-author of *The Readerville Journal*'s "Loose Canons" column. He lives in Virginia with his sons and his wife, writer Kelly Dalton, and lives on the Web at <www.petercashwell.com>. He can still hit a hook shot.

David Davis is a contributing writer at *Los Angeles Magazine*. His work has appeared in, among others, the *Los Angeles Times, Sports Illustrated,* and *The Forward*. On a good day, he can twirl a basketball on his finger.

Lisa A. Ennis is the government publications librarian at Austin Peay State University's Woodward Library. She received her MA in history from Georgia College and State University and her MS in information science from the University of Tennessee. Her publications include journal articles and contributions to a number of encyclopedias, such as the *Scribner's Encyclopedia of American Lives: Sports* and *Native Americans in Sports*.

James Fisher is a doctoral candidate in history at Kent State University. His dissertation is a diplomatic and cultural history of the Shawnee Indians in the colonial period. His is also an adjunct lecturer in history at Mount Union College and has published articles and reviews on American Indian history, the American Revolution, genealogical research methods, and the 1960s.

Doug Fox is weekend editor at the *Daily Herald* in Provo, Utah, where he has worked since 1991. A longtime follower of the NBA, Fox, formerly the newspaper's assistant and executive sports editor, covered the Utah Jazz beat for five years, including the franchise's two trips to the NBA Finals (1997 and 1998). An award-winning writer and editor, for both sports and rock concert coverage, Fox is a graduate of Brigham Young University.

David Friedman is a freelance writer. His "Digits" column examines basketball statistics in each issue of *Basketball Digest*.

Kevin Grace is an archivist and adjunct assistant professor at the University of Cincinnati, where he teaches courses on sports and society, including one on the sociology of basketball. He has published widely on America's sport culture, and is the author of *Cincinnati Hoops: Basketball in an American City* and co-author of *Bearcats! The Story of Basketball at the University of Cincinnati*. Grace is a member of the Association for Professional Basketball Research, the Society for American Baseball Research, and the North American Society for Sport History, and has been a consultant to ESPN, the History Channel, and A&E. His current research interests focus on bloodsports, sport and education, basketball fiction, and basketball barnstormers.

Kelly McMasters is a freelance writer in Brooklyn, New York. She has written articles on social history, culture, and the arts for *Glamour, NY Arts Magazine, Time Out New York,* and *Mr. Beller's Neighborhood* (<www.MrBellersNeighborhood.com>), among others. Her father is a professional golfer and PGA life-member. She is currently getting her MFA in creative nonfiction from Columbia University.

Renada Rutmanis is a recent graduate of University of California at Berkeley. She has written for such magazines as *Premiere* and *Entertainment Weekly.* She plans to begin work on a creative writing MFA in the fall of 2004. She hopes to end up back in California, where she can root (in person) for her favorite basketball team, the Sacramento Kings.

Lawrence E. Ziewacz, PhD, was a professor in the Department of American Thought and Language at Michigan State University, where he received all three of his degrees. In his career, he taught at the community college, state college, and university levels. Ziewacz was a Michigan historian, a historian of American political, cultural, and intellectual history, as well as a sports historian. His 1995 co-authored work, *Payoffs in the Cloakroom: The Greening of the Michigan Legislature, 1938-1946,* received a 1996 *Choice* award as "one of the outstanding academic books of 1995." He co-authored *The Games They Played: Sports in American History, 1865-1980,* co-edited a sports series of books for the Popular Press at Bowling Green State University, and was co-advisory editor for sports for *The Guide to United States Popular Culture.* In addition, he presented and wrote numerous papers and articles on American sports. Ziewacz passed away in December 2003.

Acknowledgments

I have incurred many debts over the past two years researching, writing, and editing this book. First, I would like to thank the writers who devoted their time and wonderful skills to this project. Without them this book would not exist. Next, I thank my family members, who provided encouragement, love, and support throughout the process.

Foremost, my parents, Linda and Jon Bowen, and my brother, Bill Coyle, have given me immeasurable support and encouragement. Without their love, this book would not have been possible. Special thanks also go to Peggy, Tom, and Megan Wilbert. My grandmother, Annabell Bergbigler, has been an inspiration since I was a little boy. I would also like to thank my in-laws, Jerry and Nancy Roda, and their sons, David and John. They have been encouraging and kind over the years.

Every word I write is in some way inspired by a group of historians who taught me how to think: Sidney R. Snyder, James A. Kehl, Richard H. Immerman, and Lawrence S. Kaplan. Their work has shown me what it means to be a scholar.

I would also like to acknowledge my good friends Chuck Waldron and Anne Beirne; Kevin and Liz Mershimer and family; Jason and Emily Pettigrew; Maria Thomas; Gene and Tina Roach; Jack and Sue Burtch; Chrissy Burtch and the girls; Bob Osmond and Marina Ecklund and family; Claudia Carasso; Dennis and Susan Jarecke and family; Mike Menser and family; Jane and Tim Goodman and family; Peter Magnani and family; Pam Boughton; Rodd Aubrey; Jessica Schroeder and family; and all my friends at Readerville.com. These people have given more than they know. A big thanks goes to all the players I have coached at Miller Creek Middle School in San Rafael, California. Thanks for allowing me to see the game through your eyes.

A special thanks to fellow historian Tom Heinrich and his family for their friendship over the years. Even though a continent separates us, I feel their closeness every day. Fritz has already gravitated toward basketball; maybe this book will help guide the way.

My deepest gratitude goes to my wife Katherine. She is my muse and soul mate. Her encouragement and understanding means everything to me.

Chapter 1

Introduction:
Basketball in America

Bob Batchelor

Basketball in America is a collection of essays that explores the intersection of the sport and popular cultures in modern America—as we have defined it—since the 1970s. Our goal is to examine basketball from a cross-cultural and historical perspective to reveal how tightly the game is now wound into American (and by extension, global) popular culture and society.

The impact basketball has had on popular culture becomes more evident day by day, particularly in comparison with earlier decades. There is even a stark contrast between today's game and the game played in the 1970s, the period initially covered in this book. In that decade, for instance, basketball drew record fans, but was undoubtedly the weak sister among major professional sports. The game was as well-known for its violence and widespread drug use as it was for the quality of its players.

Times have changed. Today, Michael Jordan is a household name around the globe. Showing the strength of the game's global ties, a record twenty-one international players were chosen in the 2003 National Basketball Association (NBA) Draft. Professional superstars have cut music CDs, starred in major motion pictures, launched clothing lines, and graced the covers of countless magazines, from *Sports Illustrated* and *SLAM!* to *The National Enquirer* and *People*.

In the amateur ranks, college basketball has taken over the month of March—from the millions of people who participate in office betting pools to the nearly around-the-clock television coverage of the dash toward the National Collegiate Athletic Association (NCAA) Championship. Across the nation, millions of young people are playing the game in school leagues, the Amateur Athletic Union (AAU), and church leagues. A park simply isn't complete without the presence of several blacktop courts with rusty rims and weathered nets.

Another stark difference is that today's game is big business. The "corporatization" of basketball begins in the amateur level and progresses up through the college and professional ranks. Nike is the most obvious culprit for critics of this influence. The company funds many amateur leagues, summer camps, and all-star events, while also sponsoring college teams, which many observers believe turns amateurs into walking billboards and quasi-professionals.

Thanks to Jordan's omnipresence, the Nike corporate swoosh may now be the most familiar logo in the world. The signing of young Ohio phenom LeBron "King" James (who dons the familiar number 23 for the Cleveland Cavaliers) ensures that Nike plans to keep it that way. The well-publicized stories about the battles between Adidas and Nike over James keeps the big-business aspect of the sport in the headlines.

Basketball players may be the most watched, commented on, and criticized, both on court and off, of all professional athletes. It is as if people intuitively understand the game's place within the fabric of American society.

For example, the media feeding frenzy surrounding the sexual assault allegations against young Los Angeles Lakers superstar Kobe Bryant became the biggest story in the world during the summer of 2003, even though American soldiers were still dying in Iraq and the national economy slumped.

Unfortunately, some aspects of basketball culture have changed very little from the 1970s to today. Heavy racial overtones cloud the feelings people have about basketball's young, rich, and predominantly black superstars. Professional players have been soundly criticized in recent years for having illegitimate children, womanizing, routinely using recreational drugs, and for a variety of on- and off-court brawls. Some observers have argued that the condemnation of pro basketball players is more intense than in other sports because of race.

Although the implication may rub some people the wrong way, it is easy to imagine that if an NBA All-Star were found dead in a hotel room of an apparent heart attack, like St. Louis Cardinals pitcher Darryl Kile, and authorities also discovered a small bag of marijuana in the room, the basketball player would have faced much more scrutiny regarding drug use than Kile did. Also, if basketball faced the same questions about steroids that Major League Baseball does, the easy connection most people make between young blacks and drugs would spark greater public outrage.

AMERICA'S TRUE PASTIME

Despite the kudos heaped on NBA Commissioner David Stern for his work marketing the game around the world, twenty years ago anyone who would have predicted that basketball would possess this kind of influence would have been granted a one-way ticket to the funny farm. There was simply no way to predict the "perfect storm" of Jordan's arrival, Nike's role in shaping and dominating global popular culture, and the explosion of a celebrity culture brought on by the information age of cable television and the Internet.

Although the popularity of basketball is undeniable, the game is in a state of constant transformation. Upheaval in the pro arena has focused on the final retirement of the sport's most popular and talented athlete—Michael Jordan. The post-Jordan NBA is struggling to maintain its growth. Ratings for the 2003 NBA Championship between the San Antonio Spurs and New Jersey Nets plummeted to historically low numbers.

At the same time, however, NBA players are trying their luck in rap, acting in movies, writing books, and trying to become household names in their own right. Thus, it's an exciting but uneasy time for professional basketball. The rise and popularity of the women's game over the past decade adds to the excitement. However, growing pains forced the Women's National Basketball Association (WNBA) to retract and caused the Women's Basketball Association (WBA) to fold after only three seasons.

Basketball in America, however, does not focus solely on the NBA and the professional game. Unlike other books, this book will include essays that cover the complete range of basketball in the United States, from high school athletics to the NBA. As a result, *Basketball in America* will entertain and inform a large number of readers who treasure basketball and the role it plays in the American consciousness.

For a variety of reasons, from the ease it can be played (little equipment needed, etc.) to the overwhelming number people participating in the sport at all levels, basketball could now claim to be America's new "national pastime." This will be the driving thesis of the anthology and serve as its underlying philosophy. The book, however, will also examine basketball from the perspectives of the high school ranks and the collegiate scene. Investigating these areas allows the authors to dig even deeper into the profound popular culture influences of basketball in the United States.

The beauty of a book examining basketball is that the subject allows for such a broad range of interpretations. The sport cuts across economic, racial, and social boundaries. Its major stars cross over into other forms of popular entertainment more than those in any other professional sport. Basketball has heroes and villains. The game is artistic and graceful while also brutal and harsh. It's still a game, but it pumps billions of dollars into the economy. These contradictions make basketball a wonderful topic through which to examine popular culture and the contemporary history of the United States.

The authors are an eclectic mix of writers, scholars, journalists, former players, coaches, self-described gym rats, and sports enthusiasts. Although they come from diverse backgrounds and have pursued different career paths, one common trait runs through them all—an undying love for the game of basketball. We hope this passion shines through each and every chapter.

BASKETBALL IN AMERICAN CULTURE

Part I of *Basketball in America* examines the game from a cultural perspective, revealing the impact basketball has had outside of the nation's arenas and gymnasiums. Through its stars, basketball has brought street life to the mainstream, popularizing things as divergent as shaved heads and multiple tattoos. Basketball has made sneakers a part of one's fashion sense and given people new points of reference for discussing popular culture.

Although many of baseball's greatest stars have lived and played in the past thirty years, such as Barry Bonds, Nolan Ryan, Greg Maddux, Cal Ripken, and Mark McGuire, no one is going around aping their styles or rapping about them in the latest hip-hop song. As great as these players are, they don't even particularly exude an image off the field. In contrast, basketball players are woven into the tapestry of popular culture as product endorsers, actors, musicians, and style beacons.

It could be argued, for example, that the nattily dressed Shaquille O'Neal helped bring back the turn-of-the-century-style suit featuring a high lapel and three buttons several years ago by sporting the look in postgame locker room interviews. Soon, the style filtered throughout the entertainment industry and eventually onto department store sales racks.

No sport can match basketball's widespread influence in shaping popular culture. The game's affinity with hip-hop and black culture obviously plays a role. In the past fifteen years, as rap and hip-hop have filtered into the mainstream, basketball has benefited from the association.

Writer and historian Bob Batchelor explores the amazing career of Michael Jordan. Rather than merely tout the numerous individual records Jordan amassed or discuss the team highlights of his six championships won as a Chicago Bull, the author looks at MJ as a popular culture icon. "Why have fans followed, obsessed, and idolized MJ for what has now been decades?" Batchelor asks.

Jordan, like few athletes before him in any sport, transcended basketball and became as popular for his off-court endeavors as for his exploits on the hardwood. Due to Jordan's success as a celebrity, succeeding generations of professional basketball players and athletes in other sports have attempted to replicate his accomplishments.

Writer David Davis examines Marvin Gaye's performance of the national anthem at the 1983 NBA All-Star Game in Los Angeles and puts the accomplishment in its proper historical light. Based on interviews with professional players at the game, broadcasters, Lakers team officials, and Gaye family members and close associates, Davis reveals the behind-the-scenes events leading up to and during the performance in the midst of the Motown star's troubled life—a last hurrah before his murder at the hands of his father a little more than a year later.

Davis skillfully places the reader in the crowd at the game, while deftly analyzing its larger significance. "Twenty years later the rendition has taken on new meaning," Davis explains. "It serves as a bridge between a straitlaced league struggling to find its identity and a global entertainment powerhouse that embraces hip-hop culture. In a sense, Gaye's anthem foreshadowed the evolution of the NBA, from the era of tight shorts to today's baggy models, from Jerry West's dribbling silhouette on the NBA logo to Michael Jordan's soaring Nike 'Jumpman.'"

Kelly McMasters looks at the "strange and serendipitous confluence of events" that led Nike to become the multibillion-dollar global shoe and apparel company that it is today. As a member of Generation X, growing up in the midst of Nike's climb to the top, she places the Nike story within its historical context while also providing insight into the phenomenon from someone who witnessed the early shoe wars.

McMasters, a journalist who has written extensively about social history, culture, and the arts, traces the rise of Nike, examining its founders Phil Knight, a middle-distance runner turned businessman, and his former University of Oregon coach and mentor Bill Bowerman. Then, she deftly shows how Nike played a commanding role in defining popular culture. First, according to McMasters, "Nike was able to hitch itself to the coattails of the fitness boom and use it to their advantage, pumping up the importance of being fit and promising a better life through a better body." Later, as the company teetered financially, Knight and his company took a flyer on the young Michael Jordan. "Nike decided to put all of their proverbial eggs in one basket," McMasters explains. "That basket was Michael Jordan." The rest—as they say—is history.

In "*Hoosiers* to *Hoop Dreams:* Basketball on the Big Screen," basketball historian and scholar Kevin Grace investigates basketball's place on the silver screen since the appearance of *Hoosiers* in 1986. He shows that "basketball has become a favored theme for sports films, clearly surpassing feature films about football and golf, and rivaling the cultural place of baseball in the national cinematic consciousness."

Sports movies work so well, Grace believes, because they embody the goals and aspirations of the nation in general—change in a land of constant transformation, the promises of both hard work and good works overcoming the odds, flights of individual achievement grounded to team rewards, and, especially, redemption. Sport serves nothing if not to somehow make amends for past or present shortcomings as we strive for victory. Basketball has become the dominant sport portrayed in movies because of the social aspects that can be explored in basketball, the personal issues that will be raised to the surface, and the dramatic movement of the game with its time-out hesitations building toward the climax.

THE PLAYGROUNDS AND BEYOND

Basketball is a game of space—the distance between you and the person d'ing you up, how far you are from the basket, and the controlled chaos of ten people operating within predetermined borders. The ability to see the game in terms of spacing often defines the boundaries of one's talent. No one in the history of the NBA could create space like Larry Bird, which allowed the Celtics great to capitalize on his deft shooting touch. On the other end of the spectrum, few players in any sport have been able to reduce space by maximizing the limits of the court to their advantage like Dennis Rodman, who uses every conceivable angle to will rebounds into his outstretched hands, almost always battling against players bigger and stronger.

Regardless of how a person learns the delicate ballet that occurs on the basketball court—whether it is in gym class or at a five-star basketball camp—as players, we hone our skills on the playgrounds. The second part of the book explores the playgrounds and what is produced from minutes, hours, and years spent on burning asphalt and in stifling gyms. This section, in a sense, explores interiors and exteriors—both physical spaces and the philosophical ones in our minds. Journalists do not usually cover this perspective in the sports pages. It is not about box scores; this part of the game starts on the court, when people are learning the game or proving themselves before their peers.

This section provides a rare glimpse behind the scenes—inside the locker room—and examines how basketball helps us identify our own individual value systems. We are given rare access to life inside a big-time Division I men's college basketball team and what it is like to coach today's high school player from an educator who is on the frontlines. It all begins on the playground, whether it is honing skills or taking in the lessons of the game that have been handed down from generation to generation. The playgrounds define basketball.

In "The Schoolyard Game: Blacktop Legends and Broken Dreams,"
Bijan Bayne dissects the playground game and urban legends who
took the game to a different level with moves and play outside the
staid box of organized basketball. He shows the evolution caused by
playground players and the effect this had on the game, which we
take for granted today. "The slam dunk, the no-look pass, and the
crossover dribble occupy a global stage," says Bayne.

Bayne, author of *Sky Kings: Black Pioneers of Professional Basketball,* explains the significance of playground hoops. And for those
of you with playground legends of your own, check out Bayne's
"Schoolyard Hall of Fame" and compare picks.

Chris Burtch resurrected a foundering high school basketball program at Slippery Rock Area High School in rural Western Pennsylvania, which had not reached the play-offs for twenty-one years prior to
his arrival. Burtch took teams to the postseason three times in his first
four years as head coach, averaging fifteen wins per season. In his
chapter "Fundamentals: Coaching Today's High School Player,"
Burtch, also a history teacher at the school, looks at how today's players have changed, as well as changes in the coaching profession itself.

Providing an insider look at what it is to be a high school coach in
the twenty-first century, he reveals, "the job of today's coach is to find
things that are important in terms of team discipline and stick with
these, while reinforcing them on a regular basis." He came to this realization after comparing his players with those he played with in
high school and college and understanding that times had definitely
changed. Unlike prior generations who routinely followed a coach's
every command, today's players do not follow their coaches without
question. Burtch's essay also includes an interesting look at teenage
grief, because when tragedy repeatedly struck the small town, the
players and their coaches relied on one another to accept and
overcome their pain.

In "Seventeen Things I Learned from Dean Smith," North Carolina
fanatic (and native) Peter Cashwell explores the life lessons he
learned from legendary University of North Carolina coach Dean
Smith. Cashwell literally had a front row seat as Dean Smith coached
the Tar Heels to two national championships, while emphasizing enduring values such as teamwork, adaptability, and fairness. "There
are obviously many lessons I've drawn from watching Coach Smith's

teams play," Cashwell says, "But none is more important than this: Play the game to the end."

Cashwell's engaging chapter proves that our childhood fascination with sports and athletics can serve as a productive foundation for the rest of our lives. Role models such as Dean Smith show us how to shape our lives, regardless of the career choices we make. Cashwell allows us to join him as he relives his boyhood memories—a litany of jumpshots and dramatic victories—awash in a backdrop of Carolina blue.

The autobiographical chapter "Socks, Jocks, and Two Championship Rings," by Michael Buchert, takes us inside the University of Florida Gators men's basketball team during two Southeastern Conference (SEC) Championship seasons, including the miraculous run to the NCAA Final Four in 2000. Buchert's unique perspective comes not from the usual suspects—the coach, one of the starting five, or even a local journalist—but from one of the real insiders at the heart of every big-time basketball program, the student manager corps.

Buchert, a self-proclaimed "NCAA jockwasher," introduces the reader to his screwy cast of fellow managers, Coach Billy Donovan, and the many athletes who led the Gators to SEC titles, including current NBA stars such as flashy point guard Jason Williams and dead-eye shooter Mike Miller. Buchert shares the tension, inside jokes, pranks, mishaps, and sheer joy of belonging to a basketball family.

Writer Renada Rutmanis looks at the influx of foreign talent making its mark on the American game in the chapter, "Foreign Players and the Globalization of Basketball." She links the NBA's successful global marketing efforts in the 1980s to foreign stars dreaming of NBA superstardom. Although some observers initially fretted about the quality of the foreign players, stars such as two-time MVP Tim Duncan and Dallas Mavericks sharpshooter Dirk Nowitzki rank among the best of their generation.

Rutmanis recalls her experience living in Central America as the Chicago Bulls looked to wrap up the 1998 NBA Championship and views this event as a defining moment in the globalization of the sport. "When I listened to that Bulls play-off game in Guatemala, the language of the announcers may have been Spanish," she says. "But clearly the language and the game of basketball had become universal."

THE PROFESSIONAL GAME

Although this book distinguishes itself from most by focusing on basketball from the blacktops to the dazzling lights of the NBA, no work would be complete without a look at the professional game.

Historically, baseball has dominated the imagination of writers and fans, probably because it evokes such nostalgia. The "national pastime" induces our romantic notions of the past and its traditions. As a result, books about the history of baseball probably (conservatively) outnumber those on basketball 50 to 1.

Despite the bookshelves dedicated to baseball, however, basketball has had a much greater impact on modern society. I would bet that a person could not make it through a single day in any decent-sized American city and not see numerous examples of basketball's effect on popular culture, whether it is baggy shorts, a player's image hawking soda, or streetball fashions that have gone mainstream. The greatest stage for hoopsters turned pop culture stars is the NBA.

In the first chapter in this section, historian Jim Fisher asks us to "imagine a player who possessed Michael Jordan's leaping ability, Julius Erving's grace and body control, Charles Barkley's strength, Larry Bird's court savvy, and Wilt Chamberlain's ability to dominate a game." That player being described is the legendary Elgin Baylor, who Fisher feels "has received little credit over the years for doing things that no one had done before. His style of play routinely bewildered his opponents, but most commentators then and now have not credited him with changing the way basketball was played."

In many respects, Fisher rescues Baylor from history's dustbin. Most modern fans only know Baylor as a front-office executive for the long-suffering Los Angeles Clippers. Even many students of the game have little understanding of Baylor's status as the player who transformed modern basketball. By bringing Baylor back to the forefront, Fisher is one of the first writers to recognize the player for all that he gave the game. Baylor, Fisher says, "Single-handedly changed the way that professional basketball was played. A game that was once slow (and often unabashed thuggery), transformed into a game of beauty. Where once method and strength were premiums, athleticism and free-flowing style dominated the game."

We begin our analysis of the evolution of the NBA with *Basketball Digest* "Digits" columnist David Friedman in "Chocolate Thunder and Short Shorts: The NBA in the 1970s." Displaying his deft statistical analysis with precision equaling a George "Iceman" Gervin finger-roll, Friedman examines the league's battle with the American Basketball Association (ABA) for hoops supremacy and the wacky personalities that fueled the game back in the disco era. According to Friedman, "The NBA and the ABA fought to sign players, to attract fans, and to win court cases that would change the shape of sports (not just basketball) forever. . . . Pro basketball was promoted as the 'Sport of the Seventies.'"

Perhaps more than at any other time in its history, the professional game mirrored society in the 1970s. The game revolved around its star athletes, but at the same time the NBA was becoming more of an entertainment spectacle. Big money and big contracts for players and the television networks caused the league to become more litigious. On the dark side, violence and drug use were pervasive and threatened the moral fabric of the sport, just as recreational drug use increased across the nation. Friedman rightly labels the 1970s "a dizzying roller-coaster ride."

Writer Lisa Ennis looks at the professional women's game in her chapter, "Crashing the Boards: The WNBA and the Evolution of an Image." Ennis traces the fate of several early women's professional leagues, and then turns her attention to the development of the WNBA, the most successful woman's league in history.

Included in her evaluation is the role the USA Basketball organization (USAB) played in marketing the 1996 women's Dream Team. "By leaving gender out of the name and the uniforms, the USAB created an atmosphere of creditability never before experienced by women's basketball," Ennis explains. "This spirit of credibility spread, resulting in renewed life for the women's game. The 1996 team went on to win gold and was wildly popular; each of the team's six games attracted over 30,000 spectators."

The future of the WNBA, as Ennis reveals, is still up in the air. Although the women's game is more popular than at any other time in recent history, there is still trouble getting a women's professional league on solid ground. Ennis' chapter will provide readers with insight into the state of the WNBA and uncover the issues that still challenge the young league.

The late Michigan State University Professor and sports historian Lawrence Ziewacz chronicles the rebirth of the NBA at the hands of a new cast of superstars in "Dr. J, Bird, Magic, Jordan, and the Detroit Bad Boys: The NBA in the 1980s." Ziewacz deftly shows how the NBA changed in the decade, not only with its newfound emphasis on a few star players and franchises, but transformations in the game itself, from the introduction of the three-point shot to the demise of center-oriented offenses.

Ziewacz, co-author of *The Games They Played: Sports in American History, 1865-1980,* traces the rise of the Magic Johnson/Larry Bird rivalry in college and its impact on the professional game, then explains how the rise of the "Bad Boy" Detroit Pistons and Chicago Bulls fits into the development of the NBA in the 1980s. Ziewacz argues that one of the enduring legacies of the game from that period is the intensity of the competition.

Award-winning writer and editor Doug Fox of the *Daily Herald* in Provo, Utah, appraises the professional game in "The Jordan Era: The NBA in the 1990s." As the paper's beat writer covering the Utah Jazz, Fox had a front-row seat during the team's two trips to the NBA Championship, each resulting in a loss to Jordan and the Bulls. Just imagine the pure joy of covering two of the game's greatest superstars on a daily basis (John Stockton and Karl Malone), and then witnessing the magic of the back-to-back NBA Championship runs against the Bulls—arguably the two most exciting in the Bulls' string of six league crowns. Fox's chapter is an oral history of the 1990s, delivered in the words of those who made the decade so great, from Michael Jordan and John Stockton to Jerry Sloan and Phil Jackson.

Fox teases the reader and all hoops junkies by recalling Jordan's winning shot at the buzzer in 1998, writing, "while most of the world relies on videotape and replays to relive that special moment in time—I can simply close my eyes, queue up my memory, and capture the greatness time and time again from my own personal perspective." Fox not only takes us inside the life of a sports fanatic and writer, but his insightful examination of the league in the 1990s will be a joy to anyone who wants to relive the magic of the Jordan era. (Note: Utah fans may want to skip this chapter, even though it is from one of their own—the memories may simply be too painful.)

In "King James: LeBron James, Hype, Hope, and the Future of the NBA," Batchelor tackles the budding legend of LeBron James, the most celebrated prep star in the history of basketball. The young man who is supposed to be the game's next messiah is poised to begin his

NBA career with the Cleveland Cavaliers, while the league searches for a new talent to replace Michael Jordan in the fans' eyes. Batchelor examines what is in store for the young star and searches for answers to questions about how James will handle life in the NBA by looking at the way he dealt with fame during his amateur career.

According to Batchelor, the stakes are high for James and the league. "The NBA needs LeBron James to live up to the hype and the hope," he writes. "The future does not necessarily hang in the balance, but finding another Jordan to showcase could revitalize the game for another generation." For basketball purists, however, the hope is that James will be given the time to develop into the best player he can be and that we can all enjoy the skills he brings to the court. The fans in Cleveland would certainly trade an NBA Championship for all the James Nike shoes ever sold.

We hope you enjoy reading *Basketball in America* as much as we enjoyed writing it. Our hope is that this book will help spark an outpouring of serious writing on the game and its place within the fabric of American society. There is much more to the game than expressed by the literature that now dominates the field—countless cheesy memoirs and hastily written biographies. Basketball has been ignored for too long.

PART I:
BASKETBALL IN AMERICAN CULTURE

Chapter 2

Michael Jordan: Icon

Bob Batchelor

I think he's God disguised as Michael Jordan. He is the most awesome player in the NBA.

Larry Bird (1986)

Sometimes I dream/ That he is me/ You've got to see that's how I dream to be/ I dream I move, I dream I groove/ Like Mike/ If I could be like Mike/ Like Mike/ Oh, if I could be like Mike.

Gatorade jingle (1991)

For many years in the 1980s and 1990s, Chicago Bulls public-address announcer Ray Clay yelled the most thrilling words in sports—and he never even got to finish his sentence. "And now, from North Carolina . . . " The mere thought of the darkened arena, laser-generated flashing logos, popping camera bulbs, and the familiar instrumental theme song competing for time with the screams of 25,000 fans brings chills.

After the hoopla, more like a rock concert than basketball game, Michael Jordan appeared in the familiar red and black warm-ups—blood red. The scoreboard, towering above in the rafters, glittered as all cameras focused on the Bulls star. The moment was quintessential Jordan—the smile, the smooth-shaved head, and the eyes . . . the intensity betraying the thousand-watt grin, like he knew what was going to happen for the next forty-eight minutes, like he could see into the future.

Put down the remote. You must watch. Tonight may well be extraordinary—MJ could post a cool 50 or hit the game-winner at the buzzer. The very notion of Jordan drew you in. Just by watching, you could be part of history. You are witnessing real-life greatness.

For so many hoops fans and former basketball players, Michael Jordan is at the center of their most vivid memories. Many people around the world have a simple belief—Jordan *is* basketball. Over the course of his magnificent career, MJ has transcended the game, becoming an American (then global) hero and true icon.

Jordan's rise as a popular culture icon is particularly impressive given the quantity of media venues that pull the average fan's attention in a million different directions each day. The competition among entertainers for airtime is as fierce in the commercial and media realm as it is for many of them on the field or the casting couch. Jordan became a megastar in a world full of second-rate and third-tier celebrities who were recognized for little more than being famous, thus diluting the notion of what greatness and fame really is.

According to historian Walter LaFeber, who examined Jordan's role in spreading capitalism on a global scale, television and the post-1970s media enabled messages to extend far beyond national borders. "Culture could move with nearly the speed of sound and reach billions of people, not just the privileged," he explained. "Jordan and Nike (and McDonald's and Disney), suddenly enjoyed the power to reach vast audiences with an efficiency unimagined several generations earlier. Jordan's corporate sponsors chose the outlets where he would be featured. Is it any surprise that they decided on certain markets that targeted sports fans (ESPN) and young, affluent buyers (MTV)?[1]

Why have fans followed, obsessed, and idolized MJ for what has now been decades? Jordan is the real thing. His magnificence on the basketball court has been undeniable, as is his legendary drive to outwork, outplay, and completely dominate the opposition. The celebrated stories about his work ethic played an important role in Jordan's folklore, enabling him to present an everyman face to the public, despite the fact that he was a millionaire as soon as the ink dried on his first professional contract.

In my own mind, the events unfold as I run through a catalog of MJ virtuoso performances. I remember watching in utter horror as a skinny, practically unknown freshman hit the game-winner against my beloved Georgetown Hoyas. That shot, so pivotal in MJ's career as motivational tool and confidence-builder, turned me into a begrudging Jordan-hater. I simply tried to forget about him for the next couple of years while he was at Chapel Hill.

When Jordan really caught my eye again, as a rookie with the Chicago Bulls, his individual brilliance required me to forgive him for sticking a dagger in the hearts of Patrick Ewing, Eric "Sleepy" Floyd, and company. Jordan's transformation into a dazzling professional player dwarfed the college player he had been, despite his stellar play for legendary coach Dean Smith. The precise offensive sets the Tar Heels ran kept Jordan in check, to a degree, leading some observers to joke that Coach Smith was the only person in the world that could hold MJ under 20 points per game.

A couple of my friends were able to maintain an anti-Jordan attitude, one in particular being a diehard New York Knicks fan, which more or less forced him to despise all things not New York. The rest of us were powerless. Jordan represented something that I could relate to—maybe his intensity or will to succeed—that superceded all the amazing acrobatics that immediately drew oohs and ahhs from fans. Watching Jordan, one immediately sensed an air of electricity, greatness, and historical importance. In a world filled with bluster and hot air, here was a figure that lived up to the hype.

Then came the commercials for Nike. The union of a hungry African-American film director (with tons of street credibility for his amazing portrayals of ghetto life in *She's Gotta Have It* and *Do the Right Thing*), a gifted athlete, and a daring shoe company could not have been better scripted. With his smile beaming into the world's collective consciousness, Jordan was soon widely recognized as more than just a basketball player. The Jordan aura took on a life of its own, thanks to the genius of the Nike marketing effort and the ties to Spike Lee. In short order, as other corporations signed him on as a spokesman, Jordan became the hottest face in advertising.

Still, looking back, who could have predicted the success? The ads were amusing. Lee's Mars Blackmon character filled the screen with a familiar face, but the simple fact was that no one wore Nike basketball shoes. Everyone I knew donned the Converse sneakers endorsed by Magic Johnson and Larry Bird. At my tiny high school in the Western Pennsylvania hills, the team boosters supplied us with a spanking new pair of Converse with a bright red logo, which matched our school colors.

In college, my roommates and I were still devoted to Converse, though many people were catching on to the red and black Air Jordans. But our loyalty remained with Magic. We even "procured" the famous dueling Magic/Bird life-sized cardboard cutout, which occupied a prized place in shoe stores across the nation. From Foot Locker to our college apartment living room, the two watched over our shenanigans for years. Couches were broken, chairs wrecked, and televisions came and went, but no one laid a finger on the towering figures of Bird and Magic. That would have meant a sure pummeling. These were our heroes.

Gradually, however, allegiances shifted. Jordan's individual skills were just too phenomenal. Trying to avoid Jordan and the Nike swoosh soon became impossible. MJ's many other commercial product tie-ins helped spread the Jordan gospel.

Like millions of wannabe high-fliers, I had the Wheaties poster of Jordan on my wall. The poster, featuring his Slam Dunk Contest take-off from the foul line dunk (fulfilling his destiny as Dr. J's "air apparent"), was a gift from a close friend and fellow playground warrior. He didn't want to give it up, but in the end realized that I liked Jordan more than he did. I still have that poster in a box in my garage. For more than a decade (to my wife's chagrin), I haven't been able to throw that thing away.

Back in high school, I remember my coach yelling at me for my tongue hanging out of my mouth, like Jordan's, though I had no idea I was doing it. Years later, even after my formal playing days ended, that simple kinship with the great one pushed me to work hard every time I stepped on the court, including hours of practice—by myself—in the sweltering humidity of Western Pennsylvania summers to be like Mike, long before the Gatorade jingle became a part of his legend.

Finally, in the 1990-1991 season (my senior year of college), Jordan led the Bulls to the NBA Finals, where they punished the Los Angeles Lakers. For me this was a defining moment. The torch passed from my former favorite player (Magic) to the new sheriff in town. Regardless of his individual brilliance, Magic just could not seem to rally his team against the young Bulls. That series was the first time I had ever seen Magic look a step too slow. Even his physical appearance seemed a bit wilted with big blue knee braces on each leg and a slew of bandaged fingers.

Jordan had just completed an amazing season, averaging 31.5 points per game, and then willed his team through the play-offs, which included a sweep of the dreaded Detroit Pistons. In the finals, MJ was a monster and almost single-handedly overpowered the proud Lakers, averaging 31.2 points per game. Even Magic could not stop destiny.

The string of titles before and after his brief retirement to pursue a career in baseball solidified Jordan's image in my mind. In those years, he seemed to love basketball even more and his passion showed in the way his individual game expanded. In the course of a few short years, Jordan's jump shot became a flawless thing of beauty and his fade-away jumper simply breathtaking. He and fellow All-Star Scottie Pippen found a new level of appreciation for each other, as if they knew that their destinies were forever entwined. The kinship between the two was awe-inspiring.

Maybe more impressive than any of Jordan's pure athletic skills, though, was the way he excelled in the spotlight, in the waning moments of a game when all eyes were on him. Anyone who has ever played knows the gnawing feeling and tightness that comes when the game is on the line, when no one is willing to take the last shot, even in a pickup game at the local YMCA. These moments define what it means to be a winner. No matter the circumstances, Jordan produced.

In early 2003, however, as he passed his fortieth birthday as a member of the Washington Wizards, many observers questioned his place among the new generation of pro basketball players. Whispers about Jordan's aching knees and diminished skills surfaced.

Almost as if answering these detractors—nobody gets condemned faster in American culture than a celebrity (especially an athlete) that hangs on too long—Jordan intensified his play after the 2003 All-Star contest in Atlanta, becoming the first forty-year-old to score 40 points in game.

Despite a horrible supporting cast—even fellow Chapel Hill alum Jerry Stackhouse could not figure out how to operate in an offense focused on MJ—Jordan had the Wizards contending for the final play-off spot in the Eastern Conference for most of the season. The Wizards, however, fell short. As a result, and because many of the younger Wizards grew disgruntled with Jordan's prodding them to produce, owner Abe Pollin cut ties with Jordan. After the season ended, Pollin stripped him of the promised position in the team's front office. The Jordan era in Washington came to a screeching halt.

Throughout a long and successful career, Michael Jordan has been called many things—most of them deeply reverent—from Jesus in basketball shoes and God to the more mundane tags routinely draped on sports stars: hero, warrior, and superstar. What he became was more than a sports figure. His fame eclipsed the all-time greats in other venues. Without discussing politics, race relations, corporate wrongdoing, or tackling other dicey topics, MJ grew into a global icon on par with presidents, royalty, and the top handful of movie stars.

Michael Jordan's influence on global culture defies reason. On paper, there is no way to fully measure Michael Jordan's influence on world culture in the past three decades. Look at it this way: there are movie stars that draw $20 million a film who do not turn people to jelly when they appear, and several sports stars have been more prolific winners than MJ, from Celtics legend Bill Russell to Yankee greats Babe Ruth and Lou Gehrig. Remarkably, however, it is Jordan (a black male in a society that is still, some would argue, wholly racist) who has captured the public imagination like no other.

THE GREATEST EVER

The sports world thrives on history and argument. Millions of words are written, and countless television and radio hours are devoted to the quest to understand sports. There may be nothing more doggedly pursued than comparing today's stars with the greats from the past. For sports fanatics, these kinds of discussions have the perfect ingredients—a nearly limitless supply of topics and (most important) no way to definitively prove that either opinion is correct. Debates over the greatest player in a given sport or across sports can go on for decades (if not centuries) without ever being concluded—a fan's dream.

Sports enthusiasts don't even have to go far back into the history books to compare stars of different eras. Another version of this argument is on finding "the next," contrasting a young star with a current great. For more than a decade, basketball's top high school and college stars have been compared to Michael Jordan. Current Cavaliers rookie LeBron James is only the latest in a long line of players who has received the dreaded "next Michael Jordan" label. Can any player—let alone an eighteen-year-old rookie—live with this kind of burden? Could MJ himself have lived up to this level of hype if he were entering the league right now?

In his autobiography, Jordan addressed the pretenders who tried to wear the "next Jordan" crown. "From all the great players the league has tried to market, most of them have blown over already. Harold Miner was blown away, Anfernee Hardaway is now swaying in the wind . . . these are athletes who have grown up through the league's promotion of them without the roots." The older, wiser Jordan then outlined what it takes to be one of the game's greats: "Marketing can jump-start a player, but it still comes down to what that player does on the court. You can't fool the public. I think the league saw my example and thought it could slide other players into the slot I created. Sooner or later that player has to make an impact in the play-offs."[2]

Michael Jordan is simply the greatest basketball player ever. At the core of his brilliance is more than tremendous athleticism. What really pushes Jordan is a competitive drive that steamrolls his opponents and compels him to win. It is a well-known fact that this competitive instinct carries over into every aspect of his life, from playing cards to cutthroat matches on the golf course. "I was always comparing myself to other players . . . where I stood, how I matched up, what I needed to work on . . . doing everything I could to stay on top," Jordan wrote in his autobiography. "It never had anything to do with money or business. The game is what mattered to me."[3]

In the course of becoming the best player of all time, Jordan has achieved a status in modern American popular culture that is reserved for a tiny handful of entertainers and celebrities in any given era. Jordan's fame has brought him hundreds of millions of dollars. His image is one of the most recognizable on the planet.

At the core of Jordan's achievements—the best thing about him, really—is that his success grew out of years and years of hard work and dedication to his craft. What propels Jordan is the extraordinary idea of transcending the game of basketball. "On the basketball court, I elevated my game to meet the demands of our team and my own expectations," Jordan explained. "The game began to become more mental than physical, the challenges more narrowly focused."[4]

It is ironic that for all of Jordan's heartfelt reverence for the purities of basketball (defense, passing, and jump shots) and its history, his athleticism and individual grace evolved (some would say, devolved) into the video game culture of modern basketball. Critics of the game disapprove of today's players for concentrating on dunking, one-on-one moves, and fancy (yet mostly unnecessary) dribbling and passing. Just like the video games kids grow up playing, the emphasis is on circus dunks and flash, rather than developing strong fundamentals.

The "Jumpman/Air Jordan" image of MJ's early career is at least partly responsible for pushing the modern game toward flash rather than fundamentals. However, placing all the blame on Jordan would be ludicrous. The Nike image sold shoes and cereal, but is far from defining the player Jordan worked to become. The crowds who packed Chicago Stadium did not see the hard work Jordan put in each summer developing his jumper, dribbling with his off hand, bulking up to remain strong through the grueling play-off runs, or mastering a deft fade-away jump shot that was essentially impossible to stop. "For all the high-wire theatrics, despite the Nike logo of Jordan as a basketball superman flying through the air lacking only a cape, his greatest moments were soft swishes released from his finger tips just beyond the foul line," said veteran sports columnist Terry Pluto.[5]

FAME

Some basketball players never seem truly comfortable with their fame, even if they have been among the greatest to ever lace up sneakers, such as Kareem Abdul-Jabbar and Larry Bird. Both men, deep thinkers who love the essence of the game itself, saw the celebrity lifestyle as a hindrance and detrimental to the sport. Some would argue that this kind of "old school" thinking was buried when the last generation of great players retired.

Subsequent generations have been quick to embrace popular culture, becoming "crossover" stars by branching into avenues outside basketball. Some critics view this trend as negative—wasting time on outside pursuits when one should be honing skills on the court. Others see the branding efforts as expanding the game into new areas and picking up new fans.

Jordan, of course, is responsible for this trend. With the help of Nike and his other endorsers, Jordan and agent David Falk recognized the power of celebrity as soon as he entered the NBA. What separated Jordan, though, was that he pursued commercial opportunities without sacrificing his dedication to the game. MJ maintained the warrior mentality, for instance, of a Larry Bird, while pursuing activities such as filming a Disney movie and shooting countless commercials. With Jordan, the special attribute that separates him from other outstanding professional players always comes back to his work ethic, which the fans appreciated, and this kept them on his side throughout his playing career.

Recognizing how important his image had become, Jordan took steps to ensure that he looked as good off the court as he did in front of the glaring lights. Throughout his career, pictures of MJ off the basketball court are nearly interchangeable. He is always exceptionally well dressed, sporting the latest designer fashions. "I remember my father telling me how important first impressions can be for some people," Jordan said. "I wanted to present myself in a way that would give people the proper impression of me. I wanted them to know I cared about what they thought. In a small way, I was able to show my respect for them, too."[6]

Obviously, given his penchant for showy sports cars and immaculate clothes, Jordan is comfortable with his wealth—lately he has added new accessories—either holding a huge cigar or clenching it between his teeth while a large gold hoop earring dangles from his left lobe. What is surprising, however, is that the public has always seemed at ease with Jordan's affluence. The fans never turned on Jordan for being a rich, attractive, well-spoken, successful black man. Every triumph simply fueled the Jordan mystique and made fans crazier for the superstar.

In 1991, when he finally won his first of six NBA Championships, Jordan also won his second league MVP, earned more than $20 million in endorsement deals, had the McDonald's McJordan hamburger named after him, appeared in a Saturday morning cartoon, and starred in a commercial with Little Richard. Did the public turn on the superstar for being overexposed? Not a chance. The next year, he signed several new commercial deals, opened his own restaurant in Chicago, and expanded his endorsement empire into Japan, Europe, and Asia. The Bulls' first title merely helped speed along the inevitable—the MJ globalization effort went into overdrive.[7]

Fame is a fleeting commodity in the modern world. The biggest movie stars fade into the background within weeks after the release of their latest film and a musician's shelf life seems to be measured in seconds, not minutes. Given these realities, the most bewildering question regarding Jordan's icon status is this—how did an African-American sports star become the most recognizable face in the world and stay on top for nearly two decades?

Maybe the answer is simpler than one would imagine . . . though trying to figure out how Jordan became a popular culture phenomenon is like digging in sand: the deeper you go, the more difficult it is to keep the hole from caving in on itself. Certainly the confluence of cable television and communications satellites beaming his smiling face and on-court exploits around the globe played an important role. The way his image has been marketed by his corporate sponsors, such as Nike and McDonald's, has also been pivotal. The MJ brand is cutting edge. But a full explanation of Jordan's position as an icon goes beyond mere advertising tricks and gimmicks. Jordan projects an undefined star quality that few athletes or celebrities possess. The short list includes the likes of Muhammad Ali, Babe Ruth, and Tiger Woods.

The answer most likely lies in Jordan's combination of athletic prowess and brand image. Bona fide heroes are in short supply in modern America. Celebrity-driven popular culture, feeding on sensationalism and short attention spans, chews up today's stars with blinding speed, and then moves on to the next big name that captures the national spotlight. In an environment exploding with new media opportunities, Andy Warhol's famous prediction about the future affording everyone fifteen minutes of fame has been reduced to about five minutes—perhaps much less. Not only do more people anticipate their turn in the spotlight, they now believe that they deserve their bit of fame.

Since bursting onto the national scene by hitting the game-winning shot in the NCAA Championship game, Michael Jordan has been not only a hero to millions of people around the world but he has redefined our ideas about competition, hard work, and dedication.

Regardless of the endorsements, the worldwide fame, and even the occasional lapse in judgment, Jordan's true brilliance has always been in the pure skill he exhibits on the basketball court. Jordan the athlete became Jordan the icon only after his exploits on the court bewildered those witnessing his greatness. No matter what, Jordan's athletic supremacy shined brighter than everything else.

The downside to Jordan's fame is that his life is no longer fully his own. He is recognized from one end of the globe to the other, making it impossible for him to escape his own celebrity. There is no privacy for a star the size of Jordan. Even his father's funeral (James Jordan was murdered in August 1993) became somewhat of a spectacle.

The demands on Jordan's time would probably drive most people insane. Celebrities don't take a special course on how to be famous or deal with sudden wealth and notoriety. "No matter how hard I try, I'm never going to be the perfect person," Jordan said in 1993. "The one time I tell somebody that I'm tired and that I don't want to sign another autograph, that person gets a whole different feeling about Michael Jordan. So my job really never ends."[8]

The bright lights extend into Jordan's relationships with those around him, including family and friends. Downtime is more like hiding than relaxing. The intensity of Jordan's fame dwarfs that of his superstar friends. However, fans won't find him walking down red carpets to award shows or generally making a spectacle of himself. Rather, spending time with Air Jordan necessitates fitting into his world. Charles Barkley, certainly no shrinking violet, said, "The one thing that's weird about Michael is that whenever we're together, we're in a hotel room, because he doesn't ever go out."[9]

Throughout his playing career, Jordan was confronted by hundreds of people everywhere he went. The walk from the locker room to the waiting bus or car was a gauntlet of fans and cameras and autographs. People who wanted something from him always made demands on his time. Now that his playing career has ended, it will be interesting to see if life changes for Jordan. At what point will the fans give him space, and will he someday come to miss the constant attention?

MONEY

Michael Jordan has never been just another amazingly rich professional athlete. MJ is an economic juggernaut, pumping an estimated $15 billion dollars into the global economy over the course of his career. In many ways, one could argue, his status as an A-list celebrity has transcended his extraordinary skills on the court.

For example, Jordan was the only African-American to make the top ten in *Fortune* magazine's 2002 list of America's forty richest people under forty years of age (his last year of eligibility). In 2002, the Wizards star ranked ninth with an estimated worth of $408 million, up from the previous year's total of $398 million. In contrast, rap moguls Percy "Master P" Miller and Sean "P. Diddy" Combs were each worth just under $294 million, while Tiger Woods clocked in at $212 million, good enough for sixteenth on the list.[10]

The idea of an aging basketball star outproducing two hip-hop entrepreneurs and Woods—the next big thing in the sponsorship world—is hard to imagine. Celebrities just aren't supposed to be able to stay hip and relevant for as long as MJ.

Stars such as Woods, NASCAR's Dale Earnhardt Jr., and Shaquille O'Neal owe Jordan a debt of gratitude for redefining the role of athletic spokesperson. He epitomized the idea of building a brand image by signing long-term contracts and using each product to publicize all his endorsement deals. Time and again, Jordan's unwavering loyalty to his products pointed the way for an entire generation of athletes. Who can forget, for instance, Jordan's decision to cover the Reebok logo on his Olympic warm-up jacket with the American flag because he was a Nike man?

"Shoes, energy drinks, fast food, cologne, a Bugs Bunny movie, upscale restaurants: Jordan had his face and his name and his money attached to them all," wrote Jay Weiner in *Business Week* after Jordan's retirement from the Bulls.

> He blazed the trail for less marketable athletes such as big, bad Shaquille O'Neal; less charismatic players such as scholarly Grant Hill; and less mature emerging stars such as "da kid" Kevin Garnett. They all took classes in the Jordan Principle: Sports sell things, and things sell sports.[11]

Michael Eric Dyson, an influential African-American scholar and critic views Jordan's rise as, "Particularly American; it starts with talent and ends with financial power." Jordan and his financial handlers, according to Dyson, used "enormous calculation" to set the star up as the quintessential American pitchman, while at the same time ensuring that Jordan would never become the stereotypical black athlete who lost his millions to scam artists and hangers-on.[12]

SCANDAL

Race has always played a central role in the history of the NBA. Whenever a scandal damages the league's reputation—from allegations of widespread drug use in the 1970s and 1980s to criticism about the number of illegitimate children fathered by professional players in the 1990s—it always has a racial undercurrent, usually supporting one of the many stereotypes held against young African Americans. Over the past decade the knock on the NBA has been that the league is filled with egomaniacal thugs, more concerned with street credibility than what happens on the basketball court.

Although many pro athletes are criticized for their off-the-field actions, NBA stars are held up as an example whenever observers discuss the sinister side of sports. Players such as Allen Iverson, Ron Artest, Dennis Rodman, and Latrell Sprewell have been flogged in the court of public opinion. Certainly some of this condemnation is warranted, but the spotlight on professional basketball players glares brighter than on other world-class athletes.

NBA players are routinely named when giving examples of all that is wrong with giving sports stars multimillion-dollar contracts. And, surprise, surprise, the supposed culprits are most often young blacks. Rarely are similar criticisms brought against white players. The idea that the thousands of white NBA players who have suited up are all choirboys, as the media makes them out to be, flies in the face of all mathematical reasoning.

As the game's brightest star, Jordan attracted his share of scandal, particularly as his celebrity broadened. It was as if after another NBA Championship and the Dream Team hoopla, people searched for defects. Gambling provided that hook. Once the news media smelled blood, they went after the basketball star and, for once, he had little control over the way his image was being marketed—used to get ratings on ESPN and sell newspapers and magazines. The stories outlined his extravagant lifestyle and detailed his ferocious gambling habit.

From the Jordan camp, the reaction happened quickly. Jordan is an intense competitor, they said. Gambling fueled that competitive drive. Soon, the extent of MJ's lifelong gambling came to light. Off the court, he placed bets on everything from Ping-Pong matches to golf matches. Golf seemed to be his sanctuary away from the spotlight and the throngs of people constantly chasing him, but it was on the links where he also wagered incredible amounts of money. Like many professional athletes, Jordan also enjoyed visiting gambling casinos to unwind. Las Vegas and Atlantic City seemed to be a natural habitat for young men who spent so much time playing cards while traveling and had enough cash to make the stakes interesting.

Public scrutiny resulted when it came to light that MJ had amassed huge debts playing golf with a variety of slimy hustlers, including $108,000 to one shark who ended up murdered. It happened that the hustler was under investigation by federal authorities at the time. They found two checks from Jordan among the man's possessions. Fans blanched when they heard stories about the amount of money he and his partners tossed around on the golf course. The stories put the league in an awkward position and forced Jordan to publicly admit his shortcomings. He told one reporter, "Was I gambling with goons who had bad reputations? Yeah, I was. Should I not gamble with goons anymore? Yeah, I shouldn't gamble with goons."[13]

Although many fans were disgusted to hear about Jordan's gambling problem and were outraged by the amount of money he tossed around (more than many people could make in years of full-time work), his reputation was not permanently damaged by the controversy. In some respects, when people learned that MJ was human with imperfections and frailties, they revered the star even more.

Jordan has endured other scandals as well. Long-whispered rumors of infidelity were confirmed in October 2002, despite an intense effort to keep Jordan's private life a secret. The basketball star, then in his final season with the Wizards, sued a former girlfriend after she attempted to extort money from him, even though they had agreed to an earlier financial settlement. Once he sued (as is nearly always the case in an overly litigious society), she countersued, claiming that the NBA star promised her $5 million when he retired. Adding to the gossip, the woman even asserted that Jordan called his wife, Juanita, "a hired hand." In June 2003, Jordan's lawyers had the suit dismissed, but the entire debacle was an embarrassment to the star.[14]

For many critics, perhaps the most unsettling controversy of Jordan's career is that he never openly and publicly used his power to provoke change politically or socioeconomically. Unlike Ali, tennis star Arthur Ashe, and other African-American sports figures, Jordan did not speak out against society's ills. When opportunities arose, such as Nike's use of third world labor or the chance to champion Harvey Gantt, an African American running for Senate from North Carolina, Jordan remained mute.

For many people, Jordan had a responsibility to his public and those who were buying the products he endorsed. Ignoring the fact that teenagers were killing one another to steal Air Jordans was hypocritical. Even under these strains, MJ eluded the kind of criticism that puts an end to a player's endorsement deals and strains his credibility. In contrast, fellow great Charles Barkley took much more heat for publicly declaring that children's role models should be their parents, not professional athletes.

Jordan's conduct as an endorser has had a profound effect on other athletes, most notably golf superstar Tiger Woods. Woods has adopted the cool, machine-like demeanor of MJ, probably the result of the counseling Jordan provided Woods when he first joined the professional ranks. Jordan has also served as a role model for former high school phenomenon and present Cleveland Cavaliers star LeBron James, giving the youngster his private cell phone number and inviting him to workouts in Chicago while MJ prepared for his comeback with the Wizards.

ICON

The global hype machine is enthralled with the dark side of celebrity. Like a rabid carnivore attacking wounded prey, the media's fascination with disgrace more or less requires that every star must eventually fall from grace. Yet, through thick and thin, Michael Jordan has remained one of the most admired people on the planet.

Jordan's popularity often dwarfed events that carried worldwide significance and bordered on the absurd. For example, at a Nike press conference held in Barcelona to celebrate the arrival of the 1992 Dream Team, a Japanese reporter summed up MJ's place in the world's collective consciousness, asking, "Mr. Jordan, how does it feel to be God?"[15]

Yes, Jordan's face is instantly recognizable worldwide. His legend, however, outstrips mere identification. He evokes images and feelings that have won over hardcore basketball junkies and casual observers alike. Jordan personifies the American Dream, but even that statement seems to come up somewhat short in describing all that he symbolizes.

Over the past two decades, Michael Jordan has transcended sports and become a popular culture icon. Unlike any other athlete of his generation (and perhaps any other athlete ever—at least all those not named Muhammad Ali) Jordan has turned into a mythical figure. People all over the globe own bright red Chicago Bulls jerseys emblazoned with the familiar 23. Millions more have bought shoes and clothing that he endorses. Though his playing career has ended, they will continue to buy Jordan-endorsed products.

Images of Jordan are burned into the pop culture landscape, from his commercials for Nike, Hanes, Gatorade, and a host of other large corporations to his starring role in the Bugs Bunny caper *Space Jam* and an IMAX film highlighting his last championship year with the Chicago Bulls.

"Unlike so many people who the Hollywood fantasy machine projected into theaters and homes who were beautiful but whose deeds were artificial, his deeds were real," explains writer David Halberstam. "In a world where so many stars and heroes were inauthentic, he remained remarkably authentic."[16]

Others view the consumer culture icon as outstripping the athlete. Journalist Phil Hersh examined Jordan's status as a cultural icon after he "unretired" in late 1993, writing, "Michael the Marketed cannot be separated from the Magic of Michael. They live in perfect symbiosis, working and playing in a way never before seen in the creation of celebrity." However, without Nike, Hersh argues, Jordan would be just another beloved sports star. "Who Michael is and what he does operate in a sort of revised existentialism, where Jordan creates himself by his actions and then becomes an exaggerated re-creation of himself in advertising."[17]

Part of Jordan's appeal is that he possesses a kind of everyman quality, despite his long list of successes. People can identify with him—foibles and all. For instance, how many young athletes have been told the story of Michael Jordan being cut from the varsity team his sophomore year of high school as a means of proving that anyone can rise from adversity through hard work and dedication? When MJ left the game at the height of his talent to give professional baseball a shot, he showed a human side, because he had trouble with curveballs—just as we all did growing up.

WHEN THE BALL STOPS BOUNCING

The most obvious question facing Jordan is "What's next?" How does one of the greatest athletes to ever grace the planet stop being an athlete?

Early indications are that Jordan will stay in the game, just as he did after his previous retirements. The natural step would have been to revert to his old front-office position and part ownership with the Wizards. However, in a move that puzzled most observers, the Wizards discarded Jordan shortly after he hung up his sneakers. The unceremonious move on the part of the Wizards was probably the toughest jab Jordan has taken since getting cut from the varsity team his sophomore year of high school.

Despite the one-man rejuvenation effort Jordan led during his two-year playing stint with the Wizards (putting an estimated $40 to $50 million into team coffers), Pollin offered little or no explanation for MJ's dismissal. The owner did, however, offer Jordan a lump sum of $10 million as a show of gratitude. Jordan declined the cash, telling Pollin that he wanted to return to his job, not get another paycheck.

In the days after, it became apparent that Wizards management polled the players about Jordan before deciding his fate. Many of MJ's teammates were still reeling from trying to live up to his standards on the court and criticized him. The team decided to drop Jordan rather than risk alienating its young players.

The irony in Wizards owner Pollin siding with his current crop of players over Jordan is that the team is a mess. The Washington franchise has been in a state of constant chaos for decades. The team has not won a play-off game in fifteen years and consistently runs budding young stars out of town, allowing them to blossom elsewhere. Even with the greatest ever on the court, the team still could not make the play-offs or finish with an even record. Still, why would anyone torpedo MJ to stay in the good graces of the likes of Jerry Stackhouse and Kwame Brown?

Perhaps the ultimate irony is that while still in the Washington front office Jordan was responsible for trading to get Stackhouse (giving up Richard "Rip" Hamilton after the budding star supposedly questioned MJ's selfishness) and risked the number-one draft pick on Brown. When he came out of retirement to don the familiar "23" for the Wizards, Brown wilted under MJ's famous glare and Stackhouse turned into a wallflower. Jordan's critics pointed to these events as reason enough for his firing. Rumors surfaced that the Wizards players turned on Jordan in the final weeks of the season. The players voiced their concerns with Pollin, who held secret meetings with several of them, including Brown, Brendan Haywood, and Juan Dixon, without Jordan's knowledge.[18]

Veteran sports columnist Michael Wilbon of *The Washington Post* provided some much-needed perspective on the situation, stating, "Regardless of whether you think Jordan did a good job as an executive, he was the most valuable asset the franchise had. He was the only reason people started to care about the Wizards again, the only credibility and legitimacy the whole organization had."[19]

With the flip-flop orchestrated by Wizards ownership, MJ is a free agent. Almost immediately, he began to field job offers, most notably from the new expansion franchise in Charlotte under the guidance of African-American owner Bob Johnson. Johnson gave Jordan an open invitation to join the club in any capacity he saw fit. Jordan ultimately turned Johnson down, but that move provides a glimpse into his thinking.

As a relatively young man beginning a second career, Jordan's opportunities are endless. Perhaps what MJ learned from the way he was mistreated by the Wizards is that to truly control an organization, you have to own it. Jordan worked quickly to put together an investment group to buy the Milwaukee Bucks from team owner and Senator Herb Kohl, up for sale in the summer of 2003. Although rumors had the deal nearly complete, Kohl announced that he was taking the team off the market, thus thwarting Jordan's ownership bid.

Whatever Jordan chooses, he will know that he gave basketball fans around the world a glimpse of what it is to be remarkable. Outside the United Center in Chicago, a sculpture of Jordan shows the superstar soaring over an outstretched arm on the way to a thunderous dunk. At the base of the statue are the most fitting and understated words to sum up Michael Jordan: "The best there ever was. The best there ever will be."

Although I'm thirty-six years old and play basketball for nothing but pride, I still hit the gym by six in the morning a couple of days a week to work on my jumper before the rest of the guys show up for pickup games. We're all old and pretty slow, but the fire still burns.

Occasionally, someone will get hot and light it up, erasing years from old bones and dusting cobwebs off treasured memories.

It all starts on the court, whether it's burning asphalt or a dank gymnasium, alone with the ball and dreams of glory. Feeling the leather on my fingertips, a soaked T-shirt, and a pair of Nikes tightly laced up, I concentrate on one thought as I fire up shot after shot— Like Mike, if I could be like Mike.

NOTES

1. Walter LaFeber, *Michael Jordan and the New Global Capitalism* (New York: Norton, 2002), p. 18.

2. Michael Jordan, *For the Love of the Game* (New York: Crown, 1998), p. 79.

3. Ibid, p. 38.

4. Ibid, p. 57.

5. Terry Pluto, "Like Mike Still a Good Thing to Be," *The Akron Beacon Journal*, February 10, 2003.

6. Jordan, p. 139.

7. LaFeber, p. 80.

8. Quoted in Janet Lowe, *Michael Jordan Speaks: Lessons from the World's Greatest Champion* (New York: Wiley, 1999), p. 139.

9. Quoted in David Halberstam, *Playing for Keeps: Michael Jordan and the World He Made* (New York: Random House, 1999), p. 318.

10. "Michael Jordan, Master P and P. Diddy Among 40 Richest Americans Under 40," *Jet*, September 2002, p. 36.

11. Jay Weiner, "What Do We Want from Our Sports Heroes?" *Business Week*, January 25, 1999, p. 77.

12. Michael Eric Dyson, *Between God and Gangsta Rap: Bearing Witness to Black Culture* (New York: Oxford University Press, 1996), p. 57.

13. Quoted in Halberstam, p. 321.

14. Lester Munson and John O'Keefe, "A Fed-Up Star Wades into an Unlovely Legal Battle with his Former Girl Friend," *Sports Illustrated,* December 2, 2002, p. 26; "Jordan Scores Victory in Court; Lawsuit Against Star Thrown Out," *Jet*, June 30, 2003, p. 48.

15. Quoted in LaFeber, p. 85.

16. Halberstam, p. 184.

17. Phil Hersh, "Should His Airness Be a Cultural Icon?" *Chicago Tribune*, March 24, 1995.

18. Steve Wyche, "Pollin Met with Players Before Jordan's Dismissal," *The Washington Post*, May 10, 2003; Mike Wise, "Jordan's Strained Ties to Wizards May Be Cut," *The New York Times*, May 4, 2003.

19. Michael Wilbon, "Pollin Clears the Air, but Muddies the Water," *The Washington Post*, May 8, 2003.

Chapter 3

Marvin, Marvin

David Davis

OH, SAY CAN YOU SEE?

When Marvin Gaye walked onto the Forum floor to sing the national anthem at the 1983 NBA All-Star game, he was in sorry shape. Mirrored aviator sunglasses hid eyes that were red from daily drug use. A lifelong sufferer of stage fright, the former Motown star had tried in vain to get out of the gig. That February afternoon in Inglewood, California, he had arrived so late that Lakers officials were prepared to replace him with an usher.

But for three minutes, Gaye pulled himself together. As a grooving backbeat echoed around him, he powered and simmered his way through the patriotic warhorse, infusing it with equal parts soul, funk, and gospel. By the time he was through, the capacity crowd of 17,505 was clapping in rhythm and twenty-four basketball superstars were swaying in place along the foul lines. Those who saw it—in person or on television—call Gaye's performance one of the most memorable moments they've experienced.

"A serenity overcame me," remembers former Milwaukee Bucks forward Marques Johnson. "His voice just took over—you couldn't think about anything else."

Some twenty years later the rendition has taken on new meaning: Gaye's anthem serves as a bridge between a straitlaced league struggling to find its identity and a global entertainment powerhouse that embraces hip-hop culture. In a sense, the anthem foreshadowed the evolution of the NBA, from the era of tight shorts to today's baggy

---

Portions of this chapter originally appeared in *Los Angeles Magazine.*

models, from Jerry West's dribbling silhouette on the NBA logo to Michael Jordan's soaring Nike "Jumpman."

The anthem also proved to be the last hurrah for a singer whose musical genius was surpassed only by his personal torment. A little more than a year after singing the anthem he would be dead, shot by his own father in the family's Los Angeles home.

AT THE TWILIGHT'S LAST GLEAMING

In the late 1970s, the NBA was in the doldrums. There was talk that several teams might fold; CBS aired the championship series late at night, on tape delay. "Back then the NBA had a negative connotation surrounding it," says broadcaster Dick Stockton. "The perception was that drugs were a problem and that the league was 'too black.'"

Despite the NBA's downbeat image, Dr. Jerry Buss wanted in. A former chemist who had made millions investing in southern California real estate, Buss had taken a bath in his previous sports foray—the Los Angeles Strings of the World Team Tennis league. But in 1979, when Jack Kent Cooke decided to sell his West Coast properties after a nasty divorce, Buss jumped at the opportunity to purchase the Lakers (along with the Forum, the L.A. Kings hockey team, and a ranch) for $67.5 million.

Buss, who had earned his doctorate at USC, was determined to inject some college-style hoopla into the pros. He hired the NBA's first cheerleading squad (the ubiquitous Laker Girls) and a pep band; "Dancing Barry" boogied during timeouts. Buss also spent heavily to field an entertaining—and winning—team, led by Kareem Abdul-Jabbar and Earvin "Magic" Johnson. Thus "Showtime" was born—and the Fabulous Forum soon surpassed Dodger Stadium as the hottest sports spot in LA.

Buss encouraged the Lakers' director of promotions, Lon Rosen, to recruit celebrity anthem singers. R&B star Jeffrey Osborne became the team's Kate Smith—"the go-to guy for important play-off games," says Rosen—and everyone from actress Molly Ringwald to sax man Kenny G. made appearances. With so many of the music industry's top players sitting courtside—including former MCA Records president Irving Azoff, agent Mike Ovitz, and producer Lou Adler (the longtime season-ticket buddy of Jack Nicholson)—the anthem became a coveted (albeit unpaid) showcase at the Forum.

"Laker games were the schmooze headquarters of all time," says former Elektra Records head Joe Smith.

The 1983 All-Star game was the first to be held at the Forum since 1972, when LA's own "Mr. Clutch," Jerry West, connected on a twenty-foot buzzer-beater for a 112-110 win. (The 1963 game was held at LA's downtown Sports Arena, the Lakers' first home and, later, the home of the Clippers for many years.) Lakers executive vice president Jeanie Buss says her father actively campaigned for the midseason contest, which at the time was a low-key affair run by the host club. "He wanted to put it on in Jerry Buss style," she says. "He wanted to show off his town."

As his anthem singer Rosen originally selected Lionel Richie, the former Commodores' lead singer who had just recorded his first solo album, a multimillion seller for Motown. When Rosen phoned the NBA for its consent, however, an official asked, "Who's Lionel Richie?"

Somewhat taken aback at the league's ignorance of pop culture, Rosen sought recommendations from Magic Johnson and other Lakers. Gaye was among the artists suggested, and Rosen tracked him down at his new label, CBS Records. NBA officials approved the selection, probably assuming they were getting a Motown act.

Born and raised in a Washington, DC, slum, Gaye had endured an unhappy childhood. According to David Ritz, author of *Divided Soul: The Life of Marvin Gaye,* Gaye's father beat him regularly and disparaged his musical efforts. He dropped out of school after the eleventh grade and failed to complete a stint in the Air Force.

He found solace through music, initially with gospel. Gaye (he added the "e" to his family name) got his professional start with a doo-wop group called the Moonglows, led by singer-songwriter Harvey Fuqua. After going to Detroit with Fuqua in the early 1960s, Gaye caught on at Motown as a studio drummer. His luscious, elegant voice soon drew the attention of founder Berry Gordy, and with songs such as "Hitch Hike," "Ain't No Mountain High Enough" (with Tammi Terrell), and "I Heard It Through the Grapevine," Gaye helped to define Motown's hit-making, crossover sound.

After Gordy moved the company to Hollywood in the early 1970s, Gaye went west. He also expanded his repertoire beyond pure pop. His masterpiece album, *What's Going On,* addressed Vietnam, ghetto life, and even pollution. (Believing it to be too controversial, Gordy

initially refused to release it.) By the end of the decade Gaye was recognized as an icon, as relevant to his generation as Bob Marley and,
later, to a new generation, Kurt Cobain.

"His goal was to make people feel, because he believed in the healing power of music," says longtime friend Cecil Jenkins. "He always
said the world needs to know that we need to get together."

For all his commercial success, Gaye lived a troubled existence.
According to Ritz, the singer was a pothead and a cocaine addict.
Both of his marriages ended in divorce, and though he and his mother
were very close, he never reconciled with his father.

By 1981, Gaye had also broken with Gordy and Motown. Plagued
by tax and marital problems, he fled to Europe. After CBS producer
Larkin Arnold helped him to resolve his legal affairs, he recorded
Midnight Love, which featured "Sexual Healing" (cowritten by Ritz).
Released in October 1982, the single went to number one on *Bill-
board*'s soul chart and stayed there for four months. That same fall
Gaye returned to LA, in part because his mother was ill.

AND THE ROCKETS' RED GLARE

The playing of "The Star-Spangled Banner" at sporting events began during World War I, but it wasn't until World War II that it became common practice. Singers were expected to perform it in only
one style: conventional. "People like Robert Merrill sang it in the traditional way," says Towson State history professor David Zang, author of *Sports Wars: Athletes in the Age of Aquarius,* "with big sound,
keeping to the notes without variation."

Gaye had been asked to sing the anthem before game four of the
1968 World Series in Detroit. Broadcaster Ernie Harwell, who selected those singers, recalls that the Tigers' front office asked him to
advise Gaye to temper his approach. "They were worried about
Marvin because of his Motown connection," says Harwell, noting
that race riots had nearly destroyed the city in 1967. "They told me to
go to him and ask him to sing it a little more traditional than he might
ordinarily. He complied to that and sang it very straight."

The day after Gaye sang the anthem in Tiger Stadium, Jose
Feliciano strolled out to center field with an acoustic guitar and a
guide dog named Trudy. What followed was a revolution in A-flat:
Feliciano's groovy, folksy rendering is considered to be the first alter-

native anthem ever sung. The Francis Scott Key classic would never be the same.

"Until Feliciano, the Star-Spangled Banner was a patriotic introduction to sporting events," Zang says. "Now it's part of the entertainment package."

Following the 1968 Series, Gaye performed the anthem before Super Bowl V in 1971 and at the Ernie Shavers-Larry Holmes title fight eight years later. For the NBA All-Star game, Gaye told friends, he was determined to stylize the anthem in his own way. He was eager to sing it in front of the NBA's best. He knew many of the players, and he loved to play basketball at his Calabasas home or in the parking lot behind his recording studio in Hollywood.

"That was his release," says confidant Dave Simmons, who also served as his bodyguard. "He was not a great player by any stretch, but we'd go for hours every day. You know how it is: All athletes want to be singers, and all singers want to be athletes."

However, Gaye's fear of performing pulled him in another direction. Biographer Ritz says that Gaye asked Luther Vandross to substitute for him, but the crooner turned him down.

So Gaye called his brother-in-law Gordon Banks, with whom he had collaborated previously. The day before the game they worked furiously, using a drum machine and guitar to mix a background tape that Banks polished in his closet studio. The result was a languid, reggae-inspired rhythm similar to the sound that drove "Sexual Healing."

"Marvin told me that he was thinking about Mahalia Jackson and how she would do it," says Ritz. "He was grooving on the gospel aspect and how he was able to juxtapose patriotism with spiritualism and sexuality with spirituality."

"He said he wanted to move the minds of men when he sang it," says daughter Nona. "He wanted people to remember what the song meant."

The crew interrupted the taping session so that Gaye could rehearse at the Forum. According to Rosen, it was a disaster. Gaye arrived hours late and unveiled a four-and-a-half-minute version that neither rocked nor rolled. "I'm thinking, *That's not the anthem I learned in grade school*," says Rosen, who is now a television producer. "I didn't know what to do."

Rosen's concern was the song's length. He tried to explain that since CBS was broadcasting live, the song could take only two minutes. Gaye kept spinning away, refusing to speak to him. Philadelphia 76ers forward Julius Erving, who had just finished practice, played peacemaker, and Gaye finally agreed to return at eleven the next morning for a run-through.

By noon on game day—February 13—he had yet to show up. "That was typical," says his oldest son, Marvin III. "People learned not to rush my dad. He wasn't going on until he was ready."

"That's why they introduced him as 'The late Marvin Gaye,'" says daughter Nona.

Frantic, Rosen secured his usual backup, a Forum usher, and told her to be ready. At 12:25 p.m., five minutes before CBS was to go on the air, he spotted Gaye making his way down the arena's steep steps, dressed in a dark double-breasted suit and accompanied by a small entourage.

The singer said nothing as he handed over a cassette.

"Is it two minutes?" Rosen asked.

Gaye nodded, and a relieved Rosen had the tape rushed to the Forum's audio engineer. Lakers public address announcer Lawrence Tanter signaled CBS's Stockton, who introduced Gaye to the crowd.

As Gaye strolled onto the court, Banks's funkified mix began to beat softly. "I thought, Man, they brought the wrong cassette," says Tanter, who was also a jazz station DJ. "I thought, He's going to start singing 'Sexual Healing' instead of the anthem."

"When the drum track started," music executive Smith says, "Julius Erving and I made eye contact and shook our heads. It was like, *What is this?*"

Gaye sang the first words in a plaintive whisper, and as he wrapped his voice around "see," he was greeted by a waiting-to-exhale holler from several spectators. The response seemed to embolden Gaye, as if he could now trust in what he'd devised. Warming to the task, allowing the music to fill the long pauses he inserted between each line, he transformed the anthem into a sultry personal plea that was at once irreverent and sacred.

"I usually said the Lord's Prayer during the anthem," former Denver Nuggets forward Alex English says, "to get myself focused for each game. I saved it for later when I heard what Marvin was singing."

Tanter and Rosen both recall hearing scattered boos, but these were soon drowned out. Gaye punctuated "the rockets' red glare" with clenched fists and bended knees, and as he swept toward the conclusion the crowd joined in, clapping with the beat.

"He did the 'Banner' at a tempo that was so soulful it was overwhelming," music producer Adler says. "Every once in a while he'd do something vocally and they'd just scream and burst into emotional applause. It was very churchlike."

Gaye ended with an exhilarated "Whoa!" then blew kisses to the audience and bowed to each all-star team. As the lights flickered off his sunglasses, the ovation was thunderous. "That's when I first understood how special my dad really was," says son Marvin, then seventeen. "It was bone-chilling how everybody was screaming."

"It was so different that it reminded me of Jimi Hendrix's anthem at Woodstock," Abdul-Jabbar says. "Marvin changed the whole template, and that broadened people's minds. It illuminated the concept 'We're black and we're Americans. We can have a different interpretation [of the anthem], and that's okay.'"

"The whole thing about Marvin was that he played alternately the good boy and bad boy," Ritz says. "He rebelled against authority: You couldn't tell him what to do. But then he'd show up and perform— and perform magically."

The game itself became an afterthought, even though it featured eight members of the NBA's "50 Greatest Players" team. Led by Erving, Detroit's Isiah Thomas, and Boston's Larry Bird, the Kevin Loughery-coached East squad led the Pat Riley-coached West team 69-64 at halftime. In the second half, Erving took control. Delighting the crowd with a monstrous dunk over San Antonio Spurs center Artis Gilmore, Dr. J finished with a game-high 25 points and won his second all-star MVP honors in the East's 132-123 victory.

Erving's performance foreshadowed glory to come: That spring, the 76ers defeated the Lakers in the NBA Finals.

After the tip-off, Rosen retreated to his office. He was certain of only one thing: He would be fired. He fielded dozens of irate phone calls and received a quiet tongue-lashing from NBA commissioner Larry O'Brien, but he kept his job. In the weeks that followed he stayed busy filling requests for bootleg tapes.

"I still have mine," says Jeanie Buss. "I listen to it whenever I want to remember that incredible vibe."

Jabbar took one other memory from the game. Riley played San Antonio Spurs guard George Gervin just fourteen minutes, dissing the superstar on the national stage. A seething Gervin vowed to torch the Lakers at the next opportunity. Two nights later, the Iceman did just that, shooting 16-24 from the field and scoring 40 points in the Spurs' 124-103 drubbing of the Lakers at the Forum.

"He absolutely killed us," Jabbar says, laughing. "He didn't miss that night."

Commissioner O'Brien retired the next year, replaced by executive vice-president David Stern. With fortuitous timing and savvy marketing, Stern presided over the NBA's meteoric ascension. First, the NBA rode the Magic Johnson-Larry Bird matchup that renewed interest in the league on both coasts. In 1984, Michael Jordan entered the NBA—and the league suddenly had the world's most glamorous, and marketable, athlete. In leading the U.S. "Dream Team" to the 1992 Olympic gold medal, Jordan solidified the NBA's international popularity.

By then, the NBA had become prime-time fare. In the 1990s, as the league morphed into an entertainment juggernaut, its image became inextricably linked to youth culture and hip hop. Kids flash their Air Jordans; Snoop Dogg wears his favorite team jerseys in music videos; Lil' Bow Wow stars in the basketball film *Like Mike*.

"Marvin's anthem was an indication that the NBA was prepared to embrace the popular culture of America, with African Americans at the center of it," says University of Southern California cinema professor Todd Boyd, author of *Young, Black, Rich and Famous: The Rise of the NBA, the Hip Hop Invasion, and the Transformation of American Culture*. "As Stern brought his marketing skills to bear, the NBA went from being mildly popular in the early 1980s to becoming the worldwide commodity it is today—an identifiable American brand as visible as Starbucks and McDonald's."

O'ER THE LAND OF THE FREE AND THE HOME OF THE BRAVE

With his anthem in the news and "Sexual Healing" selling well, Gaye seemed to be making a comeback. Less than two weeks after the game he won his first two Grammy Awards. In March, he reunited with Gordy and sang "What's Going On" for Motown's twenty-fifth-anniversary television special (best remembered for Michael Jackson's bodacious moonwalk during "Billie Jean").

That summer Gaye toured in support of the album. His live performances became increasingly erratic. He would conclude each concert singing "Sexual Healing" while dressed in a bathrobe. Then he would remove the robe, have his pants pulled down by a backup singer, and stand onstage naked except for his briefs.

After the tour, according to friends, Gaye fell into a deep depression. Through the winter and spring he crashed at the West Adams home he'd bought for his parents. He refused entreaties to return to the studio and spiraled into a cocaine-induced haze.

"It got to the point where he didn't want to be here anymore," says Dave Simmons. "At the end, he wasn't the Marvin that I knew."

On April 1, 1984, an argument with his father turned violent. Reportedly, Gaye beat up Marvin Senior. Humiliated, the elder Gay retrieved a .38 revolver, went to his son's room, and shot him twice in the chest. He died at a local hospital.

Marvin Gaye would have turned forty-five the following day. At the Lakers' next home game, Rosen played Gaye's now-famous anthem in tribute.

You can hear Marvin Gaye's All-Star Game national anthem on *NBA at 50: A Musical Celebration* and *Marvin Gaye: The Master 1961-1984,* a four-CD compilation of his work.

Chapter 4

Nike and Popular Culture

Kelly McMasters

> I never wanted to sign with Nike. I had been an Adidas fanatic
> since high school.
>
> Michael Jordan

Sit back for a moment and try to imagine a world without Nike. It
is a surprisingly difficult thing to do. Would athletes still be wor-
shipped as demigods and rock stars? Would America still be so fit-
ness-obsessed, with exercise and gym culture an integral part of our
everyday lives? More important, would we all still have at least three
pairs of sneakers kicking around in our closets?

We will never know what a world without Nike might look like, but
had Michael Jordan chosen to ignore his parents' prodding in 1984
about a certain business trip to see a certain sportswear company, the
world certainly would not look exactly the way it does today. A
strange and serendipitous confluence of events led Nike to attain its
current powerhouse position, including the surge of America's fitness
culture in the 1970s and 1980s, Jordan's incredible breakout as undis-
puted king of the basketball court, the company's behemoth marketing strengths and pushes, and, not least of all, technological innovation involving a waffle iron.

But the times in which Nike grew and prospered are no longer as
apparent. Teenagers, that hallowed twelve-to-nineteen age group catered to by marketing and advertising agents, are different than they
were twenty years ago. They understand that McDonald's, Coca-
Cola, and Nike are corporations that are vying for their attention.
Nike has continued to go after markets outside of basketball to keep
profits up and to spread the power of the brand, and is currently on the

cusp of an attempt to take over the golf market. Tiger Woods is their acting Jordan for this campaign, but although golf is currently hot, it is not, nor will it be, what basketball was to teens in the 1980s and 1990s. Today's teens are well-versed in advertising culture and understand the power of the dollar and influence of their demographic; they will demand a solid product beyond the feelings and emotions that advertising promises them. The question is, will Nike be able to continue to deliver?

IT MUST BE THE SHOES

As a child growing up in the 1980s, I can remember when Reebok was Nike's biggest competitor. Teens, those lighthouses of consumerism that lead the way through the otherwise blinding night of popular culture, typically determine what will sink or swim within corporate markets. And in the 1980s, teens lined up behind Nike or Reebok the way their adult counterparts lined up behind the donkey or elephant banners of the Democratic and Republican parties. Your choice in sneakers communicated a message about you that could be conveyed by a single glance, and in our superficial culture, kids will pay a lot to get the most miles out of that brief encapsulating moment.

In my high school, the stoners and rockers wore high-top Converse, the geeks had Reeboks, and the popular kids laced up their Nikes every morning. Of course, there were the exceptions. Every girl also had her pair of white canvas Keds that would tumble in the washing machine during dinner after each wearing to keep them sparkling white. And the cheerleaders had the cool L.A. Gear sneakers that came with a collection of plastic triangles in different colors that could be affixed to the sneaker and color-coordinated to their uniforms. By the late 1980s and early 1990s, Ponys and KangaROOS had returned to animal status, and Adidas was on the cusp of a comeback, sparked by Run-D.M.C.'s 1986 song "My Adidas." Converse was reserved for the antiestablishment groups, but these will always be a minority in popularity-obsessed teen culture. That left Nike and Reebok.

But today, teenagers are living in a completely different consumer culture. They understand that they are the celebrated demographic and that marketing executives from Manhattan to Los Angeles spend their careers trying to get inside the circuitry of their brains. They are more disillusioned and less vulnerable to the entreaties of advertising than any prior generation.

There is also a current trend in the teenage population to buy items that will make them unique and help them to stand apart from their peers, rather than the typical striving for assimilation. Kids are buying from local stores and smaller labels in an attempt to assert themselves as different from everyone else. When I was growing up, Nike was still a relatively young company that was novel and fresh. Now, teenagers' parents are apt to wear Air Jordans to the gym. This does not bode well for Nike.

HE DREAMED OF THE GODDESS NIKE

Nike did not explode into the shoe market like some infallible supernova. In fact, the company was not even born into existence with the name Nike. It began as the small brainchild of a track runner and his coach under the name Blue Ribbon Shoes in 1964.

Bill Bowerman was coaching the field and track team at the University of Oregon when he first met Phil Knight. Bowerman was lauded as one of the top coaches in his area and Knight was a mediocre middle-distance runner that Bowerman took under his wing. Luckily, Knight made a better businessman than middle-distance runner, but the two formed a special bond with Bowerman acting as Knight's mentor, and they remained friends after Knight left the university for the U.S. Army Transportation Corps.

After serving his time in the Army, Knight returned to school, this time at Stanford University, where he studied for an MBA. Still interested in athletics, Knight's final research paper explored the possibility that Japan could be a worthwhile prospect for the production of athletic shoes. At the time, Germany was the dominant force in the industry and as a result controlled much of the industry's flow and price. Adidas owned the lion's share of the athletic shoe market in America.

After graduation, Knight made his way to Japan, hoping to test his theory. During his visit, Knight met with athletic shoe manufacturer Onitsuka Tiger Company and attempted to form a business alliance and convince them to sell their products in America. According to Nike company lore, Knight realized during his presentation that the only way he would be able to convince Onitsuka Tiger to work with him was if he presented himself as the owner of a company in the United States. On the spot, Knight made up the name Blue Ribbon Sports for the company that he pretended to own and, after a successful meeting with Onitsuka, scrambled back to the United States to start it.

Bowerman entered the picture in 1964, after agreeing to a partnership involving the two men in which they would both contribute $500 as seed money. Bowerman designed many of the prototypes for the shoes and Knight distributed the inventory from his father's basement. Knight also sold the Blue Ribbon Sports sneakers out of the trunk of his car at local and regional track meets, and the runners who used them would report back to Bowerman with design flaws and suggestions.

Over the next few years, both Knight and Bowerman continued to work part-time for Blue Ribbon Sports, while Knight toiled as an accountant to pay the bills and Bowerman continued coaching. The first full-time employee was hired in 1965. Jeff Johnson had met Knight at Stanford University, where he had been a middle-distance runner. Johnson opened Blue Ribbon Sports' first retail outlet in Santa Monica, California, in 1966. The three men remained intent upon the company's goal of producing high-quality, low-cost shoes in Japan and claiming the top spot in the athletic shoe market from Adidas.

In 1970, Bowerman (according to Nike) invented the waffle sole. Experimenting with urethane rubber, he poured the liquid compound into his wife's waffle iron. This sole made Nikes lighter than their competitors and also provided more traction. This experiment altered the way sneakers would be engineered from then on. A year later, Johnson claims he had a dream of the Greek goddess of victory, Nike, which was the inspiration for renaming the company. Knight enlisted Portland University graphic design student Carolyn Davidson to create the Swoosh trademark design for a $35 fee.

The Nike Waffle Trainer sneaker was introduced in 1974 and was based on Bowerman's experiments with his wife's kitchenware. It quickly became the leading athletic shoe in America, and Nike was on its way to becoming the juggernaut we know it as today.

AMERICA'S FITNESS REVOLUTION

Americans didn't always sweat for pleasure. Personal trainers, annual gym memberships averaging $1,500, and paying $50 for a pair of jogging pants are all ideas that would have been scoffed at before World War II. It wasn't until the 1970s that the concept of organized exercise infiltrated Americans' daily schedules and being fit became a sign of status, and Nike was positioned perfectly to benefit from the incredible burst of fitness obsession that took off in the late 1970s and continued into the 1980s.

Phil Knight and Bill Bowerman may have been obsessed with running culture, but even in the years in which Nike was first conceived (i.e., the Blue Ribbon Sports years), Americans had a completely different concept of physical fitness than we do today. Even Knight and Bowerman's obsession was linked to running as a sport. Competition and organized athletics were, of course, part of America's overall understanding of culture. But running for the sake of running rather than to prepare for a competition was still an alien concept. In postwar America, athletes went to gyms. Athletes pumped iron, and athletes purchased athletic wear. The rest of America was too busy working.

In the 1950s the concept of leisure was born. Americans started questioning their quality of life, and leisure time was equated with success. Massive economic growth afforded people more time to consider their social status within their communities, and leisure became the new currency.

Sneakers remained a specialty item in the 1950s, and could be found only in sporting goods stores or in regular shoe shops. According to the *St. James Encyclopedia of Popular Culture,* the early 1960s saw the opening of sneaker stores such as The Sneaker Shop of Bridgeport, Connecticut, and in the 1970s chain stores, including Foot Locker, were introduced in malls around the country.

A running boom took off in the late 1970s. Americans who had been examining their quality of life began worrying about their health and physical appearance and started using leisure time as an opportunity to become fit. The yuppies of the 1980s suddenly found themselves with obscene amounts of money and power. Many people no longer feared unemployment, economic instability, or providing for the family—problems that plagued earlier generations of Americans.

Instead, people grew afraid of the one thing that could impede their enjoyment of their newfound riches—their health.

The yuppie generation was, by nature, competitive and also extremely brand conscious. Status took the place of leisure time as the currency of the day and the concept of self-betterment ran rampant. People weren't interested in relaxing anymore. The competitive nature drew them into the gyms and onto the jogging paths; if they couldn't compete in the office, they would compete on the track.

During the late 1970s and early 1980s, obsession with labels exploded and high-profile designers such as Calvin Klein began producing fashion sneakers. This was the first time they were introduced into the casual wear category, and by 1978 sneakers amounted to 50 percent of all shoes sold.

Nike's popularity skyrocketed during this time with the launch of the Nike Air Tailwind model, which incorporated a patented Air-Sole cushioning system. By the 1980s, Nike added windows in the sole to display the pockets of air. Sports became a cultural obsession, replacing music, which had functioned as the most captivating medium in the sixties.

In *Just Do It: The Nike Spirit in the Corporate World,* author Donald Katz quotes Nike President and CEO Phil Knight as saying that if Nike didn't spawn the fitness revolution, "we were at least right there. And we sure rode it for one hell of a ride." Nike was able to hitch itself to the coattails of the fitness boom and use it to their advantage, pumping up the importance of being fit and promising a better life through a better body.

Through marketing, Nike glamorized athletes and athleticism. The company cast sport as the ultimate measure of a person's worth and the physical body mirrored that worth. Athletes were perceived as gods, and sport was placed on the highest social pedestal. The football players had historically held the title of most popular athletes in high school and kids were judged by their shoes while walking in the hallway on the way to homeroom, but adults also suddenly found that their physical structure mattered more than ever. Being skinny was no longer enough; women now had to be buff, like Linda Hamilton in *Terminator 2.* Men who were good-looking were still fulfilling only half of the new attractiveness requirements; they needed to have a sculpted back and washboard abs to be truly successful. Everyone now strove to be an athlete.

Nike's mission statement made this even easier for people. The company claims their duty is "To bring inspiration and innovation to every athlete in the world." There is an asterisk after the word "athlete" and a message underneath the mission explains: "* if you have a body, you are an athlete." Nike thereby redefined the concept of athlete in two ways. First, Nike showed us that athletes were demigods and athlete status was a goal for mortals to strive for. The second way Nike made us understand the athlete concept, however, was by promising us that if we wanted to become an athlete, a demigod, then we could. All we needed was a pair of Nike sneakers to get us started.

THE JORDAN FACTOR

Using Michael Jordan to sell Nike products may have been the company's smartest move, but it was far from original. It was not even the first time Nike used a sports celebrity to advocate their product; tennis-extraordinaire and emotional fireball John McEnroe signed a deal with Nike in 1978, starting with signature shoes and moving on to apparel in 1986. Nike claims McEnroe's fiery personality and colorful character reflected the company's persona.

Chuck Taylor became the first athlete to endorse a basketball shoe in 1923. A high school basketball star, Taylor played professional basketball before league organizations were formed, playing with the original Celtics as well as the Buffalo Germans and Akron Firestones. Much like Nike's cofounder and CEO Phil Knight, Taylor was an athlete who happened to have a genuine interest in athletic shoes.

Unlike Knight, who started his own business, Taylor was interested in getting a sales job with Converse, a company he regarded highly in the athletic shoe business. Taylor showed up at the Converse Chicago sales offices in 1921 looking for a job and was met by S. R. Pletz, who was in charge of the Chicago sales office at the time. Pletz and Taylor immediately got along well and Taylor was hired that day, the first of many professional basketball players to become part of the Converse management team.

Taylor, like Bowerman, was interested in the mechanics of the shoe and offered ideas on how to improve the Converse basketball models. Within a year, the company put Taylor's suggested changes into effect, improving the All-Star model and making it an even better basketball shoe. In recognition of his contribution, Chuck Taylor's signature was added to the All-Star ankle patch in 1923.

According to Converse mythology, Taylor was the ultimate Willy Loman, taking his sneakers on the road and driving to small towns all over America to hawk them. Steve Stone, former Converse president, has said, "Chuck's gimmick was to go to a small town, romance the coach and put on a clinic. He would teach basketball, but without encroaching on the coach's own system. He drove a big car, a Cadillac. And his home was the back of the car. He was a pipe smoker and talked with an Indiana drawl." Taylor's commitment to Converse and basketball pushed the company's standing to its pinnacle in the basketball market. Converse would not be recognized worldwide today had it not been for Chuck Taylor.

Jordan's truest forerunner, however, was Julius Erving. Also associated with Converse, Erving's name became synonymous with Converse basketball shoes in the 1970s, when people would simply ask for a pair of "Dr. J's." Erving is Jordan's self-proclaimed idol and when Jordan was deciding what company to sign with in 1984, he thought a lot about Erving's experience. "In retrospect, they squeezed the equity out of Julius Erving without ever paying for it," Jordan recalls in his book, *For the Love of the Game.* "[My deal with Nike] was risky because no one in the industry had done anything like that. Julius Erving became identified with a specific shoe, but he was never compensated the way I was going to be."

Ultimately, compensation was the only reason Jordan decided to sign with Nike and not with Adidas, as he had hoped, or Converse, who at the time had an incredible roster of athletes attached to its name. Magic Johnson, Isiah Thomas, Larry Bird, Mark Aguirre, and Dr. J were all playing with Converse on their feet in 1984. But Jordan had been an Adidas fanatic since high school, and it was Adidas that he really wanted to sign with.

In his book, Jordan recalls preparing for the Nike meeting. He was feeling "like I was dragged out to Oregon to listen to something I had no intention of acting upon." Jordan had already spent the majority of the summer of 1984 on airplanes between awards banquets, the Bulls, and the Olympics. Jordan's parents finally sat him down and said, "This is important. You need to listen to what these people have to say." He finally gave in and traveled to Oregon, walking in to a meeting that included Rob Strasser, Phil Knight, Tinker Hatfield, Jack

George, Peter Moore, and Howard White. Jordan remained unimpressed until Strasser began detailing an agreement that would give Jordan his own shoe. But, he recalled, "I was skeptical because I didn't even like Nike shoes."

The monetary part of the agreement, however, gave Jordan plenty to like. The offer included $250,000 a year for five years with an annuity, incentives, and royalties on all Nike basketball-related items. Jordan remembered the meeting ending with him thinking, "Fine, now let's go see what Converse has in mind. Then I'm going to sign with Adidas."

After the meeting in Oregon, Jordan approached Adidas on his own. He told Adidas what Nike was offering him and made it clear that they needed only to come close in order for him to sign with them. Jordan also met with Converse at their corporate headquarters outside of Boston. He had worn Converse when he played for North Carolina and felt an obligation to listen to what they offered. In his book, Jordan says, "Their offer was pennies to the dimes Nike was offering. Their top guys were all making $100,000 a year and Dr. J wasn't even making royalties on his shoe." They refused to compromise, and so did Jordan. Adidas never even made an offer. By the end of the negotiations, Jordan's choice was clear.

What Jordan may not have realized at the time, however, was how much of Nike's future was riding on his decision. Jordan's book details Nike's poor financial state at the time, explaining, "[Nike's] stock had dropped by more than half, and was down around $6 a share in 1984. Strasser had to take a gamble. And he did. He wanted to change the entire market by betting on one person. Nike didn't have a second choice. He was a genius. It worked."

Rather than going after a group of athletes, the way many other athletic shoe companies, including Converse, were doing at the time, Nike decided to put all of its proverbial eggs in one basket. That basket was Michael Jordan, and Nike did not approach anyone but Jordan that summer. Instead of spreading their money around, they had made the decision to pump all of the money available into one star player, when they had no guarantee he would not get injured or lose his ability to perform. But Jordan was the perfect player to bet on, and as his career became increasingly more golden, so did Nike's financial status. The company's gross revenues in 1984 totaled

$986,000,000. In the year ending May 31, 2002, they topped out at $9,893,000,000.

THE MAGIC'S IN THE MARKETING

Shortly after he officially signed with Nike, Jordan started the 1984-1985 basketball season wearing the original black and red Air Jordan shoe. After the third game of the season, the NBA decided to ban Jordan's Nike sneakers because they didn't conform to the rest of the Bulls uniform. Jordan refused to change his sneakers and David Stern, National Basketball Association Commissioner, began fining Jordan. In his book, Jordan says, "I think it started at one thousand dollars a game, then went to three thousand, and eventually five thousand dollars. Nike didn't blink."

Rather than blink, Nike was ecstatic. They understood that the attention and publicity they were getting on the court for the sneakers was more effective than any of the ad campaigns they had come up with to support Jordan and his shoes. Nike paid the fines and used the ban as an opportunity to launch an entirely new advertising campaign.

Jordan remembers that the very first Nike commercial that he was involved in started with a camera shot of his head and slowly moved down his body to his feet. "When the camera hit the shoes, a big X was stamped on the screen and the announcer said, Banned! Right after that, sales went crazy."

Nike excelled at using organic instances such as the banning of the first Air Jordan shoes to strengthen its identity. Another simple example of this is their decision to promote their brand internationally without translations. In 1988, Nike announced their new slogan: Just Do It. The original intent not to translate the slogan was based on a desire to foster many international markets' love of American popular culture. But this was also a pragmatic move. Company lore holds that a Japanese executive made a presentation to Nike that outlined possible translations of the Just Do It advertising campaign. One option was a phrase close to "Hesitation makes waste." Knight refused to water down the campaign and decided that by keeping the slogan in English throughout the international campaigns, it would only strengthen the brand and promote the fact that it was American, something that at the time was considered a major selling point for Nike products in the international market.

GOING GLOBAL

Unless Nike is comfortable with topping off at an almost ten-billion-dollar annual gross revenue, the company will need to recognize the changing pattern of American teen consumers as well as international consumers. Beginning with running, the heart of Nike's program was quickly eclipsed by basketball once Michael Jordan entered the picture. Now, with Michael Jordan officially retired (yet again) and with the basketball market for all intents and purposes exhausted, Nike is looking at other markets and in different geographic places for its next attack. But will the company be able to duplicate its success?

As James Surowiecki points out in his June 10, 2002, "Turf War" article in *The New Yorker,* Nike has attempted to extend its brand into markets such as skateboard shoes, hiking boots, and rowing machines, all with little success. And when the company set its sights on taking down Adidas from the top spot in soccer shoes, Nike went into the ring prepared with celebrity sports endorsements and a strong advertising campaign. But after spending hundreds of millions of dollars on marketing, Nike still lags behind Adidas in the soccer category for the simple reason that it is pushing an inferior product. Nike's soccer shoe is "notoriously flawed," writes Surowiecki, and Nike needs to learn a lesson from this gaff that markets cannot be won by advertising alone.

Nike has also been striving to build local appeal in international markets rather than relying on the Cold War logic that anything American sells. Nike is preparing to hone in on and explore specific markets, creating handball shoes for Denmark and cricket shoes for the United Kingdom and Australia. The Just Do It slogan will still remain in English in the advertising campaigns that will accompany this international push, but now Nike will attempt to sell the international community products that will seem more organic to specific communities rather than trying to simply export American sport and push American culture.

In *Jihad* v. *McWorld,* Benjamin Barber quotes Knight as saying, "Our target consumers have been watching John McEnroe and Charles Barkley for years. The emotional ties are in place." Barber contends that Nike is not trying to export sneakers, but Michael Jordan himself. "Chairman Knight assures us [that Michael Jordan] is tied for first place in China as the world's greatest man with Chou En-lai" (one-time foreign minister and central figure in the Chinese-U.S. rapprochement). Barber quotes Knight from Nike's 1992 Annual Report: "How do we expect to conquer foreign lands? The same way we did here. We will simply export sports, the world's best economy." But Barber points out that Nike's advertising campaign does more than focus on sports. Nike is selling "the image and ideology of sports: health, victory, wealth, sex, money, energy—don't name it, just do it."

This approach may be what has brought Nike such immense success in the past, but the world looks very different post-September 11, 2001. America is no longer synonymous with unparalleled victory and infallibility. The tectonic plates of premise that Nike built their campaigns upon have shifted dramatically in the past few years, and if the company is to continue to be successful, Nike will have to recognize this and reform their advertising strategy.

Nike has undoubtedly influenced American popular culture over the past twenty years. And, like McDonald's and Coca-Cola, Nike is setting its sights globally, understanding that America offers limited potential since the company has already infiltrated and conquered. In *Jihad* v. *McWorld,* Barber quotes the late Coca-Cola CEO Roberto C. Goizueta: "How long can a company of our scope keep doubling its size? Where will the next 10 billion unit cases come from? And the 20 billion after that? The fact is, that we are just now seriously entering and developing soft drink markets that account for the majority of the world's population. These new worlds of opportunity are not only heavily populated, but also culturally and climatically ripe for significant soft drink consumption." Coca-Cola is right that climatically, where it is hot, people are thirsty. But what is Nike's equivalent here?

Sport is universal, but also geographically personal. Cubans love baseball as much as Americans, but hate the economics that plague the American game and won't respond to the same advertising tactics that Americans would. Nike has already begun to take cues from McDonald's (a company that removed beef from its restaurants in India and added a Teriyaki McBurger to its menu in Japan) and has re-searched and attempted to infiltrate local sports such as handball in the Netherlands. But this takes many more advertising and research dollars than it takes to revise a form menu of a chain restaurant.

In America, Nike is currently launching an attack on the golf in-dustry. It began in 2000 with Nike's Precision Tour Accuracy golf balls, a product that enjoyed success after Tiger Woods, Michael Jor-dan's celebrity golfer counterpart, began using them. Then, in 2001, David Duval used Nike's new line of clubs to win the British Open.

Even if Nike's golf products are made better than their soccer shoes, the company may not be as successful as they hope in the golf arena. Many young people are interested in the game, but it will never take on the raw and sexy appeal that basketball has enjoyed the past few decades.

In his *New Yorker* article, James Surowiecki explains that in the five years preceding 2002, "Nike has added three billion dollars in sales but less than forty million dollars in actual profit." Nike's stock price (NKE) has stagnated as a result of this fall in return on equity.

Nike's hegemony in the basketball market remains, but because they have already conquered this ground they don't have much room to grow. The company's plans for the golf market will most likely not be enough to pull them out of the slump of profit stagnation, and their international campaign needs to be re-skewed in light of the events of 2001 and America's decaying popular culture superpower image.

Combine all of these roadblocks with a new generation of teen-agers who are more well versed in advertising than any generation previously, and it seems that Nike's reigning era may be over. Suro-wiecki made the point that if Nike started selling light bulbs, someone would buy them. The days are over when kids will kill one another for a pair of Air Jordan shoes, and frankly, that is a good thing.

Chapter 5

Hoosiers to *Hoop Dreams:*
Basketball on the Big Screen

Kevin Grace

I

In the 1986 film *Hoosiers,* an early scene portrays basketball coach Norman Dale, played by Gene Hackman, in his role as a civics teacher at the fictional Hickory High School. He is dressed in the 1950s male teacher uniform of shirt and tie, and as a student gives an oral report to the class, Dale leans back in his desk chair with a bemused air, a well-traveled man whose teaching job in civics is to bring an appreciation of some of the outside world to Hickory, Indiana. After school, however, his teaching shifts to the basketball court, where he creates his own world and assimilates his players into a hoops culture that is just a bit foreign to them.

In the classroom scene, one of his players is giving a report on the idea of "Progress," a worldly notion, and how it affects his own life. The player is Ollie, the manager and uniformed runt of the team. His role on the basketball squad is to serve mainly as practice fodder. Ollie reads aloud to the class: "Progress. Progress is electricity, school consolidation, church remodeling, second farm tractors, second farm cars, hay balers, corn pickers, grain combines, field choppers, and indoor plumbing."

Ollie's classmates laugh at the concluding item on the list, Coach Dale chuckles, and the bell rings, ending the period. But the thought lingers as the students file out into the hall: progress. For a rural Indiana basketball player in 1952, progress has a great deal to do with how he views the game he loves. There are the material benefits to farm life in the prosperous years following World War II to consider, but there is also the movement to consolidate schools in the 1950s and 1960s, a reference Ollie makes in his illustration of how times change.

Many country schools with inadequate facilities, few science labs, and small student enrollment, similar to *Hoosiers'* Hickory High, would be combined during those years in order to improve educational standards, thus gaining something valuable in the formalized world of the classroom but perhaps losing a measure of their identities in the process. *Hoosiers* uses basketball to focus on this community identity, this progress of a small, lone, and unconsolidated school caught in the cyclone of Norman Dale's forceful practice and game strategies to roll to the state championship against the big-city school from South Bend.

The film becomes an exemplar of the sports movie in America— change in a land of constant changes, the promises of both hard work and good works overcoming the odds against success, flights of individual achievement grounded to team rewards, and, especially, redemption. Always, redemption. Because sport serves nothing if not to somehow make amends for past or present shortcomings as we strive for victory. We love this in the movies. There—on the hoops silver screen—we see redemption for past failures; redemption for our society in the face of problems such as racism, gender inequities, poverty, and crime; and redemption of the inner self.

Much of our relationship to movies is reflective of our perceived interaction with the everyday world. There is, of course, the role of cinema in providing escape from our everyday cares and concerns, and sports films certainly have a financial and cultural stake in this aspect. But more than that, sports movies reflect what we would like to believe about sports, something sociologist Harry Edwards once termed the "Dominant American Sports Creed."[1] Edwards's classic theory states that Americans desire a certain credo attached to athletic activity. That by participating in sports one attains self-discipline, acquires a devotion to teamwork, becomes aware of the value of civic responsibility and patriotism, and embraces a religiosity—all qualities that make us more worthwhile Americans. These factors about sport *may* or *may not* be true; often they are not and sometimes they are—at least enough to keep the creed alive and well. But this is what "sports" are about in American culture, and as a viewing of *Hoosiers* demonstrates, this is what we appreciate.

The small Hickory High team bonds with the community, they eventually come to work together as a unit, and each player gives his utmost. Anything else would be un-American. The movie is almost a worshipful incarnation of this dominant American sports creed. When *Hoosiers* is placed in context with the basketball films predating its release and with the films in the past fifteen years, including gritty documentaries, such as *Hoop Dreams* in 1994, as well as other feature movies, there is an immediate recognition factor of American society on the screen.

II

Since the appearance of *Hoosiers* in 1986, basketball has become a favored theme for sports films, clearly surpassing feature films about football and golf, and rivaling the cultural place of baseball in the national cinematic consciousness.[2] Filmmaker John Sayles, one of whose most popular movies was the 1988 screen adaptation of Eliot Asinof's history of the Chicago White Sox gambling scandal in 1919, *Eight Men Out,* acknowledges the importance of baseball in his life and as an influence on his career: "Baseball is the sport of my youth. It was the sport you could play when you were a kid. The ball wasn't too big for your hand, like a football or a basketball is . . . it's also the sport of America's youth, and writers and poets often evoke it as the American sport. . . . The fact is that baseball lends itself to movies because the rhythm of the sport is about a drum-roll. It's about situations where somebody is facing somebody else. It stops . . ."[3]

Although baseball clearly has a pedigree that outstrips basketball in fiction, reporting, film, and cultural references, a contemporary sense of basketball appears in the past quarter century that embraces not only the nostalgic American "values" in baseball lore but couples it with the issues of today as well. It "stops" as well. It is one-on-one. It is one kid against himself, banging the ball off the backboard or garage door, hitting the bottom of the net from the outside, and then sinking the winning shot in an imaginary championship game. Basketball can be a drum-roll too, rumbling on the court toward a deafening clash of cymbals.

The social aspects that can be explored in basketball, the personal issues that will be raised to the surface, the dramatic movement of the game with its time-out hesitations building toward the climax all serve in the recognition of the basketball court as the current Every-home in the United States. Whether the scenes are set in the small gyms and farmyards of the Midwest, the blacktop courts, or the mu-sic-blasted, laser-lighted arenas of urban America, basketball films carry a sense of immediate identification of place and action. Street-ball replaces the sandlot.

Nearly 100 commercial basketball-oriented movies have been pro-duced since 1927, when a marginal film called *High School Hero* made its appearance, and 75 percent of these were released after the 1986 *Hoosiers,* attesting that hoops have become a large part of the sports film genre.

Part of the appeal of basketball films is the wide diversity—male and female, black and white, rich and poor, urban and rural—of those who can play and enjoy the game, in greater numbers than any other sport. When James Naismith created the game in 1891, it was initially developed as a male, Christian, and mostly white activity. However, it was rapidly adopted and adapted by women in colleges and high schools. Basketball found its way into the African-American recre-ation centers, schools, and YMCAs in Midwestern and Eastern sea-board cities. The game became entrenched as a mainstay activity in urban Jewish and tenement life, again through recreation centers and the settlement houses of the Progressive Era, between 1890 and 1920.[4] In the assimilation of basketball into the nation's conscious-ness, much of the early awareness of it centered on its role as part of the educational enterprise in America. It was an easy-to-place activity in high schools and colleges, with its minimal need for space, equip-ment, and players. As Naismith found in his reasoning for developing the game, basketball was a wintertime diversion that kept the attention of students and gave them a rallying point for school spirit.

This integration of basketball with school spirit and the uplifting aims of education during the Progressive Era carried into juvenile fic-tion of the age, and would eventually find its way into film. One of the earliest recorded fictional stories on basketball appeared in 1901 by Burt L. Standish, a prolific writer of boys' sports stories in the early part of the twentieth century. The story was one of the Dick Merriwell series, titled *Dick Merriwell's Promises.* The colorful cover of the dime novel shows a group of high school boys on the court, dressed in the quilted, football-style pants still used in basketball at that time, shooting the ball into a closed-net hoop. The story is no different from any of the other Merriwell tales: young Dick overcomes deceit, bad timing, and numerous other obstacles to win an important game. He achieves the victory through old-fashioned values, and wins the favor of his classmates.

Over the next two decades, basketball as a virtuous activity and as a socialization process reached higher levels in books aimed at juvenile girls, novels in which young women become accepted in high school life by participating in the game, thus making friends and establishing a pattern for success in life.[6] These concepts of basketball then began making their way into the entertainment world, particularly in a 1907 musical comedy called *Cupid at Vassar.* The play was billed as the "American Musical College Girl Play" and promotional items featured girls playing "basket ball." From the juvenile novels, short fiction, and the theater, Hollywood would take its cue for its portrayal of hoops. In the film industry's first presentation of basketball as entertainment in 1927, it would use the traits that a half-century later would be codified in Harry Edwards' dominant American sports creed.

III

The Fair Co-Ed was released by Metro-Goldwyn-Mayer in 1927 and starred Marion Davies and Johnny Mack Brown. The movie involves a girl who goes to college only because she is smitten by the handsome man who coaches the girls' team. She spurns the concept of "teamwork" when she has a love tiff with the coach, but in true American sports creed fashion, rejoins the team for a crucial game and scores the winning points.

High School Hero actually followed *The Fair Co-Ed* in release just a day later. Written by veteran actor and director David Butler and newspaperman William Conselman, the movie was also directed by Butler. It is standard material about high school. Two rivals in the school named Pete Greer and Bill Merrill are competing for the affections of the campus lovely, Eleanor Barrett. The students are staging an amateur play, and in the process of the dispute between Pete and Bill, the play, as one expects, is ruined. They continue their battle on the basketball court, letting their differences affect their game. In the end, though, there is resolution. Although the movie is somewhat entertaining (this early basketball scene is historically interesting), it did establish an additional foothold for basketball on the screen. In 1928, a two-reel silent film titled *Rah! Rah! Rah!* was released that treated the hazing rites on a college girls' team.

A few years later, in 1931, Fox released *Girls Demand Excitement,* starring a young John Wayne in a mild look at the rivalry between the boys' and girls' teams in a high school. Wayne would appear in another "basketball" film in 1941, *A Man Betrayed* (later released as *Wheel of Fortune*), in which a small-town basketball star is murdered in the big city. This idea of heartland values versus urban evils resurfaced in many other basketball movies.

Basketball made it to movie theaters again, in *Campus Confessions* and *Angels with Dirty Faces* (both in 1938), followed by *All-American Blondes* in 1939 and in another six years, *Here Come the Co-Eds* in 1945, an Abbott and Costello light comedy vehicle that includes some basketball scenes at a female college.

Until this point, Hollywood explored basketball as it reflected school life in America, that is, the same everyday elements that made up a student's life—sports, rivalries, socialization, adolescence, and the striving for maturity—with the interesting emphasis on the cultural presence of girls in basketball uniforms. This emphasis would be diminished in the 1940s, 1950s, 1960s, and the 1970s, as female participation in competitive sport was itself diminished.[7]

In the early years of basketball in film, moviegoers did not accept the theme of the game as readily as baseball. Basketball did not have the heritage, and it was still viewed as a part of school days rather than something holding a larger role in society. As screenwriter Ring Lardner Jr. said of his father, Ring Sr., one of the great sports journalists and short fiction writers of the twentieth century: "Basketball he regarded with the distaste of a true conservative for a sport that had been invented during his lifetime."[8]

Basketball was merely evocative of the experiences of a couple of generations of schoolchildren. As those generations matured, the game became a subject for not only light comedy but also dramatic treatment. Basketball films would be approached from a variety of film interests: crime and society, fantasy and slapstick comedy, urban life, enfranchisement of women, racial conflict and resolution, and the chronicling of real life in the form of biopics and documentaries.

IV

As the game of basketball became more mainstream in American life following World War II—primarily through development of relatively stable professional leagues and the building excitement over the college game and its postseason tournaments—it was natural to expect that elements of basketball would be explored beyond the hallways and gyms of high school. In the face of this mainstreaming, one Hollywood consideration, which developed in the 1950s and remains a strong part of filmdom's approach to basketball today, is that society itself can corrupt the game.

In 1951, the infamous college basketball gambling scandals came to light.[9] For many years, with the development of the point spread system by mathematician cum oddsmaker Charles K. McNeil and the innovation of doubleheaders at Madison Square Garden, gamblers have embraced the excitement of college basketball and the financial possibilities of betting the spread. There is a long history of gambling on basketball—as the nature of sport has been of inherent interest for wagering since the dawn of competition—and the betting on games accelerated in the late 1940s.

Most of the action was centered in New York, the mecca of hoops at the time, though there were certainly colleges all over the country that were involved. The most notorious stage of the scandals came when the City College of New York, Long Island University, the University of Kentucky, Bradley University, and several other schools were the subject of investigation by the district attorney in New York City. In 1951, by the time the trials had run their course and some players, coaches, and bettors had had their lives turned upside down, Hollywood was already considering development of film treatments about college basketball gambling. Before the year was out, *The Basketball Fix* would be in theaters, starring John Ireland, Marshall Thompson, and Vanessa Brown.

This movie exploited the fascination people had with the daily media reports of the real investigation and subsequent trials: former Long Island University player Eddie Gard, in cahoots with gambler Salvatore "Tarto" Sollazzo to bribe players in New York City colleges to "shave" a few points off the score by altering their performance on the court, thus beating or dropping under the spread as demanded by the gamblers.

The importance of *The Basketball Fix* was not its entertainment quality, but its comment on basketball and society. Always regarded by the general public as pure in its "amateur" college form until this point in time, basketball was thought to be immune from the worst elements of American life. That something such as the real-life scandals could occur forced moviegoers to accept them in reel-life form as well. It was dejecting. Americans still held on to their creed of the value and importance of sport, but it was with a tenuous grasp.

College basketball gambling scandals have surfaced every decade or so since then, so it is with a somewhat jaded eye that moviegoers approach films about the college game today. In 1960, the film *Tall Story* came to theaters. For the most part a comedy about a girl (Jane Fonda) going to college to snare a husband (Tony Perkins), underlying the movie's romance was again the element of throwing a game. Perkins is set up by gamblers to lose a game against a visiting Soviet squad, throwing into the mix Cold War politics, societal wrongs, girl-meets-boy, and responsibility and loyalty to one's alma mater. Wagering of some sort has now become an indelible part of the basketball movie. Whether it is a serious drama of a compulsive gambler trying desperately to break even (1974's *The Gambler*), to paying for the services of college basketball recruits (1994's *Blue Chips*), corruption is part of the action.

In *Blue Chips,* Nick Nolte plays a college coach in a fading program with high alumni demands for a winning team. Thinking of himself as honest to the bone, he resists the coaching fraternity's practice of offering enticements to recruits and their families. But faced with the distinct possibility of losing his job, he caves in and pays a recruit to attend his West Coast school. Interestingly enough, the movie brings in for cameos such people as Bobby Knight, who has always positioned himself as a moral standard in the recruiting wars. Other notable basketball personalities also appear in the film— Shaquille O'Neal, Bob Cousy, and Larry Bird among them, and even former University of Nevada-Las Vegas and Fresno State University coach Jerry Tarkanian, long branded by the media as one of the shadier figures in college recruiting.

Nolte regains his moral balance by the end of the film, leaving mainstream viewers pleased with a neat little resolution. Corruption has been bested. Real life, however, is much messier. For instance, in our culture there has always been a consistent contrast between rural and urban. Because "urban" connotes teeming masses of different ethnicities, races, and religions, and because cities are often anonymous places perceived as permitting more expressions of personal freedom, and because larger populations give rise to more disparate points of view, we assign values to geographical society. Rural values are more homogeneous, more community-oriented, more expressive of religious faith, honesty, accountability, and hard work. In our national creed, this is the ideal image of rural life.

However, in *Blue Chips,* one of the corrupt recruits is a farm boy who accepts a new tractor for his family by the high bidder for his college services. It provides a striking counterpoint to the nostalgic rural world of *Hoosiers,* where the second farm tractor desired by Ollie as part of "progress" is as likely to be a used one as it is certain to be earned by honest labor. The script of *Blue Chips* was written by Ron Shelton, who two years before directed the now classic *White Men Can't Jump.* One of the best lines in that film—a movie about streetball hustle and bets—is when Billy Hoyle (Woody Harrelson) says to Sidney Deane (Wesley Snipes): "I don't hustle with someone who isn't honest." Oftentimes it requires teamwork to cheat. In the case of *Blue Chips,* it is father and son. In the case of *Hoosiers,* it is only the somewhat external evil of referees, acting as "homers" for opposing teams, who conspire to rob the Hickory team of hard-earned wins.

V

Hollywood's treatment of women as part of basketball has the same societal conflicts as it does with the dichotomy between rural and urban. In the early films, women were treated as girls, anxious to please one another and coyly manipulate their elders and their boyfriends. But they were still players, still competing on the court. By the end of the 1950s, they gave up their role as athletes to assume the Eisenhowerian role of going to college to find a mate, and if that mate happened to be involved in basketball, to take a supporting, and supportive, role. Thus, Jane Fonda in *Tall Story* can get away with a feigned interest in the game in order to snare a husband. Women essentially became benign cheerleaders without the gymnastics. They were the background scenery. In the 1970s, even as Title IX (1972) began to chip away at the barriers confronting competitive, athletic women that had been steadily erected since the 1920s, women were only occasionally outside the norm of supporting role. The 1978 film *Coach* features actress Cathy Lee Crosby as an Olympic athlete who accidentally becomes the coach of a high school boys' basketball team.

The more standard roles were in such low-budget films as *Splitz* (1984), an example of the drive-in movie genre that provides semi-nude sorority girls cavorting on a basketball court to prove a point, win a wager, or, simply, to appear undressed. It was great viewing fun for college boys and adolescents. In truth, the film represents a reaction against the growing emancipation of women in everyday life. College campuses of the late 1960s and early 1970s were fertile fields for social examination and the struggle for equal rights. And films such as *Splitz* covered up the issues with a mindless, meaningless appeal to traditional stereotypes.

Though *Coach* was played for comedic effect, the notion of a woman coaching a male team continues in the movies. In the 1996 movie *Eddie,* Whoopi Goldberg plays an earnest New York Knicks fan who becomes the coach through the owner's public relations shenanigans. The coach acquits herself admirably, fulfilling the desires for a comedy's standard ending. But in Rhea Perlman's role as a female coach of a New York City boy's team in *Sunset Park* (1996), the film is handled as a drama with occasional loopy situations tossed in to let the moviegoer know that the film is still about high school kids who love hoops.

The real conflict in the film is not about nontraditional gender roles as much as it is about race: the coach is white and her players are African American. She cannot possibly understand the culture of hoops that they bring to the court, their style of play, their jockeying for dominant-male status. Even though the female coach only takes the position of heading the boys team in order to earn extra money and extricate herself from the ghetto and the city, basketball is also a release from these surroundings for her players, a common theme found in such movies as *Above the Rim* (1994), *Finding Forrester* (2000), and *The Red Sneakers* (2001), the latter a Showtime cable movie also released as a commercial video.

The urban setting of *Sunset Park* contributes to the conflict and resolution of differences between the races. Perlman's players come to accept her; she maintains her standing as a teacher by asserting authority, but she is also won over by their own inner-city approaches to the game. But again, the message is that teamwork always wins out, that the players and coach are better people for being part of the game, and that the players will now go forth to educate themselves and to make positive contributions to society.

Gender sensuality, as opposed to sexuality, is also explored in the basketball films of the past twenty-five years. *Late Bloomers,* a small independent film of 1996, took on the issue of a lesbian romance between a female basketball coach and a teacher. The female athlete as a strong and sensual person, who also happened to be very good at basketball, was expressed in 2000's *Love and Basketball,* starring Omar Epps and Sanaa Lathan as the two main characters, a man and woman who are childhood rivals and friends. Both become scholarship players at the university, both try to maintain their basketball careers as they struggle at the same time to maintain their friendship, a relationship that darts at the edges of romance. At the movie's end, they reverse the traditional roles: now married, Epps supports his wife, the professional basketball player.

In a comedic contrast to *Love and Basketball,* a film such as *Juwanna Mann* (2002) seeks to celebrate the emerging appeal of professional women's basketball and at the same time stereotypes female basketball players as having a weaker game than men. To be fully acknowledged as professional athletes, they actually need a man on the team (hence the forced humor of the title); otherwise the women have only the potential of being champions. In the film, an NBA star becomes so outrageous and unpredictable in his behavior (a somewhat half-hearted acknowledgment of basketball bad boy Dennis Rodman) that he is banned from the men's league.

Desperate to continue his paydays and also to stay active in the game he loves, he turns up in drag in the women's league as Juwanna Mann. Female basketball players on the team are portrayed as insecure, man-lonely women with good, but never great, hoop skills. Even in the end when Mann's ruse is uncovered, it is only with his tacit support that the team is able to win the championship.

VI

The most dominant social factors in basketball films are the issues of race and race relations. African-American style of play has permeated the game from the street to the professional level, to the point now where it is an overriding marketing consideration for shoes and apparel, print advertisements, music, and film.[10] In fact, the first media mainstream expression of African-American play was in the American Basketball Association of the 1960s and 1970s, a relatively short-lived league that enfranchised a free-wheeling, explosive, crowd-pleasing way of moving down the court and putting up points. In trying to place the current elements of race and basketball in films within Harry Edwards' dominant American sports creed, perhaps the best fit is in the elements of teamwork and discipline, though this may be a stretch, as so much of the action revolves around the showcasing of individual talent. Usually in the end in hoops films, team wins out and a sense of community is either born or reinforced.

A clear explication of African-American culture and film is provided by media critic and scholar Aaron Baker.[11] In his writings, Baker describes the "bursts of action . . . the fast-paced flow of spectacle that has come to dominate television and increasingly the movies." These "representations reinforce the status quo . . ." of African-American basketball players.[12]

Baker looks at two particular films in depth, Ron Shelton's *White Men Can't Jump* (1992) and Jeff Pollack's *Above the Rim* (1994). In his discussion of both films, Baker looks at how African-American men use basketball in developing strategies for success. The Sidney Deane character in *White Men Can't Jump* uses streetball hustle for self-esteem and status among his peers, and to make money when his construction business is slow. On the other hand, the character Kyle in *Above the Rim* has a more complex scenario for success as he seeks a way out of the drug-infested, violence-ridden everyday life of the ghetto, while remaining true to his peers and to his own urban culture. In many ways, the screen version is little different from the lives of some stars in the National Basketball Association today: one can escape the physical confines of the ghetto, but one must also bring to the NBA a support system of friends and family, music, and clothing and accessories.

In the 1998 Spike Lee film, *He Got Game,* which stars Denzel Washington and real-life NBA player Ray Allen, the family uses the basketball prodigy as a means for their own ghetto exit. And, of course, attention is paid, in both a literal and figurative sense, to the basketball moves that showcase a player's unique talent while contributing to team wins and ever-growing financial rewards. There is also, according to Baker, the notion of film culture creating a basketball racial awareness around the symbol of Michael Jordan. Jordan, an African-American man, seems to embody the Edwards sports creed, but Baker sees further than the creed and explores the representation of Jordan as the "gap between promise and reality . . ." in African-American basketball and film.[13]

Nowhere is this more evident than in the documentaries about African-American basketball. *Hoop Dreams* (1994), an award-winning documentary, explores the real-life struggles of two young teens from Chicago, Arthur Agee and William Gates, who have great basketball talents. The film follows this pair for five years, as they move from junior high school through high school, honing their hoops skills in the hope that they can exit from their community. Life is, for the boys and their families, hoops above all. At the age of fourteen, Arthur and William dream about the NBA, the riches to be realized at that level— a level at which they can provide for their parents in luxury, where hoop dreams lead to the highest level of play, where financial security may be attained, translating to social acceptance in America, or at least acquiescent acknowledgment of two young black men. Neither boy has made it: high school was confusing and disorienting for them and their families, college hoops did not pan out as they had expected, and neither realized the NBA dream. *Hoop Dreams* is Baker's gap between promise and reality.

A different kind of film is *Michael Jordan to the Max* (2000), an IMAX movie released to video that celebrates Jordan's realization of his American dream and his career with the Chicago Bulls. Accompanied by stunning footage and a combination hip-hop and rhythm and blues soundtrack, *Michael Jordan to the Max* is the visual celebration of what Baker termed the Utopian nature of Jordan to American culture. It is not gritty, but flashy, not fraught with fear and uncertainty as *Hoop Dreams* is, but instead a career retrospective of an African-American basketball player who did make it.

In another aspect of making it in a white-dominated corporate world (basketball and its apotheosis, the NBA), we can also look at the 2000 movie, *Finding Forrester.* In the film, an inner-city literary prodigy named Jamal Wallace is also a considerable basketball talent. Jamal becomes intrigued with the reclusive writer who lives in his neighborhood, William Forrester, who decades ago wrote a still-successful novel that defines coming of age (sort of a "J. D. Salinger meets the ghetto").

To fully cultivate Jamal's literary talent, his mother pushes him to accept a scholarship to an elite Manhattan prep school, a school whose officials realize that Jamal has a substantial intellect, but they value him more for his hoop skills. What Jamal leaves in his community is an ostensibly substandard school. He must still maintain a relationship with his former schoolmates because he must, after all, return home every evening. But what he also exits from is basketball. He knows what white people (excluding the white writer Forrester) expect from him. He knows how to use this, and he does. Jamal eschews the basketball "utopia" proffered him by the elite school, and instead opts to launch his literary talents in a white world. He succeeds, and the film succeeds with white moviegoers as well as with the Edwards sports creed, because he rejects the stereotypical, "traditional" path of black exit from the community.

Whites feel safe because Jamal's success is unthreatening. Even though he is entering traditional white territory, he is still a poor, black kid, and it is known by all that the real reason he is brought to the school is because of his basketball talent, not primarily because he is intellectually gifted. Therefore, he still fits into a stereotyped black niche. The students and school administrators will grant him his success on the court because they don't feel he can take anything away from them in their larger world of wealth and privilege. African Americans can feel vindication in that a successful black life in the United States can mean more than achievement in the athletic arena. It is almost as though Michael Jordan could only use the NBA in order to become a successful businessman.

The issue of race and basketball in the movies veers off from the standard American urban dramas of *Above the Rim* and *Finding Forrester* to a contemporary retelling of Shakespeare's *Othello* in *"O"* (2001). The film, starring Julia Stiles, Mekhi Phifer, Josh Hartnett, and Martin Sheen, had a difficult journey from studio to screen, particularly after the shooting tragedies at Columbine High School. *"O"* was completed in 1999, but the violence that pervades the movie made it a controversial vehicle for theaters.

Again, as with *Finding Forrester,* a black basketball player (Phifer) has been recruited to play for an elite white school. *Othello* was Shakespeare's tragedy about pride and jealousy releasing evil begotten by fear. In *"O"*, action revolves around a white player ignored by his coach father, and his jealousy turns toward the new star, the black player who also happens to be involved in a romance with a white girl. In the bloody end, the body count mounts quickly, and there is no resolution—or even much acknowledgment—of the racial issue. It is just out there for social relevance.

The urban-rural contrast (*"O"* is set in a small Southern community) encompasses race not only in the standard for rural sports films, *Hoosiers,*[14] but in a movie such as Sherman Alexie's *Smoke Signals,* a 1998 award-winning independent film. In *Smoke Signals,* the issue is Native American versus the white world; basketball is a symbolic backdrop against which Native American culture attaches symbolism to the hoop "sphere" and the different spiritual approach taken to the game by Indians.[15]

VII

Redemption. Redemption for the past. Norman Dale uses this in *Hoosiers,* as does the Dennis Hopper character, Shooter, a Hickory hero when he was in high school until he missed a crucial basket in the sectional finals. Now he is the town drunk. Shooter uses the success of the 1952 Hickory team to redeem himself in the eyes of his son, who is a member of the team, and also with the community, as he sobers up enough to assist Dale in running the team. Race becomes a redemptive issue in basketball movies, often for white players or authority figures who use hoops to make up for past racist inclinations. In *Blue Chips,* the coach played by Nick Nolte uses his public confession to redeem his own self-respect in recruitment cheating.

Another independent film well received by the critics is 1999's *The Basket* with Peter Coyote and Karen Allen. The action takes place in 1918 in rural Washington State. Coyote plays schoolteacher Martin Conlon, an unconventional sort who loves opera and happens to know a thing or two about basketball. When two young German refugees of World War I come to school in the little town of Waterville, Conlon decides to teach his students this strange game of basketball (Conlon is, of course, from "back East," so there is again the whole rural, heartland values versus the evils of urban coasts) and thus assimilate a young German boy into the mystical athletic expressions of American culture.

The film is a lyrical, beautifully photographed production, though it falls very short on basketball history. By 1918, basketball was not an unknown sport, in either the urban areas or rural expanses and small towns of America, so the old-fashioned basketball uniforms created from magazine pictures for the small-town team do not ring true when compared with the "modern" uniforms of the city team they go against in a tournament. A single basketball is even ordered by mail. The German boy is assimilated, but the underlying story is that Conlon must redeem himself for a past indiscretion that occurred when he lived in the East: he had gambled on basketball, he had sullied this beautiful sport. He redeems himself by teaching the game, by helping it move forward in culture, carried by young, hopeful boys. Then, he can exorcise his demon of denigrating the spirit of pure American sport.

And the creed survives. On the movie screen basketball films can show our foibles, they can illustrate our cleverness and athleticism, they can document our desire to achieve and win in American culture. Basketball films are about community, in whatever fashion the moviegoer wishes to define that concept, and these films can be about resolution between the sexes and between races while allowing a particular race to rise above all, at least for the space of a couple of hours in a dark theater.

The movie screen gives us the window into what we want to believe about America and our lives. And increasingly in our culture, as basketball becomes more and more the identifiable sport for so many Americans—rural and urban, black and white, male and female—we find reinforcement for the social realities we contend with every day.

NOTES

1. Harry Edwards, *Sociology of Sport* (Homewood, IL: Dorsey, 1973).

2. See Kevin Grace, *An Annotated Checklist of Basketball Films* (Wyoming, OH: Pargoud Press, 2003). Other sources for lists and capsule treatments of sports films include Harvey Marc Zucker and Lawrence J. Babich, *Sports Films: A Complete Reference* (Jefferson, NC: McFarland & Co., 1987) and Ronald Bergen, *Sports in the Movies* (New York: Proteus Books, 1982).

3. John Sayles and Gavin Smith, *Sayles on Sayles* (Boston, MA: Faber and Faber, 1998), pp. 144, 146. Sayles did write a short story, "Hoop," (in *The Atlantic*

Monthly, March 1977), in which he approaches the concept of playing basketball as a form of theater. For specific discussion of the influence of basketball on a contemporary director, see Paul Christopher McNiff, "The Films of Ron Shelton: Redefining the Sports Genre" (California State University, Northridge: unpublished master's thesis, 1996).

4. See Steven Riess, *Sport in Industrial America, 1850-1920* (Wheeling, IL: Harlan Davidson, 1995) and *City Games: The Evolution of American Urban Society and the Rise of Sports* (Urbana, IL: University of Illinois Press, 1989). A concise treatment of the Progressive Era can be found in Arthur S. Link and Richard L. McCormick, *Progressivism* (Wheeling, IL: Harlan Davidson, 1983).

5. Burt L. Standish, *Dick Merriwell's Promise,* New Medal Library No. 446 (New York: Street & Smith, 1901).

6. See, for instance, Edith Bancroft, *Jane Allen of the Sub Team* (Akron, OH: Saalfield Publishing, 1917), Pauline Lester, *Marjorie Dean, High School Senior* (New York: A.L. Burt Company, 1917), Jessie Graham Flower, *Grace Harlowe's Sophomore Year at Oakdale High School* (Philadelphia, PA: Henry Altemus Company, 1911), and Gertrude W. Morrison, *The Girls of Central High at Basketball* (New York: Grosset & Dunlap, 1914).

7. A clear general history of women in sport is provided in Susan K. Cahn, *Coming on Strong: Gender and Sexuality in Twentieth-Century Women's Sport* (Cambridge, MA: Harvard University Press, 1994). See especially the discussion of the growing national movement in the 1920s to discourage intercollegiate competition for women.

8. Ring Lardner Jr., *The Lardners: My Family Remembered* (New York: Harper & Row, 1977), p. 22. In a way, it is with the same distaste that some sports fans approach the current extreme sports.

9. Two eloquent histories of the scandals are Charley Rosen, *Scandals of '51: How the Gamblers Almost Killed College Basketball* (New York: Seven Stories Press, 1978), and Stanley Cohen, *The Game They Played* (New York: Farrar, Straus and Giroux, 1977). Both authors were also involved in the production of *City Dump,* HBO's documentary film about the topic. In one of many interviews in the documentary, former college basketball coach and announcer Al McGuire, a New York native who played his college hoops during the scandals era, says in one of the most basic and powerful film statements about college basketball: "when you have no scratch, when you have no green, money talks and it talks loud . . ." Rosen has also looked at basketball gambling in two novels: *Barney Polan's Game: A Novel of the 1951 College Basketball Scandals* (New York: Seven Stories Press, 1998) and *The House of Moses All-Stars* (New York: Seven Stories Press, 1996), the latter an account of a Jewish barnstorming team that makes much of its money on side wagering.

10. See, for example, the "documentaries" on DVD and video such as *And 1 Ball Access: The MixTape Tour* (Nintendo, 2002). Tours of streetball performers to various American cities are accompanied by a strong hip-hop soundtrack, and are corporately sponsored by the likes of Pepsi and Mountain Dew, And 1 Shoes, and ESPN. Basketball films have even gone the "gangsta" route with low-budget, direct-to-video offerings such as *Hoop Soldiers* (2000) and *Playaz Court* (2002). The emphasis is on underground, ghetto hoops and ghetto justice. Whatever social com-

mentary might be involved, it is severely hampered by laughable acting and bad hoops.

11. Aaron Baker, "Hoop Dreams in Black and White: Race and Basketball Movies," in *Basketball Jones: America Above the Rim,* edited by Todd Boyd and Kenneth L. Shropshire (New York: New York University Press, 2000), pp. 215-239. See also Aaron Baker and Todd Boyd, *Out of Bounds: Sports, Media, and the Politics of Identity* (Bloomington, IN: Indiana University Press, 1997).

12. Ibid, pp. 215, 216.

13. Ibid, p. 236.

14. In a 1998 interview with the author, basketball legend Oscar Robertson lamented the racial aspect of *Hoosiers;* growing up in Indianpolis and attending Crispus Attucks High School (which the real-life team Hickory is based upon) won the state championship in 1954 (Hickory wins in 1952), he stated that having the climax of the film focus on a white versus black team gave moviegoers a rooting focus.

15. See also the documentary *Rocks with Wings,* a 2002 Public Broadcasting System film that chronicles more than a decade in the life of an American Indian girls' basketball team from a New Mexico reservation and also addresses the rural-urban and white-Indian racial issue.

PART II:
THE PLAYGROUNDS AND BEYOND

Chapter 6

The Schoolyard Game:
Blacktop Legends and Broken Dreams

Bijan C. Bayne

Basketball as it is played in college and professional leagues today was not always a reflection of the schoolyard game. The folklore of basketball is rife with stories of flamboyant players who were benched, pulled from games, or jeered by hecklers for exhibiting the flair associated with the playground. Almost every fan has heard a coach or broadcaster say, "That was a schoolyard play," which is generally uncomplimentary. However, a combination of trends has made the improvised play and the blind pass more acceptable in conventional games. Indeed, some scholars and purist coaches would say the pendulum has swung too far—that the contemporary game is "too street."

Basketball was born and bred in the YMCAs, churches, and men's clubs of the Northeast. From its Springfield, Massachusetts, origin, the game spread to New York and Pennsylvania. Because Dr. James Naismith, the man who invented the game, was a YMCA instructor, YMCA officials throughout the Northeast adopted the new indoor sport at the turn of the twentieth century. The new game became so popular in Philadelphia that prior to 1900, city YMCAs banned basketball, because people who wanted to play other sports could never schedule gym time.

In 1905, a black Harvard graduate, Dr. Edwin B. Henderson, founded the High School Athletic Association. This organization was established to encourage black interscholastic athletics. A year later, Henderson became athletic supervisor for black (racially segregated) schools in Washington, DC. He organized the Interscholastic Athletic Association as a governing body for "colored" secondary schools in the mid-Atlantic states. Under Henderson's direction, the track and field, football, baseball, and basketball programs in DC, Baltimore, and Wilmington, Delaware, improved significantly. In church leagues, public gyms, and schoolyards, black youngsters took to the relatively new game.

Farther north, Jewish, Irish, and Italian children played informal basketball games in the playgrounds of New York City, New Jersey, and Philadelphia. Most of these young players were first-generation Americans. The Irish and Italians flocked to courts in Rockaway, the Jewish to those along Fordham Road in the Bronx. A basket, goal, or milk crate could be nailed to a telephone pole or garage. The game was simple and required fewer accessories than other sports—no bats or gloves were needed and shoulder pads and yard markers were unnecessary. All one needed were a few willing friends, a ball, and a makeshift goal.

The best players among these city kids went on to star for colleges such as Long Island University, St. John's, Fordham, Columbia, and City College of New York (CCNY). The Philadelphians played at St. Joseph's, Penn, Temple, Villanova, and LaSalle. For the first half of the twentieth century, the premier names in college and professional basketball included Nat Holman, Barney Sedran, Moe Spahn, Red Holzman, Ossie Schectman, Sid Tannenbaum, Harry Boykoff, Hy Gotkin, Max Posnack, Rip Gerson, and Dolph Schayes. They were all New Yorkers and most were first- or second-generation Americans.

Informal or pickup basketball games became a venue for establishing one's athletic reputation. An aspiring athlete did not necessarily have to play for the settlement house or the high school to make his name known. Basketball is still the only one of the three major American team sports in which a player can garner regional or community repute strictly based on informal play.

Imagine a sandlot slugger becoming a local baseball hero in unsupervised, undocumented games. What pinpoint passing quarterback is widely heralded for feats in games of touch football? Yet basketball has such heroes, the folklore surrounding them is as colorful as that associated with the gunslingers of the Old West.

Stories about their exploits date back at least five decades in oral lore: Isaac "Rabbit" Walthour, Dick "Chink" Gaines, Connie Hawkins, Earl "Goat" Manigault, Herman "Helicopter" Knowings, Richard

"Pee Wee" Kirkland, Joe "Destroyer" Hammond, Albert King and Lloyd "Swee'Pea" Daniels in New York City; John Chaney, Guy Rodgers, Theophilous "Sonny" Lloyd, Claude Gross, Jim "Tee" Parham, Walt Hazzard, Tom "Troop" Washington, Emory Mims, George Mack, Frank "Watusi" Card, Joe Gore, and Lewis "Black Magic" Lloyd in Philadelphia; Art Daniels, Arthur Sivels, and Billy Harris in Chicago; Elgin "Rabbit" Baylor, Wil Jones, Tom Little, William "Chicken Breast" Lee, "Ducky" Vaughn, and Archie Talley in Washington, DC; Detroit's Curtis Jones; and Los Angeles' Ray Lewis. Many of these names only resound to aficionados of schoolyard basketball, although most played varying levels of the organized game. As with the legends of Jesse James and Billy the Kid, the line between blacktop fact and fiction can be a fine one.

For many, the first exposure to unconventional basketball, the palmed ball, and the slam dunk, was a Harlem Globetrotters game. In the 1930s, Trotters center Inman Jackson had a notion to use his large hands for ballhandling tricks to please crowds when games against inferior opponents were already out of hand. He could roll the ball along his shoulders and arms. He could grasp it and wave it in a defender's face, then pull it back. The funny antics sometimes diverted largely white audiences' attention from the fact that the black touring team was handily beating the hometown assortment of schoolteachers or firemen. Playground players imitated these moves, as the Globetrotters became the world's best-known basketball team.

Schoolyard basketball legends emerged from oral tradition, not recorded games or newsreels. Millions of Americans never saw Red Grange or Babe Ruth play in person, but saw their weekly highlights in newsreels at the local movie house. Most basketball fans never actually saw Earl Manigault dunk the same basketball twice while airborne, or "Jumpin'" Jackie Jackson take a coin from the top of a playground backboard in one leap. Many have read or heard of these feats (even if the coin story is attributed to several players, among them David Thompson and "Helicopter" Knowings).

Folklore is as much a part of pickup basketball as play itself. Stories are recounted at courtside. One may hear how "Helicopter" went for an opponent's head fake, jumped, and was called for a three-second violation before landing. Longtime observers tell of the shopping bags full of cash "Pee Wee" Kirkland would leave at courtside, and how much money he made playing for high-stakes wagers. Others are known not for a singular incident, but rather for being "nice."

"Nice" was a 1950s and 1960s term for exceptional talent. It was succeeded in the lexicon by "bad" (late 1960s), "nasty" (early 1970s), "serious" (1980s), "dope" (also 1980s), the always popular "the truth" (which became an actual nickname for St. John's forward Walter Berry), and the 2000s "tight." New vocabulary often enters the schoolyard from the urban society. From the schoolyard we get the expression "in your face" (1970s), which has been adopted by mainstream culture, along with many other slang sayings from the basketball playgrounds.

Schoolyard basketball, like medicine or law, has a language all its own. "Downs" (next game), "brick" (air ball or errant shot), "makers takers" (the team that scores inbounds the ball next), "run" (a game, or as a verb, to play basketball), "throw" (to block someone's shot, a term which evolved from "gate," "stuff," "pin," and "send").

A "killer cross" is a quicksilver crossover dribble. For years "jam" was not a preserve, but a dunk. Even the popular sportswear and schoolyard video product "And 1" came from the phrase shouted by a player who is claiming to have been fouled. "Stays here!" also means the speaker's team is still in possession of the ball.

As white flight, joblessness, and riots all took their toll on America's cities, the schoolyard basketball game became one of the few avenues of expression for many black males. On the court, as in jazz music, the unemployed male could earn a reputation for creativity. Improvisation ruled. Basketball is a game of deception (a metaphor for the street-smart lifestyle many players were exposed to). It is a game of head fakes, shifty dribbles, and unanticipated passes.

Although this gave its practitioners a sense of pride and self-worth they had not gained in the classroom, the habits they learned did not always sit well with coaches of organized teams. In the 1940s, the Harlem Globetrotters were the standard for tricky basketball. Palmed balls, blind passes, and fancy dribbling were their hallmarks. Those methods were approved of in the schoolyard, but not in officiated games. "No fancy-pants stuff," coaches would warn, or demand that players "Cut the razzle-dazzle" and "Stop showboating."

By the 1960s, some conservative coaches referred to this free style as "nigger ball," and not all of these coaches were white. In the 1950s

Morgan State College coach Talmadge "Marse" Hill was so straight-laced his players labeled him "The Gov" (for governor). He did not like to play young men who were showy ballhandlers. A decade later, streetball legend Earl Manigault left Johnson C. Smith College because of artistic differences between Manigault and the coach. One is reminded of Pablo Picasso dropping out of the academy in Madrid because the program was too conventional for him, or of Miles Davis leaving Juilliard because he felt he could learn more by jamming in nightclubs with established players.

Even at basketball's highest levels, observers, coaches, and officials discouraged flashy play. One of the NBA's first three black players was former Globetrotter Nat "Sweetwater" Clifton. "Sweets" toned down his game considerably as a New York Knick, not only because he was "on the spot" in a racial sense, but also so he wouldn't overshadow Knick stars such as Harry Gallatin and Carl Braun. Yet the team had a flashy white playmaker from the New York City schoolyards—"Tricky" Dick McGuire.

Others who cooled their heels in organized play were three-time Tennesee State national champion Dick "Skull" Barnett and UCLA playmaker Walt Hazzard from Philadelphia's Overbrook High School. Barnett cut back on his stutter steps in the walk-it-up-the-court NBA of the early 1960s, however, he still talked a schoolyard game. The product of Roosevelt High School in Gary, Indiana, Skull would snap, "Too late" to defenders who reached up to attempt to block his fallaway jump shot. As he released the ball, he would say "Fall back, baby."

Barnett's high school rival and collegiate contemporary Oscar Robertson said that he almost never employed flashy street moves, such as behind-the-back dribbles or dunks, in the NBA because they were unnecessary. Robertson's high school coach, Ray Crowe, frowned on such displays. Despite possessing wicked street game, in the 1960s Robertson was considered the model player most often cited by basketball coaches as the classic example of a fundamentalist with no weaknesses. Robertson stood as the graceful schoolyard product without the stereotype schoolyard game. So sound was collegian Bill Bradley's game that 1964 Olympic teammate Walt Hazzard told him, "Where I come from, you're known as 'The White O.'"

Black or predominantly black teams were held to a different standard than white stars Bob Davies (a 1950s Rochester Royal in the

NBA who used a behind-the-back dribble maneuver), Dick McGuire, and Bob Cousy. When Bill Russell's mid-1950s University of San Francisco team performed a version of the Harlem Globetrotters' "Magic Circle" ballhandling tricks during warm-ups, fans threw coins at them and called them "Globetrotters!"

As late as 1966, some sportswriters chided the Texas Western NCAA men's championship team in print for dunking the basketball, playing a "playground" style, and not being legitimate student athletes. Sports reporters and rival coaches probed to learn how the west Texas university recruited athletes from Gary, Detroit, and Harlem, as if UCLA's 1965 national champ Walt Hazzard, and prize 1965 freshman recruit Lew Alcindor (now Kareem Abdul-Jabbar) had not traveled 3,000 miles from home to play in Westwood. Of course, UCLA Coach John Wooden, a model of old-fashioned Midwestern values, was more respected by scribes than Texas Western upstart Don Haskins.

Some schoolyard hotshots never aspired to the halls of ivy. Manigault was kicked off the high school team at Ben Franklin in New York, enrolled at black preparatory school Laurinburg Institute in North Carolina to improve his academics, and did not see eye to eye with his college coach. He later fell victim to heroin addiction. "The Goat" cleaned himself up enough to earn a tryout with the ABA's Utah Stars in the early 1970s, but by then his considerable skills had diminished (a fate that befell many heroin-addicted jazz musicians). Cognizant that other urban youth were at risk to repeat his errors, Manigault founded The Goat benefit tournament in Harlem prior to his 1999 death. Jabbar considers "The Goat" the greatest player never to play in the NBA.

Curtis Jones was a ballhandling wizard at Northern High School in Detroit in the mid-to-late 1960s. Jones was a poor reader and student. A high school basketball rival of Pershing High's Spencer Haywood, Jones could dribble the entire length of the basketball court against pressure defense without once bringing the ball in front of his body. Former ABA and NBA superstar George Gervin calls Curtis Jones the best player he ever saw. Jones made a brief academic effort at an Idaho junior college in hopes of playing later at a four-year school, but he was simply unprepared. Every urban area has a dozen similar stories who were "better than" the best-known college and NBA players it produced.

Connie Hawkins is a bright man, but was a slow reader as a Brooklyn schoolchild. He primarily read comic books and the newspaper sports sections. About 250 colleges recruited "The Hawk" out of Brooklyn Boys High School. Some programs offered him free clothing, cars, and even a salary. Boys High English Department head Nathan Mazer administered an I.Q. test to Hawkins. The teenager scored a 65, and was classified as a moron. Mazer had seen Hawkins' quick thinking on the basketball court enough to know the young man was much sharper than the scores implied. For instance, he suspected that because Connie read at the seventh grade level, there were words familiar to his ear that he may not have recognized in print. Others he might only be able to define in certain contexts. Mazer worked with the 6'8" senior on spelling, grammar, and reading tests, and Hawk raised his I.Q. score to 113 (for what it's worth, President Kennedy's was 115) and his reading level to the second month of eleventh grade.

Unfortunately, few schoolyard basketball marvels had a Nathan Mazer to volunteer their own time to tutor them. Hawkins still fell prey to another schoolyard legend, former NBAer and Columbia University star Jack Molinas. Molinas took advantage of the trusting youth by asking him for phone numbers of other promising New York City high school players. When Molinas and some of those players were implicated in a college basketball point-shaving scandal, Hawkins' name came up during the investigation process as an information source for Molinas. The Hawk's University of Iowa stint ended before he could play a single college game and the NBA barred him, though he did catch on with the Harlem Globetrotters.

After two Pittsburgh attorneys fought for Hawkins' right to play NBA basketball on the grounds that he had never "shaved points" in a college game (and was unaware of why Molinas wanted the other schoolboy stars' phone numbers), The Hawk became an NBA rookie at age twenty-eight. His best years were behind him, but he averaged 24 points a game for Phoenix and made the All-Star team that season. Two years earlier he won the MVP award in the new American Basketball Association. Still, streetball savants say the general public never saw the real Hawk.

At least Hawkins finally earned an opportunity to shine in the limelight. Joe "Destroyer" Hammond's claim to fame is dropping 50 points on the likes of Julius Erving and Charlie Scott in a 1977 game in Harlem's noted Rucker Tournament—in one half! Hammond played circles around Gail Goodrich and Pat Riley in a Laker tryout as a 1972 free agent. When the team refused to pay Hammond, who had not attended college, Gail Goodrich dollars, he left camp, returning to New York.

Los Angeles' Ray Lewis was one of the surest pure shooters to ever lace up sneakers. Just ask Cheryl Miller, or Marques Johnson. "Ray Lew" was second in the NCAA in scoring at Los Angeles State in 1973. He felt he was having a better preseason than 76ers rookie teammate Doug Collins. Lewis thought he should be paid as much as Collins, a 1972 Olympian and consensus All-American at Illinois State. The Sixers disagreed. Bye-bye, Ray Lew.

Skip Wise is still lionized on the playgrounds of Baltimore. The Dunbar High School star led his Poets to a victory over an Adrian Dantley and Kenny Carr-led DeMatha High team and halted DeMatha's thirty-six-game winning streak. At Clemson, Wise became the first freshman named ACC Tournament MVP. Shortly thereafter, "Honey Dip" Wise fell victim to the street lifestyle.

Many other streetball legends make dubious choices or were never given the chance to show their true talents. When the Harlem Globetrotters came to the home of 1960s Chicago phenom Arthur Sivels to recruit him, Sivels told his mother, "Tell 'em I'm not home." After Sivels came Lord Henry Thomas, who observers say was better than his baby brother, Isiah. Lord Henry became a hustler. An earlier Chicagoan, Art Hicks of St. Elizabeth's High, was forced to leave Seton Hall during the same betting scandal that shelved Connie Hawkins in New York City. Hicks once broke a backboard at the Martin Luther King Boys' Club in Chicago.

In Boston's Roxbury section in the early 1970s, Steve Strother was a scoring terror at Dorchester High. "He's got more moves than Ex-Lax," they used to say. Stro' played at Providence, but generally did not start because he often ran afoul of Coach Dave Gavitt. When Stro' did play, he scored 30 points against America's best defensive guard, Ron Lee of Oregon (his Boston playground rival). On the courts in Roxbury, in the old Boston Neighborhood Basketball League at Washington Park, the courtside cry was "Run the Show, Stro'. Run the Show!"

All the stories are not tragic, however. Bob Cousy, Guy Rodgers, Wilt Chamberlain, and Bernard King made it. Pee Wee Kirkland turned his life around, now coaching a high school team and running a school.

Many athletes were steered straight by Harlem park supervisor Holcombe Rucker, who started the first renowned urban summer tournament back in 1946. If you ask them, Joe Hammond and others have no regrets because they made their "rep" on the blacktop "where it counts"—with no referees, no coach's favoritism, no double screens to come off and shoot—a hardscrabble, often-humbling game. Another main aspect of the playground is an emphasis on harsh verbal contests where one can lose face. In the 'yard, no matter how "tight" a player may think his or her game is, if the "heads" don't recognize it and have never seen the player "ball," one may not get chosen to "run."

Being on the losing team can be even worse, because a loss can mean no more play that day. Onlookers laugh at shots that are swatted away. Players taunt one another. They question one another's manhood. Some get "schooled" by young women. Foul calls and loose ball calls are hotly contested. Protests abound. Profanity is common. There are no trainers. If there are nearby water fountains, they are often grimy, out of order, or dispense tepid water. Then there are the bent rims, the uneven courts, and the broken glass.

The outdoor game has a gunslinger mentality to it. Talented players seek out one another. The ultimate test for two opponents, whether strangers or rivals, is a game of one-on-one (another streetball term that has entered the language at large). One-on-one represents a challenge of skills, will, and stamina.

Schoolyard "teams" also earn lofty reputations. In New York City in 1960, the streets were abuzz about the three-on-three feud between the team of Connie Hawkins, Eddie Simmons, and Jackie Jackson and the NYU group of Cal Ramsey, Tom "Satch" Sanders, and Russ Cunningham. The bespectacled Sanders once intimidated the younger Hawkins, but that summer, Hawkins played with more confidence. Cunningham was a fine college guard, but the wiry Simmons prided himself on playing well against him. Ramsey was a member of the New York Knicks, but even then, few players could sky with Jumpin' Jackie. At the time, Jackson and Simmons were All-CIAA Conference as Virginia Union teammates. In Roxbury, Massachusetts, in the late 1950s, Ed Washington (a 6'7" Boston University star and later an ABL Pittsburgh Piper teammate of Hawkins), Roscoe

Baker (a 6'2" guard from Delaware State) and Jerry Shaw (a lightning fast 5'8" guard who played briefly at Morgan State) beat all comers. A game pitting this Boston trio against Sanders, Ramsey, and Cunningham was discussed, but never materialized.

Schoolyard basketball has its hallowed locales, just as organized basketball has Madison Square Garden or UCLA's Pauley Pavilion. One legendary playground is Washington Park at Martin Luther King Boulevard and Washington Street in Boston's Roxbury neighborhood. Another, located in Harlem, is Rucker Park at 155th Street and Eighth Avenue, and "Death Valley," at West 4th Street and Avenue of the Americas (6th Ave. to locals), is situated in Greenwich Village. At Mellon Park at 5th and Shady in Pittsburgh, names such as Dick and Dave Ricketts, Maurice Stokes, Jack Twyman, Dick Groat (the 1960s Pirate and Cardinal baseball star was a Duke All-American hoopster), Ed Fleming, John Wideman, Connie Hawkins, Maurice Lucas, and Sam Clancy battled. Washington, DC's, Turkey Thicket Playground at Twelfth and Michigan may appear quiet now, but Elgin Baylor, Notre Dame president Monk Malloy, Wil Jones, John Thompson, and Wilt Chamberlain ran there back in their day. At Kingstone Park in Brooklyn in the 1950s, Solly Walker, Al Innis, Vinnie Cohen, and Duquesne All-American Sihugo Green could be found. P.S. 117's blacktop was home to early 1960s standouts Eddie "Czar" Simmons (Connie Hawkins' basketball big brother at 5'9"), Jackie Jackson, Earl Wright, Henry Halliburton, Neville Smith, and Jerry Powell (from whom Hawkins said he modeled his first head fakes en route to the basket). Over in Brownsville, future St. John's stars and pros Tony Jackson and Leroy Ellis held court. Jackson, one of the greatest shooters ever, was a target of the college betting scandals. Afterward, he had a brief ABA career. Outside New York City in Mount Vernon, youngsters Gus and Ray Williams, Earl Tatum, Rudy Hackett, and David Belton were honing their game at the Mount Vernon Center on West 4th and 7th with their friend, Academy Award-winning actor Denzel Washington.

In Philly, Earl Monroe was a high school soccer player and, at 6'2", a center of little distinction at Bartram High School. Like Hawkins, Monroe studied the moves of other players. He added these to his own repertoire, crafting a set of slippery fakes, ball tricks, spins, and wrong-footed layups that left opponents reaching for air.

Monroe did not seek a college education after Bartram. Instead, he worked in a Pillsbury factory. A buddy talked him up about Coach Clarence "Bighouse" Gaines' storied basketball program down at Winston-Salem State College, where he eventually attended. By his senior season, Monroe was shaking and baking to the tune of 41 points a game at Winston-Salem, where he led the Rams to an NCAA College Division title. These exploits earned Monroe a moniker he could never take with him into the politically correct NBA—"Black Jesus."

In his prime, Earl Monroe was considered the premier one-on-one player in the NBA. Few of his contemporaries were thought of in that regard. When Monroe was traded from Baltimore to the New York Knicks, he was adopted by a city whose schoolyard players prided themselves on the very skills "The Pearl" was known for, including jukes, spins, ball trickery, and off-balance shots. The Knicks already had a stylish guard and fan favorite, Walt "Clyde" Frazier, though other than an occasional behind-the-back dribble, Frazier's game was primarily orthodox. His off-the-court persona was the source of much of the fan admiration. Frazier was a typical 1970s star athlete, dressing with flair and driving a flashy Rolls-Royce. Connie Hawkins and Monroe were responsible for bringing the playground style to the NBA.

Philadelphia's first two NBA stars were local college products, Paul Arizin of Villanova and Tom Gola of LaSalle. They grew up playing at the Murphy Recreation Center at 4th and Shank in an Italian neighborhood. However, the top playground court for Philly players—the proving ground—was at 25th and Diamond Streets, home of the summer Baker League. The Baker League began with four summer teams in 1960. A 5'9" former Central (Ohio) State and Eastern League star named Sonny Hill was instrumental in the rise of the Baker League.

This Baker League playground is now part of the Hank Gathers Recreation Center, named after the former Loyola Marymount University superstar who died of cardiac arrest during a college basketball game in 1990. Gathers rose to superstardom from the tough streets of Philly and would probably have gone on to a wonderful pro career if his life had not been cut short.

NBA dribbling sensation Guy Rodgers was a Baker League mainstay. Rodgers netted 35 points a game as a high school player at Southwest High. The Harlem Globetrotters approached the lefty whiz, but he was advised by two of the players to bypass the lengthy Trotter road trips for the college life. Rodgers was half of Temple University's 1958 All-American backcourt. His mate was Hal "King" Lear, a southpaw shooting specialist. Each season from 1960 to 1967, Rodgers either led the NBA in assists or placed second to Oscar Robertson. He set single-season and per-game assist marks that stood for years and shared the single-game record of 28 with Celtic legend Bob Cousy.

Jerry West, Oscar Robertson, and Al Attles all considered the Philly schoolyard product the premier ballhandler in the NBA. However, despite his talent, Rodgers was overshadowed on his own team (the Warriors) by Wilt Chamberlain and in the league overall by Cousy. At 25th and Diamond, though, he had no peer. His stellar play influenced a succession of Philadelphia guards, including Walt Hazzard, Earl Monroe, Wali Jones, Andre "Bongos" McCarter, Mike Gale, Joe Gore, and Jerome "Pooh" Richardson. Perhaps Rodgers' truest recent stylistic heir is former University of Virginia star and WNBA great Dawn Staley. These players are as indebted to Rodgers as jazz legend Sonny Stitt is to Charlie Parker.

The Haddington Recreation Center in Philadelphia was the place to see Wilt Chamberlain, Walt Hazzard, the then Wally Jones, Ray "Chink" Scott, Jackie Moore, Woody Sauldsberry, and Wayne Hightower. Over the years at Queen Anne Playground at Pico and Queen Anne in Los Angeles, Dick Barnett, Sidney Wicks, and Marques Johnson all reigned. Oscar Robertson worked on his chops at the "Dust Bowl," the courts near the Lockfield Gardens housing projects in Indianapolis. In Gary, Indiana, Dick Barnett played before school and after school for hours a day, sometimes alone.

One of the greatest aspects of basketball is that it can be played alone. Many greats spend countless hours by themselves working on the off hand, shots of various lengths, and the bank shot. There is something pristine about a virgin pair of white sneaks, something pure in the softness of a jump shot settling into a white net. These sensations are heightened when one is alone with nothing more than the ball and one's thoughts. Game scenarios are often played out in the mind. Millions of players, regardless of ability, have stood out on a playground and counted down to the final shot to win the championship, "Three-two-one, she shoots, she scores!" The buzzer-beater to win the game is probably the most dreamed-about play in all of sports. Unlike baseball and hitting a game-winning home run in the seventh game of the World Series, shooting hoops on the dark, hot cement requires nothing more than a hoop, a ball, and a dream. The true greats are the ones who deliver in the clutch—Michael Jordan even starred in a commercial celebrating the game-winner. Of course, he's the expert, hitting so many big shots over the course of his career.

In his memoir, *The Haygoods of Columbus,* author Wil Haygood writes of playing long hours by himself behind Monroe Junior High in Columbus, Ohio, in the late 1960s. "Basketball called out to the lonely," Haygood wrote. He grew up on Columbus's Near East Side, where the pickup honor roll included NFL stars Bernie Casey and Jim Marshall, NBA coach Jim Cleamons, heavyweight boxing champion and Mike Tyson-slayer James "Buster" Douglas, and Ohio State legendary hoop star Herb Williams. Columbus' most celebrated schoolyard sharp was a player from the North Side, Dwight "Bo" Lamar. Lamar was a long-range gun who averaged 36 points a game at Southwestern Louisiana in 1973.

Today the schoolyard lingo has crept into mainstream sportscasts, CDs, movies, books, and other forms of popular culture. The moves that Earl Monroe had to explain to NBA officials in the late 1960s, so he would not be called for traveling or palming the ball, are commonplace in today's era at a good middle school game. Cousy, who introduced fancy dribbling to many pro fans, is fond of saying, "Now every twelve-year-old can put the ball behind his back." (And *her* back too, Cooz) The crossover dribble and the dunk are NBA staples. Maneuvers once discouraged are now encouraged. Believe it or not, dunking was once thought of as a grandstanding play that showed up an opponent. The NCAA and the high schools banned the "stuff shot" from 1967 to 1976, largely as a reaction to the dominance of Lew Alcindor at UCLA.

Texas Western (particularly 6'7", 250-pound Dave "Big Daddy D" Lattin) had rammed a few home in the team's upset NCAA title win over an all-white Kentucky team in March, 1966. Once again reflecting race relations on the basketball court, the dunk was a bit militant for those times—too "in-your-face." Thirty-odd years later when Andre Miller simply laid the basketball in on a breakaway hoop during the Rookie Game at NBA All-Star Weekend, the fans at Washington's MCI Center greeted the "conventional" play with a chorus of boos. They bought their tickets to see the sleight-of-hand of players such as flashy point guard Jason Williams, then playing for the Sacramento Kings and then Los Angeles Clippers' star Lamar Odom.

What was once avant-garde is now de rigueur. What shocked fans in 1966 is now considered tame. But, culturally, this phenomenon of evolution has a funny look many years later. Consider that Louis Armstrong was deemed extreme before people heard bebop. Teenagers who grow up to the sounds of rap stars Nelly and Nas and who model their games after those of Allen Iverson and Steve Francis play today's game. Dunks are the order of the day on ESPN's nightly highlight report *SportsCenter.*

Players want to show up on *SportsCenter,* so taunting, beating of chests, strutting, and even throat-slashing gestures are common. Sports apparel and shoe company And 1 sells videotapes of streetball highlights. Nike has used ballhandling tricksters in television advertising. The once exclusive "Magic Circle" of the Harlem Globetrotters has come full circle. Today's pro superstars are simply giving the fans what they want to see.

After Bob Cousy (dubbed "The Houdini of the Hardwood" and "Mr. Prestidigitation" by sportswriters) and Pete Maravich wowed NBA fans, the game experienced a lull in popularity in the late 1970s. An increase in drug use among players, delayed broadcasts of NBA Finals games, a series of injuries to Portland Trailblazer star center Bill Walton, and a few highly-publicized incidences of violence caused many fans to lose interest in the professional game.

Despite the waning public interest, basketball players as a whole were earning more than their football and baseball counterparts. This fact caused fan resentment. In the 1980 movie *Airplane!,* the public attitude is typified by a young boy who tells fellow air passenger Kareem Abdul-Jabbar that his father thinks Jabbar is overpaid and should play harder.

In 1979, the NCAA Men's Championship game was a showdown between Michigan State and Indiana State. Television viewers were treated to not only a team game, but a much ballyhooed duel between two 6'9" masters of the no-look pass—Earvin "Magic" Johnson of Michigan State and Larry Bird of Indiana State. Unlike Maravich— whose college and NBA teams were not champions—these players were winners. They also differed from Cousy in that they were eight inches taller and, as a matter of fact, would have been centers in Cousy's heyday.

Johnson's Michigan State team triumphed and the media took to the ebullient teen from Lansing. The brilliant passer with the winning smile entered the NBA draft. The story of his NBA rivalry with Bird is well-known. Their style of play—see the play develop two steps ahead of time and then hit the open player without telegraphing the pass—combined with their team success made the improvised play more acceptable to some coaches. Children could tell the adults, "Well, Magic does it," and adults could not retort, "But he's a loser." Nor could they continue to say, "But you're a big man. Big men play in the post." Versatile tall players entered the college ranks, such as Billy Thompson, Danny Manning, Billy Owens, and Ralph Sampson.

Though this group may not have experienced the same degree of success as other professional players, primarily due to injury, they helped advance the acceptance of the big man as ballhandler. They were not the first giants who were talented passers. "Sweets" Clifton could dish with anyone, but sublimated his game to fit the NBA standards of his time. Connie Hawkins was a beautiful feeder, but the world did not see him at his best. Bill Walton was also exceptional in this regard, but never fully recovered from a series of surgeries that began in 1978 when his Portland Trailblazers were the defending NBA champions.

Bird and Magic, with their fierce bicoastal rivalry, were hardworking and court-wise. Coaches *advised* youngsters to watch them. Players like Magic and Bird combined both street skills and a highly disciplined court game. Together they resurrected the NBA and showed that a freewheeling style would bring fans back to the game. Suddenly, the playgrounds around the country were filled with Laker and Celtic jerseys and kids were gobbling up the latest Converse high-top sneakers endorsed by the two stars.

As for the dunk, the NCAA and high school bans were lifted in 1976. Since that time, players have been weaned on footage of Julius "Dr. J" Erving (also liked by youth coaches, as a player and proven winner), David "Luke Skywalker" Thompson, Dominique "The Human Highlights Film" Wilkins, Michael "Air" Jordan, and Clyde "The Glide" Drexler. Drexler's University of Houston team was so prolific above that rim that they earned the nickname "Phi Slamma

Jamma." Like Texas Western two decades before, they reached the NCAA Finals. Houston was celebrated for its "above-the-rim" play, in stark contrast to the 1966 Miners, who were derided for aerial antics and accused of recruiting ringers from America's urban schoolyards.

The United States was a much different place in Drexler's day than the mid-1960s. The nation was more integrated in the early 1980s (even today, though, we still have a long way to go). By the time the Phi Slamma Jamma crew captured the sports world's attention, the general public had more exposure to black students and co-workers than twenty years earlier. In addition, the popularity of the dunk led to The Slam Dunk Contest becoming a highlight of NBA All-Star Weekend, even though it had been borrowed from the defunct ABA.

Today's high flyers are not as unique as they may seem, however. Playground legends, such as Sihugo Green, "Jumpin'" Johnny Green, Tom Hawkins, "Pogo" Joe Caldwell, and Gus "Honeycomb" Johnson were soaring before 1970, only with less exposure, less propensity to slam, and no *SportsCenter* replays nationwide. Often Elgin Baylor is cited as the predecessor of Erving and Jordan, though Baylor was more of a glider. Baylor did seem to hesitate in the air and release the ball at the last second. At 6'5", Baylor averaged 19.8 rebounds for the 1961 Lakers and 18.6 boards in 1962. By that time, Kelly Miller Playground in Washington, DC, had claimed him as its own.

Tim Hardaway, another no-problem player, popularized the lightning crossover dribble. His heirs include Damon Stoudamire and Allen Iverson. In the early 1970s, only Philadelphia 76ers and Washington Bullets star Archie Clark was known for his dangerous crossover. The preferred method of avoiding a close defender was a reverse dribble or, in some cases, to move the ball behind one's body where the opponent could not reach it.

And 1, hip-hop and rap music, *SportsCenter,* and the NBA now live a happy coexistence. Sneaker companies and movie studios market the schoolyard game. Ironically, the Globetrotters play conventional basketball now because they *don't* get big enough leads to go with the comedy routines. How many people can name the current clown prince of the Harlem Globetrotters as they read these words? As far away as Yugoslavia and Croatia, players as tall as 7 feet or more can execute moves and passes once the sole domain of Trotters greats

William "Pop" Gates and Reece "Goose" Tatum. A chest pass will not make the nightly local sports wrap-up show. A seventeen-foot jump shot will not bring a crowd to its feet unless it is a game winner.

Hollywood films such as *Above the Rim,* HBO's *Rebound* (about the rise, fall, and rise of Earl Manigault), and *White Men Can't Jump* honor the street game. Cable network TNT aired a documentary about the Holcombe Rucker League and Tournament called *On Hallowed Ground,* narrated not by a hip-hop star, but dramatic actor Andre Braugher.

The beat goes on—at Venice Beach in Los Angeles, in alleys in the Barrio de Belen in Havana, Cuba, and in the WNBA. The playground game has made it cool to be creative. Street sells. And, the more streetball sells, the more it will find its way into various popular culture vehicles.

Streetball is pivotal in some of the literature of novelist John Edgar Wideman, the Pittsburgh native who was once an All-Ivy basketball player at Penn in the early 1960s. The monikers keep coming: Lonnie "The Prime Objective" Harrell, Garvin "I'll Be Right Back" Opung, Ed "Booger" Smith, Jamal "Mal-Mal The Abuser" Tinsley, Rafer "Skip-To-My-Lou" Alston, Malloy "The Future" Nesmith. Tales of "Goat," "'Copter," and "Honey Dip" are still told in reverent tones. At any courtside in America, a neophyte may hear, "Young blood, you ain't seen nothin'. You shoulda seen So-and-So!" But, despite the folklore that has grown up around a playground superstar, more often than not, the local legend was waylaid by narcotics, became a scholastic casualty when trying to play the college game, or lacked the discipline necessary to follow team rules.

Pete Maravich always insisted that basketball was a form of entertainment. "Pistol" Pete, the flashiest player in the history of the organized game, died of a heart attack on a basketball court during a pickup game when he was only forty-four years old. Imagine—forty-four—the same number of points Pistol averaged per game in college, setting an NCAA record that will not die on the court. Maravich set that record by dazzling opponents with moves that would have made him "Mr. *SportsCenter,*" had he played twenty years later. Still, rival coaches labeled Maravich a "hot dog." Sportswriters at the time thought, "He only gets away with that 'cause his father's the LSU coach." Others in the South berated him for playing "n—r" ball.

Although panned by rivals and journalists, fittingly Maravich's most enduring epitaph came from a high school coach. Carl Stewart, the black coach of the great Baton Rouge McKinley High School teams, screened Maravich's magic act in an instructional film called "Homework Basketball." Stewart marveled: "He's one of us." Coach Stewart was speaking more to a culture than an ethnicity.

Marques Haynes of Langston University and the Harlem Globetrotters has likely influenced every subsequent ballhandling whiz, whether aware of him or not. Haynes graduated from Langston in 1946, and played professional basketball into his sixties. Young fans tried to copy his pet moves—sliding to the floor on one hip while maintaining his dribble, taking a knee while dribbling as defenders poked at the ball, and dribbling between the legs. The movie newsreel was Haynes' 1940s and 1950s showcase. Players such as Cousy, Fred "Curly" Neal (from Johnson C. Smith College and a future Globetrotter), Pablo Robertson (Loyola of Chicago, Trotters), Calvin Murphy, Maravich, and Ernie DiGregorio (Providence College, Buffalo Braves, and Boston Celtics) were Haynes' basketball heirs.

The early Harlem Globetrotters were the ambassadors of not only the game of basketball but also did much to expose the schoolyard game to the world. Goose Tatum and Marques Haynes did for improvisational basketball what Louis Armstrong and Duke Ellington did for black impressionist music.

Today, the slam dunk, the no-look pass, and the crossover dribble occupy a global stage. Madison Avenue and corporate America will continue to use showtime basketball to sell products. In the video age, basketball highlights influence players all over the world. Deception is the norm in basketball, so it is the game of The Harlem Magicians, "The Houdini of the Hardwood" (Cousy) and Earvin "Magic" Johnson we have come to love. The newest, and oldest, tricks will always come from the schoolyard.

SCHOOLYARD HALL OF FAME

Earl Manigault (New York City): Dropped a city record 52 in a game for Ettinger Junior High. Later a schoolboy star at Ben Franklin High. Had hops and handles. An astonishing seventy-two colleges offered him scholarships, but he fell into a life of heroin and petty crime, before later rebuilding his life.

Billy Harris (Chicago): Star at Northern Illinois University and briefly an ABA player (San Diego Conquistadors). Claims that from age sixteen to thirty he could have spotted Oscar, Elgin, Bird, or Michael 22 points and beat them in a one-on-one game to 24 points. Played summer ball versus Bulls stars Bob Love and Chet Walker.

Jackie Jackson (Brooklyn): Averaged 23 rebounds a game at Virginia Union University at 6'3". His business card read: "Have Converse, Will Travel." Later, was a member of the Harlem Globetrotters.

Skip Wise (Baltimore): The playground legend was an inspiration for future NBA stars Muggsy Bogues and Reggie Williams, among others.

Curtis Jones (Detroit): A high school hero, Jones experienced a stereotypical fall from glory.

Pee Wee Kirkland (New York City): An All-CIAA star at Norfolk State, he scored 219 points in a prison game.

James "Arkansas Red" Allen (Arkansas): Scored 60 points in a college game against Grambling and NBA star Willis Reed.

Harry Davis (Durham, NC): Father of NBA's Hubert Davis and brother of NBA's Walter Davis, and a better player than both of them.

Ray Lewis (Los Angeles): A New York Knick scout once rated him higher than UCLA's Bill Walton during an NBA preseason camp in 1973. Possessed incredible court vision.

Bobby Knight (Hartford): The former Knick and Globetrotter was an extraordinary ballhandler. He still plays, although he is in his seventies.

Wil Jones (Washington, DC): Considered a marksman. He set a Colonial League single-game mark of 56 points at American University in the early 1960s. He later coached Earl Jones at the University of the District of Columbia.

James "Fly" Williams (New York City): Williams once scored 63 points in the Dapper Dan Classic, a noted high school all-star game versus a team that featured NBA legend Moses Malone. He averaged almost 30 points per game as a freshman at Austin Peay to lead the NCAA.

Steve Strother (Boston): Drafted by the Houston Rockets in 1975, despite not starting much of his college career. Considered the greatest schoolyard player in "The Bean" since Providence All-American Jimmy Walker.

Connie Hawkins (Brooklyn): Played Iowa's All Big Ten star Don Nelson one-on-one when Hawkins was just an Iowa frosh—Nellie barely scored. Later became the ABA MVP in 1968.

Chapter 7

Fundamentals:
Coaching Today's High School Player

Chris Burtch

Despite the obvious similarities, coaching high school basketball in the new century is different from coaching the sport thirty, twenty, or even ten years ago. Those of us who played the sport in the 1980s, 1970s, and before, remember the idea that the coach was unquestionably the boss and the things that he said or did were just simply the way things were.

My parents knew very little about what went on at our practices, and my biggest concern was that my coach would call my father to tell him that I was either in trouble or that my work ethic was lacking. Looking back at my experience as a high school basketball player, this notion, at least in part, kept me motivated to work hard. More important, it also went a long way in keeping me out of even more trouble than I got into. I know that many of the players whom I played with in high school and college feel the same way.

For a variety of reasons, many of which will be discussed later, the basic notion of coach and/or teacher as authority figure has changed in some fundamental ways since then. First of all, today's high school players do not simply accept without question everything a coach does or says as the way it is.

A prime example of this was the experience I had my first year as a varsity coach. We used to do a drill with our players that both my high school and college coach did with us. The goal of the drill was simple: it was to run down the court after the ball, get to it before your partner and dive on it with reckless abandon. As a player I hated this drill, but I assumed it made me tougher, so I did it with my teams.

When my best player got hurt in the drill, missed a game, and was hobbled for weeks, I sensed a growing rebellion on my hands. I talked to my captain about this after practice one day and his comment was meaningful. He said, "Coach, that drill does absolutely nothing to make us better. All it does is beat us up and make us want to kill each other in the locker room."

He was, of course, absolutely right. Since then, I have reserved the drill for early season situations when I believe a team needs to get tougher. But the thinking process of my captain illustrates one of the fundamental challenges a high school or small college coach faces today that our predecessors did not: their players scrutinize each drill to ascertain whether or not it is worthwhile.

As a player, I simply never considered whether a drill was beneficial; I just did it because the coach told us to. It is easy for my assistants and I to see which drills my players believe are worthwhile and which ones they do not by their intensity level. In our best drills, the ones which directly improve our players' performance in our offense sets or in our defensive schemes, the players go hard and approach it with a lot of intensity every time. In the drills that do not necessarily directly improve our team or individual skills, they simply do not go as hard, no matter how much screaming and yelling we, the coaching staff, do. There are drills that I do not use anymore because I have learned through my players' attitudes and actions that they are not worthwhile.

The coaching definition of discipline has changed in many ways as well. Ten years ago, being on a disciplined team meant playing for a coach who would not allow earrings, tattoos, or anything that expressed individuality. My experiences in both high school and college was that while team rules such as this were set in stone, being disciplined enough to know what a good shot was and/or how to hold onto a lead late in the game were not as important.

Today, we live in an age in which nearly every professional or big-time college athlete that we see on television is adorned with jewelry, tattoos, and gold teeth and uses language to match this attitude. So once again, the job of today's coach is to find things that are important in terms of team discipline and stick with these, reinforcing them on a regular basis.

My players, for example, will buy into the idea of how important it is to be disciplined in terms of shot selection, working the clock at the end of a game, and keeping their cool with opposing players and officials. But in this day and age, the coaching staff finds it much more difficult to take issue with things such as earrings, tattoos, and other objects that express individuality. Quite frankly, the rules that my coaches set in stone were often trivial and did not have much to do with the game itself. With today's athletes, I would much rather teach them to hit an open cutter for an easy layup or know the correct pass to beat a press than worry about whether they wear earrings or have garish tattoos.

In the summer of 1999, I learned a valuable lesson from a highly successful coach, who happens to be one of the two or three high school coaches for whom I have the most respect. His teams are, without question, the most disciplined teams in Western Pennsylvania. When I am around this coach, I try to absorb as much as I can.

On this particular day, the first morning of a summer team camp run by legendary Pennsylvania coach George Abraham, we were scheduled to play his team. His players were shooting around when we arrived. I was shocked when I walked into the gym and realized that many of his players had earrings and tattoos. He wasn't there yet, so I figured they would take out the rings and cover the tats when he got there. He came, we played the game, his players were their usual disciplined selves, and they absolutely shocked me with their work ethic. The players, however, did not take their earrings out or cover their tattoos. It didn't seem to detract from the team's discipline at all. In fact, he was harder on his players then I remembered him being in my playing days.

At lunch, we talked a little about today's athlete and the changes in players over the years. He basically felt that there were battles a coach had to choose to fight and others that simply were not worth it. He felt his team would be as disciplined as he made them. In the end, they would play hard if he demanded it, earring or not. That message is simple and fits right in to the theme of the difference in coaching today's athlete.

The outsider's perception of today's athlete is that of a spoiled, coddled brat who only "plays when he wants to." But ironically, I have come to believe that in many ways my players and today's players in general need my assistant coaches and I more than our predecessors did.

In my first two seasons as the school's varsity coach, the focus of the team and the school was winning games. We had a gifted player, one of the best to ever play at the school, as well as a good supporting cast. We generated a great deal of excitement in January and February of my first year when we won eight out of our last twelve games and made the postseason for the first time since 1984.

The winning continued the next season. Living in a small college town, it was fun to watch as the whole area got absorbed in watching our star player, Ben Zajac, break scoring records. Playing outstanding basketball as a team and utilizing Zajac's individual abilities, we cruised into the play-offs.

I was amazed at how it seemed that the players came to rely more and more heavily on me and the other coaches to keep their lives as normal as possible as things got more and more insane around us. During the stretch run of that second season, I had more players come to me with off-the-court problems than that of my previous eleven seasons of coaching put together. Many of these problems stemmed from the fact that in a school that had averaged six wins per year for the previous fifteen seasons, many people involved in these kids' lives started looking for ways to bring them back down to earth.

The day after we beat perennial powerhouse Sharon High School for the first time in school history, a teacher gave a player of mine a discipline card for eating an apple at 7:15 in the morning. At the time the player was sitting at his locker in an empty school studying chemistry. He had eaten an apple every morning all year up to that point with no problems. All of a sudden, basketball players were perceived as arrogant.

It became a challenge to make sure that my players understood that this was an unfortunate by-product of flourishing in a place where the team had not been previously successful. Most people involved with the school and the community were incredibly supportive and proud of us, so we had to address this problem without making the players feel as if everyone was out to get them. I had to work very hard at keeping the cocoon that surrounded our team intact through all of the press coverage, administrative pressures, and playing in front of crowds that were twice as big as crowds we played in front of the previous year. These things, which seemed to be such monumental problems at the time, paled in comparison to the situations that we as a team, a coaching staff, and a school faced the following year.

The season started normally enough, with a cautious optimism that despite the fact that Zajac was gone, we could win the county and maybe even compete at the district level in the play-offs—if we could get to the play-offs. The fact that Zajac and his 2,000 points and 1,000 rebounds had graduated was problem enough, but we were also faced with the problem that we had absolutely no inside presence at all. We had to figure out how to go from getting all of our points inside to getting none of them on the blocks.

We opened the season at a tournament that we had won the previous year, playing an outstanding team from Ohio in the first round and then playing the host team in the consolation game. We battled in both games, but those were top-flight high school basketball teams and, at that point in the season, we were not. It is difficult to try to convince proud and competitive high school athletes that a loss is not the end of world. That, however, became the challenge of the early part of the season for the coaching staff. When we followed the tourney with losses at two state-ranked opponents, we were in full-fledged crisis mode and it was only the beginning of December.

We had a team meeting at that point and really brought back the focus to the little things—the fundamentals—such as throwing the pass with the correct hand, going off of two feet on layups, really selling out on defense, and working the offenses until we got a high percentage shot. We followed the meeting with perhaps our two best practices. After that, the season turned around quickly.

We went out and won six of our next eight games, including a nice win to conclude 2001 in the consolation game of a holiday tournament. With no game for six days, and league play coming up in mid-January, I decided to try something I hadn't done in my coaching career up to that point—give the team a few days off. We traveled home that night and I had a sense that we had really turned a corner as a team. My captain, Zach Sarver, indicated to me that the team felt the same way. Looking back on that night, we had such a sense of fulfillment and excitement about the rest of our season. It's funny how fate sometimes steps in to change everything.

DEALING WITH TRAGEDY

Late in the afternoon, while watching an unremembered game film on New Year's Day 2002, the phone rang. That moment is frozen in my mind. I can still remember the sound of my daughters playing in the next room while a fellow history teacher and friend, Sidney Snyder, informed me that four Slippery Rock students had been killed in a car accident that afternoon. One of the students had been a teammate of my sophomores as a junior high player and another had been a cameraman and manager for our team the season before. My thoughts immediately went to the parents of these kids. After the shock began to wear off, I wondered how my players were dealing with this.

I did not know what to expect the next morning when I arrived for shoot-around. To my surprise, many of the players were already there, more than an hour earlier than the scheduled time. I always considered one of my strengths as a coach to be communication, but I can honestly say I had no idea what to say to my team. Not much could be said. The players quietly began to get into their shooting groups and start the drill.

My assistant coach, Bob Book, and I just watched in amazement as the guys worked at the drill and went through it with determined zeal. We talked after the shoot-around and I had them take a moment to re-member their friends. We changed and got on the bus to go to our game at Greenville. I don't think I've ever been as proud of a team as I was that night as I watched us play through a lot of emotional pain—and at times tears—while valiantly battling to beat a good Greenville team.

There is nothing like watching people get through grief and pain together. It soon became apparent that the misfortune had made the players and coaches rely on one another even more heavily. I realized how therapeutic playing the game of basketball was for the players.

Our squad opened league play with a very satisfying win against a good Hickory team, and the thought of actually winning the league began to be a real possibility. But as it turned out, the ties that had been forged by going through the early season adversity and the hor-rific tragedy would be severely tested through the next few weeks.

We played Grove City, the early season favorite to win the league, in the second game. We were in control throughout the contest, but some costly mistakes, bad decisions, and missed free throws late in the fourth quarter allowed the Eagles to steal one on our home floor. Understandably, the next day was rough. Some finger pointing and bad blood occurred among the guys.

We played another home game the next night, knowing that playing so soon after a devastating loss could be a disaster or the best thing for us, depending on how the team responded. I talked before the game about composure and putting things behind us and going out and playing our best basketball under difficult circumstances. As we had seemed to be able to do all year, we bounced back and beat a talented Oil City team that night. It didn't take the sting away from the loss to a league rival the night before, but I spoke to the team about resiliency and how adversity can build character. Coming back from such a heartbreaking loss to beat a good team could be a great learning experience for us.

The team slugged through the middle part of the season, winning a tough league contest at Hickory and then having to swallow another very difficult loss to Sharon. The character of our team and our identity was quickly becoming that of a group of overachievers who worked hard and played a very physical game against teams with more individual talent.

The only thing separating us from first place was the one-point loss to Grove City and a two-point loss at Sharon. We were frustrated but had a sense that, at 2-2, we could still win the league if we could limit the mistakes that had plagued us in those losses.

Just when the team (and the school, for that matter) started returning to some shred of normality, tragedy struck again. Once again, concerns about wins and losses seemed small.

After the Sharon game, we were told that one of our cheerleaders had contracted meningitis and would probably not return to cheer again that season. At first, her condition seemed to be getting better. After the initial shock subsided, we were told that she was resting comfortably and even planned on returning to school soon.

Senior Night is a special occasion for the players who have put in many years of sweat for the program and themselves. The night is filled with celebration and each graduating senior player and cheerleader is honored on-court with their parents in front of a packed house.

The Senior Night game was going to be a tough battle—a non-league game against Western Pennsylvania powerhouse George Junior Republic. The salute to our seniors was smothered by another horrible tragedy for our community. I will never forget the feeling I had in the pit of my stomach when Cory Hake, Slippery Rock's Athletic Director, stopped me on the way down to the locker room after the game. He told me that another one of our own had died. Although our prayers had been with the cheerleader, she succumbed to meningitis.

In eleven years of coaching I had never cried in front of my team. My gut instinct told me that displaying such emotion was being overly dramatic. Faced with yet another tragic death, however, I could not fight off the deep feelings of sadness. I remember telling my team how proud I was of them, how much I loved them, and then just breaking down right there in the locker room. Unfortunately, it would not be the last time I would break down in front of my team that season.

As a team, we went to the funeral home the next day. I stood at the end of the line as the players came out of the viewing, one by one. I can remember each of their reactions—some wept uncontrollably, others were stoic but obviously in pain. I tried to be there to comfort all of them.

That effort—trying to support a group of young men who had encountered more tragedy in a short span than many people do in a lifetime—is perhaps the most difficult thing I have ever done in my life. I'm not sure if they realized this, but I was trying to console a group of confused, sad, and angry young men when, at the same time, I was as angry and sad as I've ever been in my life. Ashley Anderson's death didn't make sense, particularly when we had been given such an optimistic prognosis. On a deeper level, I wondered how the school, students, and community would rebound from another death of one of their own?

That night the team had to play a scheduled game at Grove City, our longtime rival and nemesis. We traveled the handful of miles to Grove City and played valiantly, but simply didn't have enough left to win a game of that magnitude.

Relations had always been a little strained between the two schools, because of the intensity of the rivalry. However, that night, Grove City's head coach, Don Fee, came in after the game and, in tears, talked about how much he admired our players' effort that evening. Considering the fervor of our rivalry, this was a tremendous display of class and sportsmanship. Coach Fee's words also put the day in context—basketball seemed to be so important, but it was really just a game.

* * *

The level of media coverage of high school sports has changed dramatically over the past decade. When I played at Slippery Rock High School, each game received a couple of paragraphs in the local newspaper. Now, the sports pages of several papers are filled with long stories and game analysis. The Internet has also provided an outlet for anyone who can dish out a little money for a domain name and a monthly hosting fee.

Despite the emotional burdens weighing heavily on the team and the courage it took to show up and play hard against a talented Grove City team, we took a beating for the loss. I had to quietly accept it when I picked up the paper the next day and read about our cold shooting and lack of execution.

As a result of this experience, I have become much more defensive of my players. Reading or hearing negative comments about them is difficult to take under any circumstances. Often the kids are caught up in media hoopla that has little to do with the way they play and a lot to do with personalities and personal alliances. Realizing that people who aren't around the team on a daily basis are sometimes going to take potshots forces today's coach to be more cognizant of the media and its effect on players.

I don't think that high school coaches or players will ever face the media onslaught of those at the collegiate and professional levels, but protecting the kids from the press is important in our information-rich society. Even in a small community such as Slippery Rock, where everyone pretty much knows everyone else, dealing with prying eyes and wagging tongues is on the job description of today's coach.

We finished the league season with another very tough loss to eventual league champ Sharon. Once again, our toughness and intensity kept the game close. In the end, however, the much more athletic and talented team pulled away. The loss to Sharon was another bitter pill to swallow in a season full of bitter pills.

Despite the tough loss, the team still had one more game, a game that my players had been looking forward to all year. We had been invited by George Junior Republic's coach Bob McConnell to play the first game of a double header against a great Lisbon, Ohio, team before they played the number-one team in the country—Akron St. Vincent-St. Mary and prep phenomenon LeBron James. In addition to giving us the opportunity to see a future NBA superstar up close, the Lisbon game would be played in front of a packed house at the Beegley Center, which seats about 8,000 spectators, on the campus of Youngstown State University.

The game itself seemed to mirror our entire season. The team came out a little tight and flat and fell behind early. We were forced to claw our way back into the game and actually had a shot to tie the game with a three-pointer at the buzzer, but it fell short. As tough as the Lisbon loss was, the next two hours were perhaps the most enjoyable of the season. We watched two incredible teams go at it the entire game.

The experiences we had been through truly made me appreciate my players. It was a treat to not only spend time with them away from being their coach but also to watch them enjoy the talents of St. Vincent's James and George Junior stars Benson Callier and John Brown.

Adding to the magic of the night, George Junior pulled off the upset, which made our players feel pretty good. We had played George Junior tight earlier in the season, but eventually succumbed in a 12-point. A sophomore on my team had bought that week's *Sports Illustrated,* which featured James on the cover. Seeing James on the cover of every sports fanatic's Bible made the whole experience more exciting.

Riding home on the bus that night, I reflected on the season—tough league losses, great wins over teams such as Meadville, Oil City, Titusville, and Hickory, and the absolutely unthinkable tragedies we had all experienced. It was difficult to make sense of everything and still too many emotions at the surface.

It always takes me about a week to feel somewhat "normal" after a season, and after this one, it would certainly take longer. I recall waking up on Saturday morning, exactly six days after our last game, and thinking to myself that I actually felt good about some situations that were bothering me a few days earlier. How quickly that would change.

At 9:15 a.m., Bob Book, my assistant coach, called to tell me that a sophomore on our team, Jason Yakima, had been killed the night before in a car accident, along with another Slippery Rock student. Two other players, also sophomores, were in the car, but had escaped with only minor injuries.

I remember thinking that it couldn't be true—I felt an incredible numbness, which slowly turned to anger as the weekend progressed. For the first time in my life I went into shock. Several people called me over the next few days. These conversations, including a relatively long one with our girls' head varsity coach, John Tabisz, I simply don't remember.

This young man was the kind of player that every coach covets. He was always in the gym working on his game, arriving early and staying late; a good student and an even better citizen; beloved by all on our team and in our school. He and I always joked about him being the first player to send in his summer camp form—every year for five consecutive years.

At school on Monday, all the sense of normalcy that the teachers and administrators had tried to keep while dealing with the other tragedies was gone. Health care professionals, local priests and ministers, psychologists, and others assembled at the school in an attempt to help the students get through yet another incredible loss.

As with the other losses, we faced this one as a team, particularly since it was one of our own that passed away. The players and other coaches were in and out of my room all day. The conversations ran the gamut from reminiscing about our teammate to teasing each other. Other times we just congregated, gaining strength from the collective unit. Sometimes we cried together. The members of the team, the coaches, and other family members and friends pulled together over the next few days. By doing this, we were able to survive the loss.

We went as a team to the viewing hours. The most humbling experience of my life occurred when this incredible kid's dad told me that I had made his son a better person and that he was just crazy about being a member of the team. I just hugged his mom and stood there and cried like a baby on her shoulder. Once again, my assistant coach and I went through the line first and then stood at the end and tried to comfort each player as he came through. How we made it through those weeks and months, I will never know.

I do know that watching his family, his teammates, and his friends trudge through and find reasons to smile and try to recover was an incredible inspiration to me. It seems strange to say, but at that moment, I realized how important it was to be a basketball coach. The experience was more than just preparing offenses and defenses designed to utilize the team's best talent and it was more than designing off-season drills to improve their individual skills. Coaching must come from the heart. Making an impact on players' lives is an awesome responsibility that should not be taken lightly.

In the end, players are probably not going to remember individual moments of games or practices. Later in life, however, long after they have hung up their sneakers, they will have a sense of how the sport helped them develop as individuals. As a coach, a persona will have an affect on the player's growth as an individual. This is much more important than winning and losing games.

THE FUTURE

As a group, the coaches did not know what to expect from the team the following year. Six terrific senior players had graduated. A bigger question mark was how the team would gel after all the adversity it had been through on and off the floor the previous season. We returned two varsity starters and the members of a 15-5 junior varsity team, but there would be many questions heading into the new season.

As the team makeup changed, so did my inner circle. Coach Book asked for a year off and was replaced by my longtime friend Jeff Steele. Such a transition always has the possibility of becoming a distraction. It did seem to Jeff and I, however, that there was a forging together because of all we had been through, which made us a much stronger unit in many of the summer and fall league games that we played in preparation for the new season.

It is extremely important to have your team playing league games and working on skills in open gyms and camps in the off-season, but often this can be frustrating because you play many summer and fall games without many of your players, who are participating in other sports. At Slippery Rock, the football, soccer, baseball, track, and basketball coaches basically share the same handful of athletes. Often, the schools we play in our conference do not have the same problem, but it is a situation that we as a coaching staff must work through without complaint.

After the previous season's adversity we could never again take anything for granted, and I approached the 2002-2003 campaign that way. I have become convinced that if a coach is going to succeed with today's high school players, he or she must be willing to be humble enough to share these players, but still be willing to put in time with those who come into the gym.

EPILOGUE

The 2002-2003 Slippery Rock Area High School varsity basketball team posted a 16-8 record and once again returned to the district play-offs. Many of the players wore black wristbands to commemorate their fallen comrades.

Chapter 8

Seventeen Things I Learned from Dean Smith

Peter Cashwell

I became an optimist over a seventeen-second span. Actually, it took several minutes of real time, but the game clock counted down only seventeen seconds. That's not many—fewer than it takes CBS to air a TV commercial—but these were long ones, far longer than the rushed, abbreviated seconds I live with nowadays, that ticked by on the day after I turned eleven. Each one was long enough to leave a lasting impression, to teach a lesson, though I didn't know it at the time. I was young, and excited, and the teacher of those lessons wasn't even in the game. He was sitting on the sidelines, watching, already aware on that March afternoon that optimism doesn't always get you far. The green light may wink across the bay, but experience teaches us that it will almost certainly remain out of reach.

Almost.

But I cling to that "almost" as if it were a lifeline, and I cling because of that impossible seventeen-second span. I'm forty now, easily old enough to be cynical, but I can never quite let go of my optimism. I just can't. Coach Smith would never forgive me.

0:17

I grew up in Chapel Hill, home of the University of North Carolina, where it is hard not to learn about basketball. My journey began in 1971, when my parents took my little brother David and me to New York City to see UNC's team, the Tar Heels, play in the National Invitational Tournament. I was only eight, but I still recall the nighttime lights playing along the mass of the Empire State Building, the clattering sound of the train ride from Connecticut, and the sight of Bill Chamberlain, a rangy 6'5" forward, lighting up Madison Square Garden for 35 points to lead UNC to the title.

By the time we got home, the team had made a grammatical shift from third person to first—*they* hadn't won the NIT, *we* had. Dad saw the writing on the wall and found season tickets for David and me, back in the days when you could still find seats in Carmichael Auditorium. Ours were folding chairs on the floor behind the north basket, but so far off to the side that when a player shot from in front of the home bench, we couldn't see him. We didn't care about the poor sight lines, only that Carolina basketball was blossoming before us. And blossom it did, for the next decade and a half. We saw the Tar Heel legends: Jones, Davis, Ford, Worthy, Jordan. We also saw the journeymen, the players whose contributions might come only on spot duty, or even in practice, but we knew their names then and know them still: Mickey Bell, John Virgil, Woody Coley. They were Tar Heels. We felt honor-bound to remember them.

In 1972, led by Chamberlain and junior college transfer Robert McAdoo, Carolina made it to the NCAA Final Four in Los Angeles, and Mom and Dad took us to California a few days behind the team. I recall little about the games (UCLA won it all—again), but I know exactly how I felt about UNC basketball by then. Mom snapped a picture of me on the morning of our departure for home; in it I'm wearing the coonskin cap I had bought at Disneyland, and my face is lit up with an expression of awe and joy that I've since only seen in photos of me holding my newborn children. Dad is bending down to tell me that we're flying home on the same plane as the Tar Heels.

0:16

There was a lot to love about our team. For one thing, we had cool uniforms. The V-necked jerseys, unlike most other teams' tops, didn't look like undershirts, and the shoes simply reeked of cool: canvas high-top Converse All-Stars, the stars on their inside ankles set against a field of brilliant Carolina blue. Yes, we had our own special color, a color *named* after us, which distinguished us from teams with commonplace colors such as red, orange, or royal blue. Years later I would discover that people outside North Carolina called it "sky blue" or "powder blue," but to this day I look at a bright October sky and see "Carolina blue" on the label of the celestial crayon that colored it.

We also loved the Heels because they won. All kids prefer to root for a successful team, and Dave and I were no different. We identified with the Tar Heels because we hoped their superiority on the court would somehow prove us superior as well. What we began to notice over time, however, was that our team's superiority didn't hinge on the players. We always had good players, mind you, but they weren't the *same* players from year to year. Something else, we realized, must be at work. We knew that Carolina players had certain habits—for instance, scoring a basket and then pointing at the teammate who had made the assist, or briefly huddling together at the foul line just before a free throw, or holding up four fingers and spreading the court— and we knew that somehow these habits added up to winning the game. David and I had always assumed that was the way basketball was meant to be played; what we soon realized was that these practices weren't in the rule book, but had been specifically introduced by the coach, a guy by the name of Dean Smith. Perhaps, we reasoned, the Tar Heels' success had something to do with him.

We were right, of course, and wrong. Dean Smith would be the first to point out that he himself never set foot on the court for UNC. Still, a coach's contributions can be measured to some degree by what his team does on the court and, of course, by what he does for his team *off* the court. Smith guided his players into the NBA, into college coaching jobs, and even into his home; in 1987, the parents of sophomore center Scott Williams died, and Smith served as his surrogate father thereafter. Over his thirty-six-year career at UNC, Smith spent so much time looking out for others' interests that it seemed shocking when he put his own interests first for once. In 1997, he decided the game wasn't fun for him anymore and he quit. Of course, even in doing something for himself, he figured out a way to help a friend: he waited until just before the start of fall practice to announce his retirement, all but guaranteeing a promotion to head coach for his longtime assistant Bill Guthridge.

Perhaps Coach Smith would prefer to let someone else take the credit, but I'm afraid he must shoulder at least some of it: no other coach in the history of college basketball has led his team to 879 victories.

0:15

Cicero once said, "If you aspire to the highest place it is no disgrace to stop at the second, or even the third," but for nearly two decades, his wisdom was ignored when it came time to discuss Dean Smith. No one had expected him to succeed at first, of course; no one had expected him to be UNC's coach at all. Smith, who had assisted the legendary Phog Allen at Kansas and Bob Spear at Air Force, had come to UNC to assist Frank McGuire, not to replace him. In 1961, however, it became known that some Carolina and NC State players had become involved in a point-shaving scheme, and McGuire decided the time was ripe to leave for an NBA job. With the team going on probation, established coaches probably didn't see UNC as a terribly appealing opportunity, and UNC's Chancellor, William Aycock, took a chance on Smith, who was a few months past his thirtieth birthday.

Things didn't begin auspiciously. In his first year, the Tar Heels went 8-9 overall, as one might expect of a scandal-weakened program with a rookie head coach. But no Dean Smith team would ever again have a losing record. One team came close: in his third season, the Heels went 12-12 for the year and 6-8 in the Atlantic Coast Conference, a fifth-place finish that marked the low point for Smith in ACC play. From that point on, his teams would create one of the greatest streaks in college basketball history: for thirty-three straight years, UNC would finish no lower than third place in the toughest conference in the nation.

It was a streak that many Carolina fans, myself included, would come to accept as a birthright. Even in an "off" year, UNC would finish in the top three, just as the sun would set in the west and the flowers would bloom in the springtime. What we never considered was the fact that there were seven (later eight) other schools in the conference, and we had to beat at least five of them every year in order to maintain our position. It was an attitude that, while widespread, was grossly unfair to the team and its coach.

What was worse was that some fans actually *complained*. Throughout the 1960s and 1970s, despite a record of success that had become all but monotonous, Dean Smith was criticized for being "unable to win the big one." The string of top-three ACC finishes, the Final Fours in 1966, 1967, 1968, 1972 and 1977, the NIT Championship in 1971, the Olympic gold medal in 1976—these weren't big ones?

Apparently not. Each trip to the NCAA tournament seemed only to increase the size of the monkey on Smith's back. When the injury-depleted Tar Heels stumbled into the championship game in 1977, mostly on the iron will of guard John Kuester, the monkey was fully the size of Al McGuire, whose Marquette team held Carolina off to win the title. In 1981, when a smooth-shooting forward named Al Wood led the Heels to the title game, the monkey had grown bigger and angrier and looked a lot like Bobby Knight, whose Hoosiers relegated Smith's team, once again, to second place. By the time Carolina got to the 1982 championship game in New Orleans, the monkey astride Smith was far larger than even such giants as Georgetown coach John Thompson, or even the Hoya's outstanding freshman center, Patrick Ewing; no, this monkey was big enough to climb onto the roof of the Superdome and swat biplanes out of the sky.

Thompson, a close friend of Smith's who had assisted him at the 1976 Olympics, had to feel awkward—how could he deny Smith yet another chance at the title that would silence his critics? For his part, Smith had to feel both desperate to win and somewhat regretful that a victory would have to come over Thompson. Neither coach, of course, did anything to hold his team back; if anything, Ewing seemed more aggressive than usual, swatting away Carolina's first five field goal attempts and being called for goaltending on every one. The game see-sawed along, with junior forward James Worthy leading the Heels and Ewing anchoring the Hoyas, but Smith had to be thinking about the monkey—when would it finally jump off? *Would* it jump off?

It loosened its grip with seventeen seconds left in the game, when senior point guard Jimmy Black faked a pass to his right and whipped the ball left to freshman shooting guard Michael Jordan. Jordan elevated, as he would so many times in his career, and calmly flicked the ball through the net. It was 63-62 Carolina.

The simian weight on Smith's back wasn't gone yet, however. Georgetown still had plenty of time to work the ball inside to Ewing for a high-percentage shot, or pop an open jumper. But with only ten seconds left, an errant pass cold-cocked the monkey for good. Hoya guard Fred Brown was standing near the top of the key when, for no apparent reason, he flipped the ball into the hands of a player standing out of position near the right hash mark: James Worthy.

Worthy, obviously shocked, held the ball for an instant and then drove madly toward the UNC goal. He was fouled before he could get a shot off, and he missed both his free throws badly, but the damage had been done: the monkey was no more. Thompson, who made a point of embracing the dispirited Brown, congratulated his friend with obvious sincerity. Smith, for his part, gave his fiercest hug to Black—a senior point guard, the pinnacle of humanity in Smith's way of thinking—and left New Orleans a free man. The greatest "second-best" coach in the country was a champion at last, and the streets of Chapel Hill would be painted Carolina blue by morning.

0:14

In September 2002, as the ACC approached its fiftieth anniversary, the Raleigh *News and Observer* ran a column in which Caulton Tudor made the case that Dean Smith was the greatest coach in ACC hoops history. Ned Barnett responded with an argument that Duke's Mike Krzyzewski was the best. Barnett's primary argument is framed thus: "[C]oaching is ultimately about how a leader confronts challenges, develops and inspires talent and achieves the highest goal in his field. Against those measurements, Krzyzewski prevails" (*News and Observer,* September 26, 2002).

Okay, fair enough—Krzyzewski has unquestionably been able to alter his style in order to overcome challenges. Nonetheless, I think Barnett's argument actually serves Smith's case better. Consider that Smith started coaching in 1961, when college basketball was radically unlike today's game. There was no shot clock, no three-point line, and no arrows for alternating possessions—every tie-up was settled by a jump ball. Freshmen were ineligible for varsity teams, the NBA did not draft underclassmen (let alone high school players), and the NCAA Tournament involved only a handful of teams. Dunks were legal, if unspectacular, though they would go through a brief period of being illegal. Perhaps most bizarre to a modern basketball fan was the fact that the ACC had no black players. So how did Smith handle the changes that came his way?

He took a direct hand in making some of them. In 1966, he began recruiting black players, an act of no little courage in a South only one year removed from the violence of Selma. Though the Tar Heels failed to dislodge the UCLA Bruins from their viselike grip on the

NCAA title, the fact that UNC sent three straight teams to the Final Four after Charlie Scott's arrival on campus suggests that Smith adjusted to the new situation pretty well.

Indeed, before 1975, getting into the NCAA Tournament at all was a great accomplishment. Until that year, only one ACC school could go to the Big Dance: the winner of the ACC Tournament. As Tudor astutely points out, this arrangement made the ACC Tourney the biggest pressure cooker imaginable—more so than the Final Four, in many ways, because the teams were such intense rivals, fully aware of one another's strengths and weaknesses. At the ACC Tournament, Maryland-State, UNC-Duke, or UNC-State games were like wars, but Smith's teams won five such winner-take-all championships, plus eight more after 1975.

Freshmen became eligible to play in 1972, and though Smith always preferred experience over raw talent, he was willing to make exceptions for first-year stalwarts such as Mitch Kupchak, Walter Davis, Phil Ford, Mike O'Koren, and Michael Jordan. With first-year players playing substantial roles, Smith got teams to the Final Four in 1977 and 1981 and the championship season of 1982. The final points of that title game were scored by a tongue-waggling freshman, but Smith must have been pleased that the dominant performance in that championship game came from the veteran James Worthy, who scored 28 points to earn MVP honors.

Unfortunately for UNC fans, but fortunately for the Los Angeles Lakers, Worthy would skip his senior season to turn pro. Two years later, Michael Jordan would do the same. What did Smith do? He adjusted, just as he'd had to do in 1972 when junior college transfer Robert McAdoo left the Heels after one season, and just as he would do in later years when J. R. Reid, Rasheed Wallace, Jerry Stackhouse, and Jeff McInnis also left UNC early under his watch. So long as he felt the player would benefit from entering the draft, Smith wouldn't stand in the way. With every unexpected change in personnel, Smith would adjust.

He had made adjustments on the court all along. Despite the effectiveness of his trademark four corners delay offense, Smith had long pushed for a shot clock, and in 1985 the NCAA finally introduced one, along with a three-point shot the next year. Forced to abandon the four corners, except for brief, half-hearted spreads that he still used to shave the clock by twenty or thirty seconds, Smith could easily have rested on his laurels and let his program slide into mediocrity. Instead, he kept tinkering with his offensive and defensive schemes, kept hitting the recruiting trail, and after a decade of changes won his second NCAA title in 1993.

In his final season, at age sixty-six, he was back in the Final Four. One can only wonder what the 1961-model Smith would have made of a game featuring the 1997 Tar Heels. How would he react to watching point guard Ed Cota, a bald, tattooed, African-American freshman, drain the shot clock to the ten-second mark, then suddenly serve up a perfect alley-oop? What would he think upon seeing the ball snared by another black player, a sophomore named Vince Carter, and seemingly thrown down from the stratosphere? I think the young Smith would be stunned for a moment, but then he would say to himself, "Hmm . . . I bet we could set that same shot up as an out-of-bounds play. . . ."

Yes, I believe that adaptability is indeed one of the things that makes a great basketball coach, and Mike Krzyzewski is one of the very best ever. But if I had to find a coach to help me adapt, repeatedly, to changes that dwarf anything that's happened since 1980, I'd want Dean Smith.

0:13

A coach from Kansas and a player from New York broke the color line in North Carolina basketball. It helped that the player had transferred to Laurinburg (NC) Prep, giving him a chance to see firsthand what life in the South would be like, and giving UNC's recruiters a good chance to study him and consider their options. In 1966, Smith decided to offer him a scholarship—the first offered to a black player by any ACC school—and Charlie Scott became a Tar Heel.

Scott's coming to Chapel Hill was more courageous than we might realize today. Though it likes to consider itself the South's most progressive state, North Carolina in 1966 was still segregated, and it played games in other places where an integrated team was still an offense to (white) fans' sensibilities. Playing against South Carolina in Columbia, for example, Scott had to endure taunts and racial slurs from the Gamecock supporters. He sometimes received hate mail, and even a few death threats, but none of these affected him as much as the events of 1969.

In the summer of 1968, after just one season of varsity ball, Scott had been a gold medalist for the U.S. Olympic team. In his junior year, he averaged 22.3 points a game and led the Heels to their third consecutive ACC tournament title with a 40-point explosion against Duke. In the NCAAs, he scored 32 points and knocked in the game-winner to beat Davidson and send UNC to the Final Four again.

In the spring of 1969, however, the media named John Roche ACC Player of the Year. Roche, a talented player who would go on to a brief ABA career, was a sophomore at South Carolina—of course a *white* sophomore—and was also the only unanimous selection to the all-conference team. Moreover, despite the fact that UNC and UNC alone had represented the conference in the NCAA tournament for the past three years running, Roche's coach, Frank McGuire, was named ACC Coach of the Year—not Dean Smith.

Scott spoke out angrily against what he saw as the racism of the awards, even threatening to leave UNC. He eventually chose to stay for his senior year, but he was unrepentant about his comments. As he put it, "I don't consider it so much an injustice to me as an injustice to black athletes and black people everywhere. I've been trying to tell them there is no prejudice in the ACC—how do you explain this?"

The explanation, of course, is that there *was* prejudice in the ACC, and that Scott and every black person he'd spoken to had known it all along. His anger, however, was also expressed on behalf of at least one white man—the coach who had brought him to the ACC in the first place and whose remarkable success had gone unrecognized. That Smith had lost the coaching award to McGuire, who five years earlier had left him in charge of a UNC program on probation and gutted of talent, was an even greater twist of the knife.

Smith's reputation as a coach is so enormous today that we have trouble imagining him without it. When we picture him recruiting Charlie Scott, we can easily make the error of picturing him as the gray-haired dean of college coaching, his gold medal around his neck, his 879 victories tucked neatly under one arm, his reputation following him around like a zeppelin on a string. But when he drove to recruit Scott, Dean Smith could have fit his coaching reputation in his glove compartment with room for a map of the routes to Laurinburg. He had been a head coach for only five seasons. He had never won an ACC title, never been to a postseason tournament. All he had done was get the Tar Heels out from under their probation, recruit a few good players, and get the team over .500. He had no institutional capital at UNC, and no particular goodwill among Carolina fans; only a few years before, after a loss at Wake Forest, he had been burned in effigy. In 1966, Dean Smith as we know him barely existed.

But we know him now largely because of what he did in 1966.

Smith had long been an advocate of civil rights. He committed time and money to the cause of equality, often in cooperation with the Reverend Robert Seymour, the progressive-minded pastor of Chapel Hill's Binkley Baptist Church. In offering Scott a scholarship, however, he took a stand that he could easily have avoided, a stand that was both extremely visible and irrevocable. Had the university or the fans reacted angrily to the idea of a black player, Smith's career as a coach could have ended overnight. Had Scott's tenure at UNC been less successful on the court or off (appropriately, he was a dean's list student throughout his four years), Smith still might have been made a scapegoat. But Smith knew Scott would be exactly the player, and exactly the man, who could help him do what was right for the team, for the university, and for the cause.

The day after Smith's retirement, Michael Wilbon of *The Washington Post,* in appreciation of his efforts—*all* his efforts—wrote two perfect sentences: "Dean Smith, by far, is a greater man than he is a basketball coach. And he is on any short list of the greatest basketball coaches of all time."

0:12

Today basketball is a global obsession. The NBA is loaded with players from Canada, Germany, Croatia, and even China, and kids wear T-shirts with Michael Jordan or Kobe Bryant's names on them even in Southeast Asia and sub-Saharan Africa. With figures such as Dirk Nowitzki and Pau Gasol taking the court for their home countries, a typical all-star team of Americans will be hard-pressed to be competitive in an international tournament, let alone contend for the championship.

Thus, it is hard to remember that there was a time when basketball was a purely American game. The game was created in the States (albeit by a Canadian) back in 1891, and every international tournament may as well have had PROPERTY OF UNCLE SAM stamped on it for the next eighty years. Basketball's first Olympic gold medal was not awarded until 1936, but it went, of course, to the United States. For nearly four decades, the United States held an iron grip on the sport's greatest international contest, winning seventy-one straight games in Olympic competition.

At the Munich games of 1972, however, a veteran squad from the USSR got the chance—three chances, actually—to make a last-second basket that put the United States on the short end of the score at last. The final layup was made after the officials had put time back on the clock—twice—to keep the Soviets' hopes alive. The American team, furious at this perceived injustice, refused to accept the silver medals they believed the referees had conspired to give them.

Thus, when the next Olympiad rolled around, winning a gold medal was a Cold War imperative. If the 1972 Games had been a Sputnik-like victory for the Soviets, 1976 would have to be the equivalent of America's putting a man on the moon.

The man chosen to land this particular Eagle was one who at the time had not won an NCAA tournament title. He had sent a player to each of the last three Olympic teams, but he himself could offer no championship more impressive than his lone NIT title from 1971. *Couldn't the U.S. have gotten John Wooden?* some wondered. Or, since he at least had an NCAA championship to his credit, maybe NC State's Norm Sloan?

But the choice was Dean Smith, who promptly decided that the best way to win for the red, white, and blue in 1976 was to make sure the blue was the proper shade—a *paler* shade. Despite the fact that UNC's Larry Brown (1964), Charlie Scott (1968), and Bobby Jones (1972) had been Olympians, most observers were shocked when Smith chose *four* Tar Heels to represent America in 1976: point guard Phil Ford, swingman Walter Davis, center Mitch Kupchak, and power forward Tom LaGarde.

It's clear now that these four outstanding players fully deserved their Olympic berths; LaGarde had already represented the country in 1975's Pan-Am games, Kupchak was an All-American who had been named the ACC's Player of the Year for 1976, and both Ford and Davis would go on to win NBA Rookie of the Year honors. At the time, however, Smith's decision struck many as outright favoritism, a bias as strong as that exhibited by the officials in Munich and, worse, one that might derail America's hopes of retaking the gold in Montreal.

Certainly Smith knew that Tar Heels alone could not beat the world. Still, his other choices for the team showed that he preferred to coach players with whom he was familiar—specifically ACC players, one each from NC State, Duke, and Maryland. The stars of the team, however, were Notre Dame's Adrian Dantley and Indiana's Scott May, who were themselves 40 percent of the non-ACC contingent.

Regardless of his reasons, no one could argue with Smith's results. Dantley led the team in scoring and May in rebounding, but Kupchak and Ford were starters and major contributors; Kupchak was third on the team in scoring and second in rebounding, while Ford led the team in assists and ranked fourth in scoring. When Marquette's Butch Lee led a fired-up Puerto Rican team to within a point of the biggest upset in Olympic basketball history, it was Ford who sank the winning free throws. Though the USSR had been upset in the semifinals, meaning that there would be no rematch of the 1972 title game, the United States was nonetheless perfectly happy to play the final against a Yugoslavian team it had already beaten once. Behind Dantley's 30 points, the Americans reclaimed the gold 95-74.

0:11

Dean Smith's signature creation was the four corners offense, a delay game that Carolina used for decades to exploit the college game's lack of a shot clock. If the Heels could grab a second-half lead, any lead, the point guard would hold up four fingers, his teammates would scatter to the far corners of the frontcourt, and the shouting would begin; opponents' fans would boo and catcall, while Tar Heel fans began whooping with joy at the prospect of another victory.

Those four fingers almost always signaled a UNC victory. The point guard would dribble around in the center of the square, taking time off the game clock, playing keepaway, looking for an easy drive. If the defense threatened him, he would pass off to a teammate; if they tried a double-team, he'd look for a big man cutting backdoor. The four corners was devastatingly efficient, the ultimate expression of Smith's fondness for the high-percentage shot. Once the four fingers went up, the Heels' points would come from either layups or free throws. In the hands of a master ballhandler and floor general such as

Phil Ford, the offense was balletic, but it was a rare fan of Duke or State who could appreciate the dance.

There was one loss to Duke, however, in which the four corners helped give Duke a 47-40 victory. In that now-notorious game, the Heels held the ball against the heavily favored Blue Devils through most of the first half. Duke went up 2-0 after the opening tap. Because of a few turnovers and fouls, plus one extraordinarily ill-advised airball thrown up by center Rich Yonakor, by halftime the Heels were down 7-0, a score that must have led some casual fans to believe that the game under discussion was football. In the second half, Smith let his team play the Blue Devils straight up, and straight up was how they stayed; each team scored 40 points in the final twenty minutes. The game provided hard evidence that the Tar Heels could actually stand toe-to-toe with their powerful rivals; it was also evidence that even Homer, or his basketball equivalent, could nod off once in a while.

0:10

Smith made a few other mistakes, but not all were public. One private error was taking up smoking. The pressure-filled environment of coaching, along with North Carolina's low cigarette prices, probably contributed to what became a physical and psychological addiction. Lighting up on the bench was of course out of the question, but as soon as a game was over, Smith would celebrate in the hallway near the locker room with a quick cigarette. He struggled with quitting through most of his career, and was open with his players about the struggle. Not until he began suffering nosebleeds did he finally draw a line and give up the cigarettes.

Some of his mistakes were more public, such as when he allowed himself to be dragged into a no-win argument with the Cameron Crazies. The Crazies were the horde of often irritating but always creative Duke students who packed Cameron Indoor Stadium and made life miserable for visiting teams. UNC fans and even players have been known to consider some of their catcalls funny, such as the one that greeted Tar Heel guard Steve Hale when he came into the game after recovering from a collapsed lung: "IN-Hale, EX-Hale," chanted the crowd, and even Hale, a premed student, had to smile.

Other taunts from the Duke fans (or "Dookies," as they're known around Chapel Hill) were not so civil, such as the signs mocking Mike O'Koren's acne. O'Koren's response was to jab a finger at the scoreboard, where Duke was trailing.

The taunt that crossed the line from Smith's point of view was one that made fun of UNC power forward J. R. Reid. The Crazies mocked him by chanting "J. R. *Can't* Reid," and Smith started a slow burn. Reid was a solid student, the son of two educators, and the only reason Smith could see for singling him out was the fact that he was black. Given Smith's dogged loyalty and attitudes toward racism, it's not terribly surprising that he would jump to his player's defense. Unfortunately, his defense only dragged others into the fray. Smith was not about to publicly reveal a player's test scores, but he did announce that Reid's and Scott Williams's combined SAT scores were greater than the combined scores of two of Duke's big men, both white. The innocent Duke players, naturally, were not happy to have their SATs made the subject of public debate, and Smith wound up looking rather foolish by dignifying the Crazies' chant in the first place. It was a mistake, but one made from a sense of loyalty and a passion for racial equality—wrong, but done for the right reasons.

0:09

One thing that separated Smith from his rivals was longevity. He became UNC's head coach in 1961; every other ACC coach from that year was gone within a decade, and few of their replacements lasted long. By the time Smith's career ended in 1997, NC State, a highly successful program in its own right, had gone through five coaches and was a year into the tenure of the sixth. Virginia's Terry Holland was gone, and Lefty Driesell, who had come to Maryland with great fanfare in 1970, had left in 1986 in the wake of Len Bias's death. Many of these contemporaries were highly respected coaches, and two of them—Norm Sloan and Jim Valvano, both of NC State—even brought home NCAA titles during Smith's career.

But in most observers' eyes, only one ACC coach ever offered Dean any real competition: Duke's Mike Krzyzewski. Coach K arrived in Durham in 1980 and set about restoring the school's somewhat faded basketball glory. By any measurement, he exceeded expectations and then some. He got Duke to the Final Four in 1986,

1988, and 1989, but these were just warm-ups. In 1990, Christian Laettner and Bobby Hurley led Duke to the championship game, but the Blue Devils were blown out by Nevada-Las Vegas. The following year, strengthened by the addition of Grant Hill, they avenged that loss in the semifinals and won Coach K his first NCAA title. Then, in 1992, Laettner, Hurley, and Hill led Duke to a second consecutive championship, something no team had done since John Wooden's UCLA juggernaut came to rest in 1973.

That all this had been happening less than ten miles from his office had hardly escaped Smith's notice. UNC's teams were still rock-solid, full of NBA-quality players such as Brad Daugherty and Rick Fox, and still finished in the ACC's top three every year. After the 1982 season, however, the Heels seemed snake-bitten in the NCAAs. They still had great players and a great coach, but despite three regular-season ACC titles and one ACC Tournament championship, they could not seem to get past the Elite Eight. And when the Heels finally managed to get back to the Final Four in 1991, they fell to UNLV in the semis and then had to watch as the title went to their archrivals.

But it was after the 1992 season when the Research Triangle *really* started buzzing, much as it had before Dean's 1982 breakthrough. Duke had been to five straight Final Fours, and had won the past two. UNC had been to exactly one in the previous decade. Had Smith lost his touch? Could he find a way to compete with Krzyzewski, a coach younger than he by some sixteen years, but who already had twice as many NCAA titles? Did he have an answer?

Apparently so. Smith's 1993 squad went 34-4 and won their coach another championship to match Coach K's pair. Their achievement (and Smith's) was perhaps even more impressive when one considers UNC's starting lineup in the championship game: Eric Montross, George Lynch, Brian Reese, Donald Williams, and Derrick Phelps, not one of whom ever earned an NBA All-Star berth. The opponents in the 1993 championship were Michigan's legendary "Fab Five" of sophomores, led by future pro stars Chris Webber, Juwan Howard, and Jalen Rose. The Heels had talent, but they won by playing an almost perfect game of fundamentally sound team basketball.

The Carolina-Duke rivalry was far from settled, however. In 1994, Duke returned to the Final Four; in 1997, Smith led UNC there for the last time. Smith had won his record 879th game in the regional finals, but the Heels fell to eventual champion Arizona. No one knew then that Smith had coached his last game; it was a decision he didn't make until the following fall.

When Smith retired, he and Coach K were tied with two national championships each, but the debate rages on, even today, about which coach was superior. Krzyzewski's third NCAA title, earned in 2001, his twenty-first season at Duke's helm, has only added fuel to the fire, a fire that still smolders across North Carolina more than five years after the coaches had their last meeting at courtside.

0:08

There is at least one other stat—the most important stat, either side might well argue—in which both Smith and Krzyzewski excelled: their programs' graduation rates. UNC's basketball lettermen graduated at a better than 96 percent rate during Smith's tenure, while Krzyzewski's crew has done so at better than 93 percent to date.

It's also worth considering that all these coaching statistics were achieved in the toughest basketball conference in the nation; both Smith and Coach K had to win games from powerful programs with their own NCAA aspirations, such as NC State, Maryland, Virginia, and Georgia Tech. And consider that Duke and Carolina met every year, at least twice a season, sometimes three or four times, in each of the seventeen seasons in which both Smith and Krzyzewski were coaching. If they hadn't had to beat each other so often, each coach's victory total might be padded by a good thirty games.

Kryzewski's three-to-two lead in NCAA championships is an undeniable annoyance to all UNC fans. It is unlikely, however, that Coach K will match Dean's win total; he's fifty-five at this writing, and even if he averages twenty-five wins a year for the rest of his career, he won't pass Dean until sometime in 2015. Then again, he'd be only sixty-eight then—Dean retired at sixty-six.

In the end, however, any hope of settling the question statistically is defeated by the fact that Smith did all of the above over a thirty-six-year career at UNC, while K has been a head coach only twenty-six years, and only twenty-one of those at Duke. In many ways, it's premature even to have this argument.

Some see the argument as not just premature, but fundamentally misguided. They have a point. Even if it were possible to settle the question of how good coaches are by appealing to statistics—statistics from games in which the coaches set no screens, score no points, and grab no rebounds—one group of people can argue, quite legitimately, that Smith and Krzyzewski are at best the second- and third-best college basketball coaches of all time. To them, it's like arguing whether Mount Mitchell or Mount Washington is the higher mountain—no matter which you pick, the shadow of Everest looms over them both. As any UCLA fan will tell you, John Wooden casts an awfully big shadow for a guy his size.

0:07

I grew up listening to George Carlin, and am unafraid of hearing or using any of the "seven words you can't say on television." Dean Smith, by contrast, does not curse. Not during games, not during practices. So far as I know, Smith doesn't even swear when he hits his thumb with a hammer. I'm certainly as addicted to four-letter words as Coach Smith ever was to cigarettes, but I must confess admiration for a stand he once took against one such word.

The stand took place in Carmichael Auditorium during a game against Virginia, led by the seven-foot four-inch Ralph Sampson, a player gifted with both size and skill. The Cavaliers were one of the toughest teams in the country during the early 1980s, and on this particular afternoon, they were giving the Heels fits. At one point, a call went against Carolina and the fans erupted in frustration.

Contrary to the "wine and cheese" image that has grown up around UNC fans, who admittedly pride themselves on maintaining a certain sportsmanlike decorum, they can display a nasty streak, and they were eager to show it to the Cavaliers that day. Sampson had angered some UNC fans by his decision to seek his fortune farther north. Virginia Coach Terry Holland had further angered them by naming his dog "Dean" and telling the press he'd done so because of the animal's whining. And of course there was the fact that UVA was in a good position to beat the Heels on their home floor. No, there wasn't much reason for anyone in Carmichael that day to love Virginia.

Still, it was something of a surprise when the crowd began chanting. Carolina crowds weren't known for spontaneous chants; they tended to wait for the instructions of a cheerleader. No cheerleader had started

this chant, however—a loud, clear, and angry cry of "BULLSHIT!
BULLSHIT! BULLSHIT!" that echoed around the auditorium.

Play had been stopped, and people were on their feet, so David and
I were screened off from seeing what was happening at the scorer's
table, but it was pretty apparent whose voice came over the PA system—only one man in the room had that particular Kansas twang in
his voice.

"Stop that!" cried Smith into the announcer's microphone. "Let's
beat 'em the right way!"

There was a moment of uncertainty—hadn't Dean seen that call?
Didn't that call *deserve* to be cussed at?—but then suddenly a cheer
sprang up. Yeah! This was Chapel Hill, after all. Why should we sacrifice our dignity? Why should we feel so threatened by not getting a
call? We didn't need the referees in order to win. We should be cheering for the Heels, not against the refs.

Within seconds, the crisis had passed. And Carolina did beat 'em
the right way.

I still don't think there's anything especially wrong with profanity
in general, and I use it with relish when the occasion demands. But I
admire Coach Smith for suggesting that some things we *can* do aren't
necessarily the things we *should* do—that some occasions, even simple ones such as basketball games, deserve our best behavior.

0:06

If, as Voltaire observed, God is a comedian playing to an audience
too afraid to laugh, then He has something in common with Dean
Smith. In sports, and in college basketball in particular, and in ACC
basketball in still more particular, there is a tendency to overdrama-
tize. What is unquestionably a game is treated as though it were Ar-
mageddon, or at least a major troop engagement. Smith recognized
the absurdity of this, but it was sometimes hard to tell, perhaps because he also recognized that even a game deserves to be played as
well as possible. As a result, some of his funniest lines fell on relatively deaf ears. "If you make every game a life-or-death proposition,
you're going to have problems," he once observed after a game. "For
one thing, you'll be dead a lot."

I only occasionally encountered Coach Smith around town, but I
vividly recall the afternoon one summer when I was shooting baskets

on the courts outside Phillips Junior High in Chapel Hill. I was in my late twenties, out of shape, and a long way from my Carolina Basketball School days, but I was there, practicing free throws and layups while I waited for some friends to arrive for a pickup game. A car pulled into a parking spot just outside the gym, but I could see immediately that it wasn't one of my friends, none of whom could afford that beautiful BMW. I was quite surprised, however, when the driver turned out to be none other than Coach Smith, clad in a light blue windsuit. He was heading for the gym, which was almost certainly, I realized, where some of the current Carolina Basketball School players were practicing. As he passed by my court, having no idea who I was, he nonetheless noted my footwear—my ancient and well-worn Air Jordans, a vision of ugliness in black, red, and white.

"Those shoes helping you jump?" he called out, smiling.

I was astonished to find myself replying in kind. "Oh, yeah," I said. "I'm getting up six, seven inches."

He laughed and went into the gym. I stood, ball on hip, marveling. I'd made Dean Smith laugh! If I did nothing else with the rest of my life, I could at least say that I'd accomplished one good thing, and all it had cost me was a little self-mockery.

Coach Smith himself wasn't above a little self-mockery, either. At one university function, my mother happened to be seated next to him at dinner. Mom is one of the universe's great conversationalists, and before long she had engaged him by complimenting his daughter, who had been my counselor at day camp the previous summer. Obviously proud, Smith happily received all my mom's comments about his daughter, agreeing 100 percent that she was bright, kind, and attractive. Then he got a twinkle in his eye.

"Of course," he said, "She can't do *this*." And he stuck out his tongue. Not at my mom, mind you. He stuck it out to display his most prominent feature, one that his daughter had not inherited, but one which he could easily lick—his nose.

0:05

In the good old days of college basketball, there was an assumption that any player coming to Chapel Hill would be staying a while. There were a few guys, usually highly decorated high school stars shocked by their lack of playing time in UNC's veteran-friendly system, who transferred to other schools after a year or two, but for the better part of Coach Smith's career, players were part of the family for four years.

The term "family" is an exaggeration, but not that much of one. Former players who had gone on to coaching or the NBA would nonetheless appear in Chapel Hill from time to time, taking on current players in pickup games whose intensity was legendary. The rims on the outdoor blacktop court at Granville Towers, the players' dormitory, became bent and dented by the force of the dunks thrown down by new kids showing their stuff, or by All-Stars demonstrating that the new kids' defense still needed some work.

Carolina players still look out for each other, and for their competitors. It is likely not a coincidence that the Washington Wizards hired Michael Jordan as an executive and quickly brought in UNC products such as Hubert Davis, Brendan Haywood, and Jerry Stackhouse, not to mention Duke standout Christian Laettner and Maryland's fiery Juan Dixon. Other franchises that have seen clusters of UNC alumni occupy their front offices and rosters would include the Lakers (with Mitch Kupchak in the President's office and James Worthy and Rick Fox on the floor) and the 76ers (with Larry Brown, Dave Hanners, and John Kuester on the bench, and Billy Cunningham, George Lynch, Eric Montross, and Stackhouse on the court).

If UNC players have historically tended to view themselves as part of something bigger, it's hardly accidental. Carolina freshmen, even the ones who started—*especially* the ones who started—were forced to accept that view from the beginning. First-year players had to remember that the team always came first, and they had to contribute to the team in such mundane ways as carrying the film projector. When the game started, a freshman might get more playing time than a senior, but in Coach Smith's eyes, the senior's four-year commitment of time and effort was worth at least as much as anything the freshman might have in his box score.

Smith did his best to reward his veterans for that commitment, and scheduling was often the means of providing that reward. Each senior class would have had to have spent four Christmases away from home during its tenure; Smith eased the pain by making sure that one of those holidays would be spent at a tournament in Hawaii and one at a tournament in Europe. In addition, the Heels tried to schedule a game in or near each senior's hometown, giving his friends and family the chance to see for themselves how he'd contributed to the Carolina program. Moreover, if a former player got a college coaching gig, as Jeff Lebo, Buzz Peterson, and Randy Wiel did, it was a near-certainty that his team would get a game against UNC; it might result in a lop-sided loss at the hands of the current Carolina team, but it would again be an acknowledgment that his years in Chapel Hill were still valued. When a player signed with the Heels, he signed for life.

Not every player found this appealing, of course. Some came to Carolina, found Smith's system a bad fit, and headed to other schools in search of a better one. (It is perhaps noteworthy that none became household names after leaving.) It was more common for a blue-chip recruit to turn UNC down in advance, as prep star Kenny Anderson did. Anderson opted for Georgia Tech, saying he didn't want to be "another horse in Dean Smith's stable." In 1990, Smith settled for an-other point guard, Derrick Phelps, a defensive standout who in his ju-nior year anchored Carolina's NCAA championship team. Anderson, who left Tech after two years and still earns a good living in the NBA, may not regret his decision, but his comment shows that not all play-ers understand that great weights are pulled not by individual horses, but by teams.

0:04

I first heard the joke more than a decade ago—after Michael Jor-dan had left the University of North Carolina, after he had led the last squad of American collegians to win Olympic gold in men's basket-ball, after he'd become NBA Rookie of the Year, after he'd dropped a jaw-dropping 63 points on the mighty Boston Celtics and been granted deity status by Larry Bird. I laughed at it, of course, because there's a certain unexpected twist in the punch line, but even then I knew that the underlying assumption was in error.

Who was the last person to hold Michael Jordan under 20 points a game?

Dean Smith.

The assumption was that Jordan was like the Genie in Disney's *Aladdin,* a pale-blue miracle worker who could have exploded off the Carolina bench to wreak havoc on the opposition in all manner of impossible ways—but that his controlling coach kept him bottled up inside a carefully-constructed lamp called the "UNC system," preventing him from working his magic.

I knew better. Even Disney knew. The Genie himself says that the magic and the constraints are inextricably linked—"phenomenal cosmic power, itty-bitty living space."

Dean Smith didn't keep Jordan in that lamp. Dean Smith *put* Jordan there.

Mind you, Michael had some pretty magical qualifications of his own. Coach Smith didn't make him 6'6", or give him that vertical jump, or light that competitive fire under him. He didn't show Michael how to make the fade-away jumper after his knees had begun wearing down. He certainly didn't create that protruding tongue—heck, he did his best to make Michael keep it in his mouth.

Jordan was a superb athlete, a driven competitor, and a gifted ballplayer, and he would have been all these things without the influence of Dean Smith. I don't doubt that he could have become an NBA All-Star with a different college coach, one whose system allowed him a scoring average higher than 17.7 points per game. I do believe, however, that Michael Jordan would have been something very different without those three brief years in Carolina blue.

The Jordan image is all about flight, about soaring toward the basket with the ball poised for a slam, but the beauty of that image shouldn't distract the viewer from the substance of Jordan's game. And that substance begins with defense.

Jordan's many honors include one that might escape casual notice, but which I'm sure didn't escape his old college coach: he earned All-Defensive Team honors nine times—a record. Indeed, he was the NBA's Defensive Player of the Year in 1987-1988, a year in which he was also the league's scoring leader and MVP, and he led the league in steals three times—all during seasons when he also won the scoring title. His 2.42 steals per game makes him the third-best thief in league history, and he is second only to John Stockton in career steals. In one 1988 game, he had ten steals, one short of the all-time record; that same year, he made eight steals in a single *half.* He was even a pretty good shot-blocker for a guard; in his remarkable 1987-1988 season, he averaged 1.6 blocks per game—not that far off the 1.78 career average of seven-footer Sam Bowie, whose greatest claim to fame remains the fact that the Portland Trail Blazers passed on Jordan in order to draft him instead.

Curry Kirkpatrick wrote that "[A]s a freshman Jordan didn't especially like playing defense," but after his sophomore season, he was "easily the best defensive guard in the land." The statistics back Kirkpatrick up. For the season, Jordan averaged 2.16 steals a game, nearly double his average as a freshman. The change in his defensive status wasn't merely statistical, however, as he revealed three games into the season. UNC was struggling, desperate for a win, but Tulane came to Carmichael unafraid of the defending NCAA champs, and they gave the Heels all they could handle. With time running out and UNC down by two, Jordan hit the tying basket—but not on a pass from an assist-minded senior point guard. Instead, Jordan created his own opportunity. After being called for an offensive foul with five seconds left, Jordan deflected Tulane's inbounds pass, stole the ball, and heaved up a desperate shot to send the game into overtime—the first of three, after which UNC finally went to the showers with a 70-68 win. Jordan would finish the game with four steals, tying what was then his career high, but it was only an inkling of how his defensive skills had improved.

He provided more evidence in the Tar Heels' ACC opener against Maryland. With his Terrapins in possession at the end, but down by a single point, Lefty Driesell craftily called an inbounds play for one of his team's lesser-known offensive threats, his son Chuck. Chuck got the ball and drove unopposed to the basket, giving his father what must have been a moment of pure joy: the prospect of a victory over Dean Smith, in Chapel Hill, delivered by his own flesh and blood. But the moment was a brief one—as Chuck released his shot, out of nowhere came a leaping Jordan to bat the ball away and preserve the Carolina victory.

Against third-ranked Virginia a few weeks later, defense again made the difference. Ralph Sampson, the Cavaliers' 7'4" star, had led his team to a 16-point cushion, but then Jordan led the top-ranked Tar Heels in a furious second-half rally that left them down by only a point with a minute left and Virginia in possession. Perhaps "Cavalier" is a name of ill-omen for a team that needs to hang onto the ball with care, because as Rick Carlisle dribbled the ball upcourt, Jordan swiped it. One sudden dunk later, Carolina was on top. Virginia had one last shot to win, but when it missed, Jordan was there to seal the win by leaping to grab a defensive rebound—over Sampson.

From that point on, every basketball fan in America knew that Michael Jordan was not just a scorer, not just a clutch shooter, but something else entirely. Plenty of players could average 20 points per game, just as plenty of players could hit a game-winning shot if someone else could get them the ball in scoring position. But Jordan—Jordan was a magician. He could not only hit the shot, but could first make the ball disappear from his opponents' hands—poof!

0:03

If there's one thing guaranteed to send a kid into ecstasy, it's direct contact with an idol. My brother and I were lucky enough to regularly get such contact with Carolina players. Sometimes our parents would make it happen. Mom and Dad were always eager to have us travel with them to see the team, so we'd sometimes thrill to the realization that we were on a bus with Jeff Wolf, or at an airport baggage claim with Jim Braddock. Once Mom even attended a charity auction and bought for us a basketball lesson from Tar Heel big men Rich Yonakor and Chris Brust.

Such encounters were exciting, but highly unusual. Our usual way of getting contact with a Tar Heel was far simpler and quite literal: we would wait for one to land in our laps.

The sort of hardworking player known as a "gym rat" is known for throwing himself to the ground after loose balls. In Dean Smith's system, every player was supposed to have some rat in him. David and I saw this rattiness up close because of our seats' location on the floor of Carmichael. If a rebound went long, or if an entry pass were deflected, there was a good chance that the ball would head toward our corner, and where the ball went, a Tar Heel followed. Scrappy guards such as John Kuester regularly flew into our seats in pursuit of loose balls, but so did highly recruited talents such as Walter Davis, whose 6'6" frame gave us such a thorough dousing with sweat on one occasion that we stayed damp until after we'd returned home.

Truth to tell, sweat was something of a fetish item for us. It represented something important: hustle. We were both ballplayers, and we knew that although talent was handed out unevenly, hustle was something any player could achieve. If a player sprinted back on defense, filled his lane on the fast break, or kicked a leg out to block a pass, he was making a statement: he wasn't coasting on his ability, but squeezing out every last bit of basketball in his body.

Sweat was the fresh-squeezed goodness that came from hustle, and David and I admired it. If we couldn't get it deposited directly, we might get it in a used wristband; David, being more outgoing than I, chased down the bemused Davis after one game in Carmichael and asked for his Carolina blue sweatband. To our astonishment, he got it, and he wore it without cease for what seemed like years afterward. Whether it still lurks in some unknown box in my parents' attic I don't know, but I feel certain that wherever it is now, it was never washed.

0:02

Obviously I've drawn many lessons from watching Coach Smith's teams play, but none is more important than this: Play the game to the end. Or maybe it's not the most important lesson, but it's the one that was driven home the hardest. And I know exactly when it was driven home: on March 2, 1974, the day after my eleventh birthday, in Carmichael Auditorium.

David and I were in our usual seats deep in the northwest corner of the floor, and Duke was making our day miserable, despite the fact that the Devils had a losing record and the Heels were 20-4. Even in those days, everyone knew that a Carolina-Duke game was a battle of equals, regardless of ranking or record. Earlier in the year UNC had escaped with a win in Cameron Indoor Stadium when Bobby Jones had dropped in a last-second layup, but we had no hopes of a similar conclusion that afternoon. Duke was ahead by eight points, 86-78, when Jones went to the foul line to shoot one and one. Only seventeen seconds were left on the clock.

Jones hit both shots, and the Heels, still gamely determined to fight it out, immediately applied pressure on the inbounds play. After the panicked passer sent the ball in, Walter Davis ended up with possession and found John Kuester for a layup. Suddenly down by only four, UNC called time-out with thirteen seconds left.

There was a small bubble of hope forming in my stomach at this point, but I tried hard to keep a lid on it. We were still two possessions behind—the three-point shot was a decade away—and the clock was against us. At the same time, I had to consider two things: one, that Dean Smith was a brilliant designer of defensive plays, and two, that we'd just scored 4 points in four seconds.

The strategy after the time-out didn't change much: try for a steal on the inbounds pass, and if that didn't work, foul. The Heels were unable to intercept the pass, but they may as well have done so— Duke guard Tate Armstrong inexplicably missed the catch and lost the ball out of bounds. UNC inbounded successfully and put up a shot, and Jones was able to tip the ball into the basket; the Heels were within two with six seconds remaining.

Unfortunately, the Blue Devils weren't about to lose a third straight inbounds pass, and the Heels were forced to foul Pete Kramer, who went to the line for a one-and-one opportunity with four seconds on the clock. I wasn't optimistic. Surely after so many miracles had already been granted the Heels, we had no right to expect anything further.

We didn't have the right, but we got it anyway—Kramer's first shot missed, and UNC's Ed Stahl grabbed the rebound. Instantly every pair of hands sticking out of a white jersey formed the letter T. After the time-out, UNC had three seconds to put the ball in play and try to make up the final two points.

Predicting the economy of miracles had now become bewildering. Would the basketball gods give us so much, only to yank away the final opportunity to tie the game? Or would they decide to quit throwing good fortune after bad? David and I were nervous as cats down in our corner. We had every reason to believe that we and we alone were responsible for what happened next. Did we need to be sitting down? What position had we been in when Stahl had grabbed the rebound? Should we get back into it? We knew something was *meant* to happen, but our own role in bringing it about remained unclear.

Coach Smith, meanwhile, had calmly drawn up a play that was vintage Carolina, but with a twist. As expected, he put the ball in the hands of a trusted senior, Mitch Kupchak, who stood beneath Duke's basket and pitched the ball fifty feet to an unexpected target: freshman swingman Walter Davis, who turned, dribbled, and with one second left launched a shot from the east sideline, almost on top of the hash mark.

I can see the ball to this day, arching high and spinning across the sky-blue beams in Carmichael's ceiling. It wasn't coming right at us—we were too far toward the corner—but I could tell that it wasn't going quite straight. Davis's whippet-like body, stretched to its fullest, came to rest on the court at almost the same instant that the ball struck the backboard, just inside the square, and caromed through the hoop.

I've seen a photograph of the shot from behind Davis, and my brother and I are just visible in the corner, leaning forward, our mouths open, our eyes tracking the ball. David is still seated, I'm already rising, and the ball still hangs in the air. Yet even without the photograph, that moment would have remained frozen in my memory—the longest single second of my life. The cry that burst forth from 8,800 throats in the seconds afterward was the most joyous sound I have ever heard.

Even when, eight years later, another senior passed to another freshman, who hit a jumper to win a championship, the sound that echoed from New Orleans to Chapel Hill did not approach the one that burst forth from Carmichael Auditorium when I was eleven years old. Jordan's jumper against Georgetown gave us something we'd hoped for, something we'd even expected, or felt we deserved; when he sank it, we cried out almost in relief. But Davis's bomb was nothing of the sort. There was no relief in our cry—the overtime was still to be played, and the game could still be lost. But for that moment, we were lost in a joy that lifted us from our seats and sent us into the embrace of every person standing anywhere near us. We'd been down 8 points with seventeen seconds left. We could have expected nothing, we deserved nothing—and yet we were granted our fondest wish.

0:01

So, to this day, I keep watching. Until the bitter end, until the buzzer sounds and the referees leave the court. I don't give up, because Coach Smith and the players who loved him taught me not to. Most of the time I'm rewarded with nothing more than frustration. But still I remain, staring like Jay Gatsby at the green light across the waters, because I have stood in its glow once already, and I have faith that I may do so again.

Chapter 9

Socks, Jocks, and Two Championship Rings

Michael Buchert

So this is it. This is the stuff that ends up on the cutting room floor of those perennial *Sports Illustrated* exposés claiming to offer the "exclusive and uncensored" take on our favorite franchises. This is sacred ground, unpolluted by sportswriter sharks and Vegas bookies, where nineteen-year-old giants get to be nineteen-year-old kids. It would be difficult for anyone to mask intimidation here, stashed away in the bathroom corner of a shoebox of a locker room at Jacksonville Coliseum, just within earshot of my official introduction to life on the road. We are nearing midseason, and the Florida Gator men's basketball team finds itself down by four points at halftime to a drastically undermanned but home-standing Jacksonville University Dolphin squad.

Head coach Billy Donovan is letting his guys have it, detonating some strategically placed, and sometimes innovatively so, four-letter bombs as he attempts to relate the severity of the situation. Just on the other side of the paper-thin wall that separates us, I cringe and almost duck instinctively as he rips into them. Growing up the son of a high school football coach, I learned at an early age when not to bother Dad for spare change. With the only exit clear across the locker room, I had no intention of placing myself in the line of fire now.

"Those guys are killing you on the glass; they're first to every loose ball. . . . WHERE ARE YOU *[expletive]?*"

By now this is old hat for athletic trainer and Rolling Stones super-fan Chris "Six" Koenig, having been with the team when former head coach Lon Kruger led the unfathomable run to the Final Four in 1994. A true renaissance man, Six coordinates all aspects of the team's

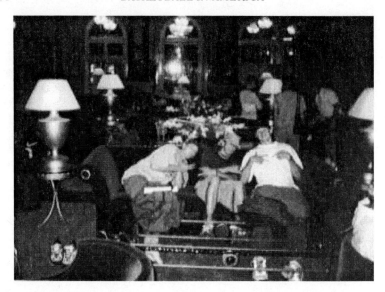

"Seine language." Brett Nelson, myself, and Matt Bonner settle in at the Concorde St. Lazare hotel in Paris after a long flight. The team played five games in eight days while traveling across Europe in the summer of 2000.

travel accommodations, including pre- and postgame meals, in addition to his obligations in the training room.

Until now, my duties as a freshman manager had prohibited me from straying too far from the laundry room, so what I had once naïvely regarded as a microvacation had slowly evolved into anything but a holiday. First, at shoot-around this morning, I expertly managed to leave the basketballs back in my hotel room, forcing major Division I players to mime their way through plays for an hour.

This small oversight had conferred a very real sense of impending doom upon the remainder of my first road trip. You can imagine my relief when I was assigned to film the game from the top row of the arena, relatively out of harm's way. That rickety wooden platform is exactly where I would be now, if it weren't for those three Gatorades I had sucked down during the first half.

As Coach Donovan continues his rampage, Six finishes washing his hands in the sink. Dipping down to splash water on his face, he turns to the side, catches my eye, and grins.

"Oh yeah!" He mouths the words, flaring his tongue out, à la Mick Jagger.

"What's the deal? Why's he so mad?" I whisper.

Six shakes his head, flashing a toothy smile.

"It's showtime, baby. Fake juice," he says, launching a Gatorade towel at me before strutting back out into the danger zone.

Fake juice, n. (slang) 1. A motivational tool utilized by coaches to impress an apocalyptical sense of immediacy upon players. For example: "For these next twenty minutes of basketball, your entire life is on the line!" 2. Usually expressed at unnecessarily high volumes and accompanied by excessive hand clapping. Can also refer to any sort of falsely enthusiastic verbiage meant to raise the morale of a team. For example: "Oh yeah, baby! It's a beautiful day to get better!"

Most commonly found at early morning or midnight practices, the juice is an implicitly understood necessity in sports. Coaches begin each year with a surplus of the stuff, only to have the veteran players sarcastically regurgitate it back at them once the monotony of practice sets in around midseason.

The shouting from the locker room quiets considerably for a few seconds. I glance daringly around the corner. He must be finished.

"THOSE *[expletive]* ARE LAUGHING AT YOU!!"

Maybe not.

"I refuse to go back out there with a bunch of cowards. I need soldiers! You guys have absolutely no sense of urgency right now! WAKE UP!!" Donovan growls.

Gary Zetrouer, my boss and head manager, steps into the bathroom. Beads of sweat dot his forehead as he struggles to catch his breath. This job is in his blood, and he will leave after this, his maximum-allowable sixth year as student manager at UF, to join the NBA's Orlando Magic in a similar capacity. Although seemingly oblivious to his quirkiness, Gary can sometimes breathe fresh air into the dreadfully long workdays, so I tolerate the requisite half-dozen pictures of his girlfriend that decorate our hotel room on the road.

"Have you been in here the whole time?" He is not a happy camper.

Though I try to avert my attention from him, quickly absorbing all fifty square feet of the bathroom, I can hear the give and take of his exaggerated breathing.

"YOU *[expletive]* ARE GOING TO WONDER WHY YOU EVER PICKED UP A BASKETBALL!!" Coach has now progressed to the always-effective scare tactics.

"Dude, I am not walking through that." I was not walking through that.

Gary laughs, rolls his eyes, and walks to the urinal. "It doesn't look like you've got much of a choice. You've only got ten minutes to get back up there. Just stop being such a baby. What's he going to do, eat you?"

I had never known Gary to squander a chance to remind me of his vast jurisdiction, and tonight was no different. Of course, I have to get back upstairs right now, and not a second later. Defeated, I brush past him and ease my way into the doorjamb. Propping myself against the opposite wall, I watch Coach Donovan as he scrawls feverishly on the chalkboard. He turns back to the team and stands deafeningly silent, violently rolling the piece of chalk in his loose fist. The word *HEART* screams from behind him. Still leaning, I decide to seize the opportunity and make a run for the door. Just as I move, Coach Donovan turns the volume back up.

"IT'S ALL ABOUT HEART . . ."

By the time I realized that I had accidentally flicked off the lights, I was halfway out the door. I turned around, barely making out the players, assistant coaches, fellow student managers, and Coach Donovan, all peering through the darkness in my direction. In those few agonizing seconds of blackness, I imagined Billy Donovan scribbling a quick mental note to rid himself of that rookie manager of inconsequential name from Orlando. My first road trip with the Florida Gators would surely be my last. I had just effectively dimmed the lights on my once-promising career as an NCAA jockwasher.

"CAN SOMEBODY PLEASE TURN ON SOME *[expletive]* LIGHTS?"

I spent four years with the Gator basketball team, and some of my most beloved memories are blanketed in darkness.

As you can tell from my initial road trip, my first season with the team was erratic, to be sure. In spite of this, however, there were a few moments when I felt that I was about to be a part of something unparalleled.

Coach Donovan had arrived in Gainesville just one year prior. Although "BillyBall" had begun to generate some excitement on campus, basketball season was still widely regarded as an intermission to Steve Spurrier's main attraction at The Swamp. The University of Florida lived and breathed Gator football.

On paper, Coach Donovan knew that he had inherited a team with potential, but infusing his intense, breakneck personality into a group of what were, in effect, his stepchildren proved far more challenging on the court. Still, his first Gator team managed to set nine school records; jumping from worst to first in SEC 3-point field goal percentage. The team finished the 1996-1997 season with a record of 13-17, failing to make the postseason. Still, a foundation had been set in place that had the potential to propel the program into the upper echelon. Although few knew it then, Coach Donovan was about to unveil a secret weapon that would change the face of Gator basketball forever.

I first met Jason Williams at a Gator basketball camp in the summer of 1997. Gary Zetrouer called me and suggested that I work a few of these youth camps to get acquainted with the players and staff, so I left for Gainesville the day after my high school graduation. No parties. No self-congratulatory excursions to Europe. My mother waved from the driveway as my 1993 Ford Ranger pulled away, losing the battle as she fought back tears that had flowed so joyously just a day before. I didn't have time to feel much of anything. Tomorrow's wake-up call was at 5:30 a.m.

It was late on the first night of camp, and several of the players had gathered on the practice court to scrimmage in front of the kids. It was amazing to witness the campers' reactions to every move their heroes made. A twisting lay-up by 5'11" senior guard Eddie Shannon got them on their feet. Sharpshooter Greg Stolt's endless barrage of three-pointers even had me cheering. But then, *it* happened.

Tattoos adorning each arm of his lanky, unassuming frame, JWill grabbed a loose ball and burst out from a pack of defenders just below the free throw line, tossing it a few feet ahead. He was alone in the open court, so I merely expected him to show off and dunk for the kids. Instead, just after he passed half-court, Jason bulleted the ball behind his back toward the sideline. It was all too quick, and unquestionably illegal, but in one sweeping motion the ball ricocheted off the carpeted walls with a resounding *THUMP,* bouncing right back to Jason in perfect stride, before he rose, tilted, and dunked it. Coaches

"A man of many hats." I performed with the Dazzlers Dance Team on Senior Night as we closed out our season against Kentucky. The team was remarkably supportive of this side project, and it was truly a thrill to take center stage in front of 12,000 screaming fans, including my parents.

stopped talking, campers' jaws dropped, and even some of the players fell to the gym floor, rolling and laughing. I almost had to remind myself to breathe.

Although he has gained popularity among NBA fans for his unique style of improvisational playmaking, Jason has always been a fervent student of the game, leading by example with his fierce competitiveness. Because he shared Coach Donovan's winning mentality and innate passion for basketball, their interplay, at least in front of the team, was usually relatively understated. It seemed that they were constantly aware of each other's expectations, and although Jason occasionally ventured into murky waters on the court, he never strayed too far from shore.

Jason's creativity, not unlike a painter's or dancer's, flourished in the nurturing environment that Coach had been cultivating since Assistant Coach Donnie Jones introduced them at a summer camp several years earlier. Finally, in an early February game against the Kentucky Wildcats, the protégé delivered a masterpiece on a nationally televised stage that legitimized the legend of JWill.

With ten games left on the SEC schedule, the Gators strolled into Rupp Arena and put on a clinic, embarrassing one of college basketball's greatest dynasties for much of the game before winning 86-78 in front of a surprisingly fickle home audience. After hitting two deep three-pointers in the midst of a lopsided Gator run, Jason buried another bomb that CBS commentator Brent Musberger estimated from "Churchill Downs!"

Filming the drama from a shaky piece of scrap metal that jutted out above the lower level, I was stunned to hear the Kentucky faithful booing their team—one of the most storied programs in the history of college basketball—just ten minutes into the game, and laughed audibly when they actually began cheering for us in the second half. JWill was nearly flawless in leading the Gators to their first victory at Rupp since 1989, finishing with 24 points, 6 rebounds, 4 assists, 4 steals, and countless new fans.

The postgame celebration continued as we boarded the airplane and headed home. It seemed that the team was finally coming together, poised for a run at just the sixth NCAA Tournament invitation in school history. With the improbable win, a group of individuals suddenly realized its limitless potential when it played as a cohesive, confident unit. The morale in the locker room over the next two weeks reflected the guys' newfound belief in one another. Something big was happening.

On February 17, just two weeks after the epiphany at Kentucky, Jason Williams was dismissed from the team for violating the university's substance-abuse policy. At lunch a week earlier, Jason had joked with fellow manager Brian Barton and I that his days as a Gator were numbered, but we had learned to take much of Jason with a bit of caution.

Walking to practice later that day, our friend chewed on a straw and told us dirty jokes in his trademark West Virginia twang. I remember laughing so hard that my eyes began to water. There were never any tearful good-byes or ceremonious farewells; one day Jason just wasn't there anymore. The Gator family had an irreparable hole in its heart. The team never recovered. The swagger and confidence of the group disappeared with its flashy leader, and the Gators lost five of their last six games before being discarded by Georgetown in the first round of the NIT Tournament.

New season . . . new players . . . newly renovated arena. By the time Midnight Madness kicked off my second year as a manager, the virtual drama of the previous season had long-since vanished in the memories of Gator loyalists. Coach Donovan's unyielding determination on the recruiting trail had generated a top-notch freshman class, not to mention unparalleled national buzz and lofty preseason expectations.

In light of the all the hoopla, the athletic department was beginning to flex its bulging biceps in support. Athletic Director Jeremy Foley snapped his fingers and gave the O Dome a proper makeover, replacing the outdated bubble top with a state-of-the-art roof, and because true beauty lies within, began the addition of $17 million worth of high-tech, crowd-pleasing goodies to the interior. Still, by the time the house lights dropped just before midnight on October 15, 1998, a single spotlight on professional wrestler Ric Flair, the premier of the laser light spectacular had been reduced to mere background eye fodder.

The crowd of 8,500, mostly consisting of recently emancipated undergrads testing ever-escalating alcohol tolerances, welcomed McDonald's All-Americans Mike Miller and Teddy Dupay, as well as fellow prep stars LaDarius Halton and Udonis Haslem, with adoration previously reserved for Gators of the gridiron. As I stood with the team at center court, striking up false conversation with manager Bob Pozatek so as to seem important, I realized that what I had once regarded as a lame postsecondary pep rally had quickly evolved into a celebration of a budding dynasty.

Florida basketball was beginning to feel fun again, and the fans were eager for more after the early promise of last season. Proving that sometimes better ingredients really do make a better pizza, the squad won seven of its first eight games heading into the Christmas break, poised to open the eyes of more than a few unsuspecting SEC opponents.

Decembers in Florida are traditionally warm, but Christmas in Gatorland is pure hell. Sure, you are briefly liberated from the daily grind of sleeping through General Psychology and scrambling to copy your neighbor's already second-generation homework assignment, but two-a-day practice on December 26 is hardly my idea of a vacation proper. You spend most of your hours between workouts in bed, visions of $25 per diem dancing, and quickly tire of waking for the sole purpose of wiping other people's sweat from dirty gym floors you didn't feel like sweeping.

The college town that bounced with the frenetic energy of 45,000 students just days ago now boasts a limp population of nineteen. Soon you learn to embrace your new role as the shortest human on campus. Still, the nearly three full weeks of virtual house arrest helps one to appreciate the few days of bickering siblings and incessant Nat King Cole that await you at home. Even the seeming splendor of a catered Christmas dinner at Coach's house makes you nostalgic for the marvelous mush of Mom's pumpkin pie. I never particularly enjoyed "The Twelve Days of Christmas," but three are far worse.

On one particularly frigid 73° December morning, I sprawled myself out on the equipment room floor, barely visible beneath the five or six-dozen stray athletic socks I was attempting to reunite. Although it was difficult to motivate myself to rummage through someone else's "clean" undergarments (*sometimes* we actually used detergent!), it was even more difficult to get me to stop. I was in a groove, content to be working quietly without the incessant *THUD THUD THUD* of so many bouncing balls, but I knew that it was just too good to be true.

"MIKE! MIKE! You gotta com'n here and check dis out!"

Stott Carter had been a manager for a year when I arrived. I must say that he had come a long way since he first introduced himself with a mouthful of venison jerky, but he was still far from shedding the permanent sunburn tinting the back of his neck. A native of the backwoods of Gainesville, Stott had come to the team after a serious ankle injury had ended his promising playing career. He planned to absorb enough basketball knowledge at UF to strike out on his own one day as a college coach.

"Dude, you gotta see what LD got fer Chrismuss!"

He had dashed into the equipment room a burst of energy, but the half-empty gallon of Sonny's iced tea by his side didn't keep me guessing for long. Still, he typically reserved this sort of enthusiasm for Stone Cold Steve Austin or The Rock, so I was a little curious.

"Lemme guess. Coach just added *another* practice today?" I didn't bother to look up from my socks.

Before Stott could respond, a piercing shrill came from the locker room, where the players convened before practice. I knew instantly that the sound had come from LaDarius Halton, a freshman guard, but I wasn't quite sure of its impetus.

Okay, enough with the socks.

"What is going on in there?" I jumped to my feet, scooping the remaining misfits back to their eternal damnation in the sock bin.

"LD juss won five thousan' dollurs ona scratch-off teecket!" Stott's expression now was probably not too much unlike that of those poor deer just before he drew back his bow and arrow.

"Yeah, right. Where did he buy it from?" I asked. My year with the team had taught me that while anything was possible with these guys, you really couldn't believe a word they said.

"He didn' buy it. Teddy gave it to 'im."

Oh God. If you are given to believing in the mystery of reincarnation, then you might say that Teddy Dupay was once Napoleon Bonaparte, a medieval jester, and a bulldog in his previous lives. His insatiable desire to win makes up for his diminutive basketball height (5'10"). Teddy was a coach's dream. His willingness to dive for a loose ball or take an elbow to the face made Teddy a crowd favorite, but those who knew him best never forgot that devilishly sneaky side to him.

In contrast, LaDarius was one of the nicest, most playful guys on the team, an art student whose compassion and geniality was rare in many athletes with an enormous amount of talent. (He scored 76 points in a single game as a high school senior.) He possessed the curiosity and wonderment of an eight-year-old, the kind that might believe in the magic of a lottery ticket. All was definitely not right.

Typically before practice each day, it is difficult to hear yourself think over the *BOOM BOOM* of Jay-Z's latest and greatest thundering from the locker room. The near silence that struck me as I entered today confirmed that something was up. The players, all except LaDarius, were sitting quietly by their lockers as if they were back in second grade in search of extra recess time. Jay-Z had apparently taken the day off. All eyes were on LD, who was pacing frantically back and forth over the massive gator head emblazoned in the carpet, his cellular phone pressed to his ear as he spread the good news.

"YEAH! YEAH! . . . Naw, Ted gave it to me . . . Uh-huh!" LaDarius' lips fought themselves to form words through his huge grin.

As LD hung up the phone, jumping and high-fiving, I noticed Coach Donovan and Assistant Coach John Pelphrey craning their necks around the corner. As the crowd and LaDarius' excitement began to grow, I realized that things were about to get real bad, real quick. Most of the players were up now, applauding and egging him on. I could tell that some of them felt bad, or at least were thinking about feeling bad. Teddy had remained quiet at his locker, feigning resentment that his gift had been the $5,000 winner, but now he rose to join the celebration.

"Hey, LD, let me see the ticket!" Teddy was smiling now.

"All right, Ted, but don't try anything funny," said LD.

"Come on, man. That's messed up." The guys could hardly control themselves as Teddy kept it going.

As Teddy reached for the ticket, LD pulled it back to his chest and took a few steps backward.

"Nah, man. This is my money! I'm not letting anybody touch it!" LaDarius was playing right into his hands.

Teddy glanced over to Coach Donovan, grinned as he dropped the bomb.

"Hey LD, read the back of the ticket, man. Where do you have to go to cash it in?" Teddy smirked.

The team gathered around him, bracing, as he read silently. Teddy stood to the back of the crowd, his face red flush.

"LD, what does it say?" He poured salt into the wound.

As I watched LaDarius' eyes drop to the bottom of the ticket, I knew that he was going to require some serious counseling.

"Winning tickets must be validated by the TOOTH FAIRY! WINNING PRIZES MAY NOT BE CLAIMED ANYWHERE, SO FORGET ABOUT IT!"

Everyone erupted in laughter as LD plopped down onto the black leather sofa, wailing. Teddy walked over to console him, but quickly reconsidered. The damage had already been done. As LD sulked to the court that day for practice, the players put their arms around his limp frame and playfully rubbed his clean-shaven head, encouraging and joking.

He had come so close to winning, to being a champion for a day, but his moment had been snatched from beneath him. These moments when the guys allowed themselves to leggo their egos were few and far between, but they often provided a glimpse of mortality into these athletes who otherwise seemed superhuman. I genuinely felt for LaDarius that day, and I think that at least a few of the players felt the same, if only for a second. After all, in the game of basketball, seconds can last forever.

After coming within just a game of winning a share of the regular season Southeastern Conference title, the team received its first invitation to the NCAA Tournament since 1995. We were sent to Seattle for the first round. It was thrilling for me just to be there, but Coach Donovan was far from satisfied with the *ALSO RAN* that many sports analysts had already affixed to the side of the team bus. The Gators didn't do much to change that perception in the first game against Pennsylvania, as they came out sluggish and barely recognizable, trailing by double-digits at halftime. The Quakers were a scrappy bunch from the Ivy League Conference, known for their high basketball IQs and sharp fundamentals, and they seemed destined to play the role of Cinderella in Seattle.

Fortunately, senior Greg Stolt's inspired three-point shooting got the rest of the guys going, as they used their athleticism and full-court press to wear down the opponent and advance. Two days later, the Gators took on Weber State. Once again, it wasn't pretty. Overcoming a truly remarkable 32-point performance by Weber State's Harold "The Show" Arceneaux, the team scratched and clawed its way to an 8-point victory in overtime.

After two wins in Seattle, Florida advanced to the Sweet Sixteen in Phoenix to play the true Cinderella team of the tourney, the Gonzaga Bulldogs. In only the third Sweet Sixteen appearance in UF history, the guys played with a great deal of composure and poise, overcoming a horrendous shooting night to lead by three points in the game's final minutes. Still, after two phantom Florida turnovers in the final 20 seconds, Gonzaga's Casey Calvary tipped in a missed shot just before the buzzer, effectively dashing our hopes for a shot at winning the NCAA Championship in St. Petersburg.

In the locker room after the game, it was difficult to watch the pain and disappointment stream down the players' faces. I felt terrible for them. After trudging through over an hour of anguishing interviews and press conferences, many of the players and coaches left America West Arena, longing for the solace and comfort of a home they hadn't seen for almost two weeks. Checking for both stray luggage and straggling 6'10" power forwards, I popped my head into the locker room one last time. In the next to last locker, Teddy Dupay sat with a towel over his head, sobbing, but he wasn't alone. After surveying the rest of the otherwise vacant locker room, I stopped short of flipping the final light switch. I met LD's reddened eyes, and he nodded and smiled slightly.

Patting Teddy gently on the back of the head, LaDarius said, "C'mon, Ted. It's time to go home."

In each of his first three seasons as head coach at the University of Florida, Coach Donovan had managed to redefine the standard for success by recruiting players who possessed genuine passion for the game of basketball. But although the freshman class of '99 had generated a whirlwind of publicity around the burgeoning program, the subsequent batch of talent arrived in the summer of 2000 in the midst of a maelstrom of championship-speak. Brett Nelson, Matt Bonner, and Donnell Harvey had all earned McDonald's All-American honors as seniors in high school, and the relatively unheralded Justin Hamilton had already shocked many with both his intellectual and physical maturity.

Before even the first whistle blew on my third season with the team, *ESPN The Magazine* recognized the O'Connell Center as one of the most terrifying places in the country for opposing teams, dubbing it "The House of Horrors." The Florida Gators opened up the new season by blasting the Florida State Seminoles by 35. Then the team won ten of their next eleven games, heading into SEC play. Still, the new millennium would bring great uncertainty, great challenges, and more than a few great things.

"A family affair." Walking out with my parents to meet Coach Donovan at midcourt on Senior Night, I realized the impact those amazing four years as a part of the Gator basketball family would have on the rest of my life.

New Year's Day in the world of college basketball is a far cry from the unending hours of football viewing and barbecuing that I had grown accustomed to as a kid, and a 7 a.m. practice on January 1 goes a long way in regulating the amount of sparklers a guy can fire up the night before. Still, many college basketball teams find solace as they leave December behind; the first day of the New Year brings a clean slate, where the wrongs of yesterday can be transformed into the victories of tomorrow.

Head coaches all across the country wake up to the fresh air of in-conference play, where the games *really* start to matter, and you can almost feel the temperature rise as the bad blood of rivalries starts to boil. After cruising through less fortunate competition during the first few months of the season, the team that many were predicting to dance all the way to the Final Four in March was ready to sink its teeth into more sizeable prey. The Florida Gators entered SEC play with a chip on their shoulder and were determined to gain something that had been as elusive as a championship ring: *RESPECT.*

Road games in the SEC are a lot like going to the dentist—you go only because you have to. Most gyms are sweltering and claustrophobic. Bloodthirsty fans who despise you and everything you represent seem to hover on top of you. Still, and perhaps because of all this, respect is earned here. For a visiting team in the SEC, a victory in a rival's backyard sends a message: WE DO NOT FEAR YOU!

After a dramatic overtime loss at Tennessee, the Gators had a chance to do just that as they traveled to Bud Walton Arena in Fayetteville. The Arkansas Razorbacks were a dominant team at home, and Florida had never won a game there. Ever. Things were not going to be any easier on this night, as senior guard Kenyan Weaks had been restricted to a liquid diet for the past few days. Team leader Mike Miller was ailing from a sprained wrist suffered in practice earlier in the week, and wasn't sure if he would be able to go. The student sections were even rowdier tonight, and the guys knew that they were in for a true Hog, er, dogfight.

Overcoming a consistent shooting night by NBA-bound Joe Johnson, the guys were able to wear down the Razorbacks with persistent and crowd-quieting offense. Mike Miller scored 19 points and grabbed 8 rebounds, fighting through pain to lead the team. Kenyan and Donnell Harvey led a swarming defense that frustrated Arkansas throughout the night, and the Gators left for home one win closer to gathering some hardware. Two weeks later, the team clinched their first SEC Championship since 1989, and, yes, a nice-sized helping of respect.

The NCAA Tournament Selection Committee rewarded Florida's brilliance during the regular season by sending the team to Winston-Salem as the fifth seed. Before practice one day as the team readied to take on the twelfth-seeded Butler Bulldogs, I challenged Mike Miller to a game of Horse, eager to display my marksman-like range from the outside. After some inventive, if not unfeasible, makes and miscues found the score tied at S, I decided to get back to fundamentals, squaring up to the rim from two feet away. Mike laughed as my ball swished through, implying that a superstar of his caliber was far too good to miss a layup. As his shot rolled errantly off the back of the rim, I shook my head, saying nothing. It was my first victory in two years.

In Winston-Salem, with the Gators trailing 67-68 with three seconds remaining in overtime, things did not look good. Butler had frustrated Florida for much of the game, using a methodical, ball-control offense to diffuse the Gators' full-court press. As manager Quentin Ball and I sat watching from seven rows behind the bench, I couldn't help but think of the next day's headlines. *Florida Stunned!! ... Bulldogs Take Bite Out of Gators' Run to Final Four!!*

I only remember Quentin sprinting past me, past the security guards, over the railing, and on top of the pile. Taking a pass from Teddy Dupay, Mike Miller had stumbled into the middle of the lane and dropped in, yes, a layup, as the buzzer sounded. The players on the bench erupted, jumping on top of Mike and screaming. The coaches were beside themselves, leaping into the air like school children. Senior Brent Wright cried, as his season was so close to coming to an end. The Gators had survived, and in the process ensured a place in the NCAA tourney history books. This was one to remember.

The team rode a wave of success throughout the remainder of the tournament. Before I knew it, I found myself on one end of a hallway in the bowels of the Carrier Dome in Syracuse, with legendary Duke Head Coach Mike Krzyzewski standing stoically on the other. I had watched Duke's success in the 1990s on television; seen arguably the greatest game of all-time unfold as Christian Laettner crushed Kentucky's dreams. Only this wasn't television. The Florida Gators were about to meet up with the most successful program in college basketball's past decade, the #1 ranked team in the nation, and I was right in the middle of it all.

It was as though they had been there a hundred times before. Drilling long-range shot after shot while maintaining superb defensive focus and offensive patience, the Florida Gators picked the Blue Devils apart for forty minutes. The shock from Duke's bench was as palpable as the euphoria from ours. The guys were truly amazing throughout, thwarting several second-half comeback attempts by the Blue Devils en route to an 87-78 win. Preparing the locker room minutes after the final buzzer had sounded, I was expecting a loud, raucous celebration to come storming through the doors at any second. Instead, I barely heard them come in.

Filing in one by one with towels hung low over some of their heads, you might have thought that the Gators had lost by 20. I caught Brett Nelson's eye, smiled.

"Yeah, man! C'mon, we won!!" I jumped up and down, nearly knocking him over.

Brett looked at me, barely there, and then slipped away, taking a seat next to his teammates.

Brent Wright, a junior forward, was not in the mood to celebrate either. Not yet.

"Hey, y'all! This doesn't mean *[expletive]*!!" He barked.

"Three more to go, boys! Three more to go!" shouted Mike Miller.

Only they weren't boys anymore. Those eighteen- and nineteen-year-olds, all green and selfish and arrogant just months ago, were gone now. The Duke Blue Devils had come up against an impenetrable, well-oiled machine on this night, hell-bent on destroying anything in its way. After disposing of Oklahoma State with relative ease in the Elite Eight, we packed up and headed for Indianapolis to grapple with another storied dynasty, the North Carolina Tar Heels. The Gators had navigated the road leading up to the Final Four with cutting precision, and were ready to see their journey right through to the promised land.

It is deceptively calm inside the eye of the storm that has become the NCAA Final Four. Somewhere between the shameless hawking of tacky screen-printed T-shirts and incessant armchair prognosticating, there is a game to be played. Coach Donovan, alert almost to the point of extreme paranoia at times, had been sure to keep his players focused and shielded from any and all outside interferences upon arriving in Indianapolis.

After checking into our hotel, Coach dispatched one of his henchmen to the managers' rooms to lay down the law. Thirty minutes later, all telephones had been confiscated from players' rooms, and a strict 10:30 p.m. curfew had been imposed. Each manager was assigned to two rooms and ordered to keep watch in the hallway until 2 a.m., just to be sure. Because he, too, had played in the Final Four while at Providence, I suspect that Coach's apprehensions were founded, and the guys didn't put up much of a fight.

Surprising at it may seem, neither did the Tar Heels. In a game that had promised to be a first-rate shootout between two hot teams, Florida dismantled UNC's championship hopes with a punishing, full-court assault that had their players dragging with ten minutes remaining in the game. As they had throughout the tournament, the deep, talented Gators had run their opponent ragged to the point of exhausted submission. They advanced to the championship game for the first time in school history by defeating the Tar Heels 71-59. Michigan State, yet another team that had seen great success over the past few seasons, would be a formidable foe for these young Gators, but you can be assured that they weren't going to go down without a fight.

On the bus en route to the biggest game in Florida basketball history, we watched a news clip from back home to get the guys revved up. Because we had been on the road for so many days, there was a general ignorance of the "BillyBall" phenomenon that was taking place in Gainesville. Fans ran wild through the streets of Gainesville, leaping onto cars, dancing. A trio of sorority girls got a little overexcited during one particular live interview.

"THE GATORS *[expletive]* RULE!!" Said a brunette in a navy blue Gator T-shirt.

"TEDDY DUPAY IS SO HOT!!" Added a beer-bottle-wielding blonde.

It was obvious that the Greeks had been partying. We were all stunned—moved, really—at the seeming rock-star status that the team had obtained back home, but that was nothing compared to the star power that turned out in Indianapolis for the big show. While walking to my seat just behind the Florida bench, I passed Laker great and Michigan State alumnus Magic Johnson. I think I spotted a member of *Nsync in an elevator, but was too ashamed to tell my little sister that I didn't know his name. Still, I could never have been prepared for what would happen next.

I wouldn't have noticed him if it weren't for the half-dozen bodyguards flanking him as he ordered a hot dog from the concession stand. A crowd was beginning to amass, so I quickly joined them to get a glimpse of the legend. Shaking violently from his bout with Parkinson's, yet somehow still managing to move so gracefully, Muhammad Ali stood mere feet away, in the flesh. His presence was harrowing and awesome at once, but you couldn't take your eyes off him if you wanted to. He just wouldn't let you. Sensing the crowd, the Champ waved us in closer, smiling. He reached into his pocket and slowly removed a red handkerchief, trembling. He held it out for us to see before stuffing it into his great right fist, shaking. Suddenly, in one lightning-quick instant . . .

"SNAP! CLAP! MAGIC!"

It was gone.

I was changed.

Somehow, in light of the debilitating disease that had diminished him so, "The Greatest of All Time" had summoned the presence that had won the Rumble In the Jungle and endeared him to millions. As his bodyguards parted the crowd and the Champ shuffled out of sight, I tried to digest the past 60 seconds of my life. I will remember them for sixty lifetimes.

Oh, and then there was the championship game. After fighting through some understandable nervousness at the outset, the Florida Gators began to find the rhythm that had fueled their run to the championship. Still, the veteran Michigan State Spartans, led by seniors Morris Peterson and Mateen Cleaves, were nearly perfect in heading to the locker room up 43-32. Coach Donovan was forced to make some adjustments to try to disrupt MSU's offensive flow, while somehow finding a way to increase the overall tempo of the game to wear the Spartans down. It would prove difficult.

The Gators opened the second half with a burst of energy, cutting the lead to six with 16:18 left in the game. After Cleaves went down with an ankle injury, Florida looked poised to mount a comeback. With momentum shifting to the Gators, Cleaves hobbled out from the tunnel in melodramatic fashion, calling upon his minions à la Hulk Hogan. It was a sickening display, but effective.

After Cleaves returned to the game with just under five minutes to go, Michigan State went on a 16-6 run that sealed the title for the Spartans. As Mike Miller walked off of the court, helpless, I assumed that he would be back here again, battling with his teammates. Today just wasn't the day for the Gators. Michigan State won the game 89-76, and Mateen Cleaves took home the MVP trophy, along with a bag of ice for his "sore" ankle. We boarded the plane the next morning, eager to return to the comfort of our own beds. It had been the greatest Florida basketball season ever.

My final season as a manager for the Gator basketball team was much like my four years at Florida. It was over before I knew it.

Mike Miller and Donnell Harvey declared for the NBA Draft in the summer of 2000, ensuring that they would never again put on a Gator uniform. Although it was disappointing to see them go, they were able to capitalize on their terrific play during the nationally televised run to the Final Four, and both were drafted in the first round.

A string of bad luck and a flurry of injuries weakened an already depleted squad due to Mike and Donnell's defections. Florida lost senior leader Brent Wright to a broken foot just before beginning SEC play at South Carolina, where a desperation shot from half-court sent the Gators home with a loss. The team was 1-3 in conference play when rival Georgia came to town. Down by one with less than a minute to play, acrobatic guard Justin Hamilton grabbed a steal and sprung toward the basket with a defender just behind. As he leaped toward the rim, Justin tore his ACL (anterior cruciate ligament), and the Gators lost the game and yet another scholarship player.

In light of the adversity that seemed to follow Florida for much of the season, the team made an improbable run to the SEC Championship by winning eleven of its last twelve games. After Florida had gone more than a decade without a conference title, Coach Donovan's squad had captured two rings back to back. Surging at the just the right time, Florida earned an unprecedented third seed in the NCAA tournament, and Gainesville was buzzing again as its beloved boys traveled to New Orleans to take on Western Kentucky.

After disposing of their first-round competition with little fanfare, the Gators looked ahead to the Temple Owls, whose defense at tournament time was traditionally stifling. Despite a day of rest, the team came out flat in the first half against the Owls, failing to score a single field goal in the last eight minutes before intermission. The deficit proved too large for Florida to overcome, and its season, as well as my career with the Gator basketball team, came to an abrupt, quiet end.

My story is not about glamour or superstardom. Where I'm from, heroes aren't carried out on the shoulders of their teammates. Where I'm from, *I* doesn't even exist. In this place, everyday people just like you and me clasp hands and pray for mothers and fathers, for humility and courage. In this land, your sweat is anything but no sweat, and you quickly learn that the game of life doesn't slow down for anyone.

Where I'm from, the least you know about your friend is the number on his jersey that elsewhere defines him. You learn to take advantage of each second, each quarter, and each game, to depend on each person, each brother, and each other. Where I'm from, if you are one of the lucky ones, you learn not to trust the tricky magician, because at any moment . . . SNAP! CLAP!

MAGIC!

Chapter 10

Foreign Players
and the Globalization of Basketball

Renada Rutmanis

I spent the summer of 1998 in a little town in Guatemala. Much to my disappointment, the Chicago Bulls were not able to win in the NBA Championship in four or five games, and I thought my rather remote location in a foreign country would prevent me from seeing them successfully complete their second three-peat. Little did I know.

Despite the excitement of the World Cup that year, my host family invited me to watch game six, which was being televised around the world. My host family didn't even know the names of the teams, but they did know they were rooting for the guys in red and for Michael Jordan.

This year was different, however. They were not just watching an American team playing an American sport. The Bulls had two notable foreign players in Toni Kukoc from Croatia and Luc Longley from Australia. Even the great Bulls, led by the otherworldly superstars Michael Jordan and Scottie Pippen, became part of a growing trend around the NBA. Each team, it seemed, stocked itself with a couple of foreign players.

What became a trend in the late 1990s does not seem to be slowing down anytime soon. In the early 2000s, many of the best players in the league are foreign-born, including reigning MVP Tim Duncan and German sharpshooter Dirk Nowitzki. When I listened to that Bulls play-off game in Guatemala, the language of the announcers may have been Spanish, but clearly the language and the game of basketball had become universal.

HISTORY OF FOREIGN PLAYERS IN THE NBA

Foreign players have always been a part of the NBA. In the very first game of the 1946-1947 season, an Italian-Canadian named Hank Arcado Biasatti played for the Toronto Huskies, a team that would last only one year.[1] Although it would not be until 1996 that Canada would get its own team again, foreign players continued to infiltrate the league.

Depending on the needs of the league and the current political situations around the world, the number of foreign players and their makeup would often change (it was nine years after being drafted before Arvydas Sabonis felt the political climate had changed enough to let him come play in America). Lithuanian Sarunas Marciulionis, who first played for Golden State in 1989, was the first player from the former Soviet Union to sign a professional contract.[2] In 1996, Horacio Llamas became the first Mexican-born player to play in the NBA when he was drafted by the Phoenix Suns. Currently, approximately one-seventh of the players in the league were born outside the United States.[3] This number will only increase as foreign talent flocks to the hoops Mecca of the NBA.

Part of the reason for more international players coming into the league may have been its quick expansion in the late 1980s. Charlotte and Miami each received teams in 1988, and the following year they were joined by Minnesota and Orlando. Then, in 1996, teams were opened in Vancouver and Toronto as the NBA expanded into Canada (the Vancouver team would later be moved to Memphis). This meant there was space for many additional players all at once, and many teams looked overseas to fill their rosters with the best talent. According to the NBA, teams now spend as much as 20 percent of their scouting budget on overseas scouting. In 1988, seventeen NBA teams sent scouts to the pre-Olympic tournament, whereas none had attended the same event in 1984.[4]

In addition to more openings in the league, there was also more openness between the United States and what had once been either isolated countries or enemies. In 1987 the NBA invited the Soviet National Team and Tracer Milan of Italy to participate in the first McDonald's Open tournament, a tournament for championship teams of international clubs.[5] In 1988 the Atlanta Hawks became the first NBA team to make a trip to the Soviet Union.[6]

The league as a whole also started to reach out to the rest of the world. During the 1990-1991 season the NBA became the first major American sports league to play regular season games outside North America. That year the Phoenix Suns and Utah Jazz opened the season by playing two games in Tokyo. Games were played in Japan in 1992, 1996, and 1999, and the NBA has also held games in Mexico seven times.[7]

Although basketball continued to grow as an international sport throughout the years, many people credit the 1992 Dream Team with boosting international interest to an entirely new level.[8] Of the twelve players who represented the United States in Barcelona that year, ten would later be named to the NBA's list of the Fifty Greatest Players. This team showcased the very best of American basketball to the rest of the world.[9] Before participating in the Olympic games, the team toured Europe, drawing hoards of fans wherever they went. Even players on opposing teams were often in awe of the original Dream Team, and would sometimes ask for autographs while on the court.

HISTORY OF BASKETBALL AROUND THE WORLD

As basketball became a worldwide sport, it needed a mechanism for organizing itself on a universal scale. FIBA (the International Basketball Federation) was founded in Geneva, Switzerland, in 1932, and had eight founding national federations.[10] It now has 206 member national federations and governs all international competitions, including the World Championships and the basketball portion of the Olympics. Basketball was played as a demonstration sport at the 1904 Olympics in St. Louis and was first played as a medal sport in 1936 at the Berlin Olympics.[11]

In 1989, FIBA decided to allow "open competition" in Olympic basketball.[12] This paved the way for the creation of the Dream Team because it allowed professional players, rather than just amateurs, to participate. But it had another impact as well. Players from other countries were now able to play professionally in the United States and remain eligible to play for their respective countries every four years during the Olympics, which was especially important for players who did not want to abandon ties to their homelands.[13] The Olympics allowed players to show national pride and talent, while playing in the NBA gave them the chance to play against the very best the world has to offer.

Besides players coming to the United States directly to the NBA, there has also been an influx of players coming to play at American universities. In 1984, there were twenty-five international players in the NCAA Division I basketball league. By the 1999-2000 season, almost 400 foreign players were participating.[14] More and more international students are coming to play college basketball in the United States, making them more prominent as draft choices. NBA executives, however, now regard European leagues and their players to be on a higher level than the NCAA.[15] As more and more American players try to jump directly from high school to the pros, many teams find that foreign players have had more professional experience and coaching.[16]

SOME NOTABLE FOREIGN PLAYERS

Patrick Ewing

Patrick Ewing was born in Kingston, Jamaica, and later attended Georgetown University. In his freshman year, Ewing led his team to the 1982 National NCAA Championship game. In 1983-1984 season, the team won the NCAA Championship for the first time, and Ewing was named the tournament's most valuable player. That summer he played on the U.S. Olympic basketball team that won the gold medal. The following year Georgetown reached the NCAA finals once more, and the National Association of Basketball Coaches named Ewing the college player of the year. Ewing was the number-one pick in the 1985 draft by the New York Knicks. On November 19, 1996, Patrick scored his 20,000th point, making him known both for his size and defense as well as for his scoring.

Drazen Petrovic

Drazen Petrovic grew up in Sibenik, a small port city on the Adriatic Sea. Drazen was only eighteen years old when he became the best player in the country, taking his club Sibenka to a national championship. Drazen finished his rookie year with the Portland Trail Blazers with 7.6 points per game and was traded to New Jersey, where he exploded onto the court and became one of the premier shooting guards in the NBA. With an average of 20.6 points per game and shooting 51 percent from the floor, Drazen took the title of best shooting guard in the NBA. Drazen participated in the 1992 Olympics, which was Croatia's first Olympic basketball appearance. Drazen and Croatia took home the silver medal. His career was sadly cut short when he died in a car accident the following year.[17]

Arvydas Sabonis

Arvydas Sabonis was born in Kaunas, Lithuania, and drafted in 1986 by Portland, but he continued to play in Europe until 1995, when he came to America and joined the Trailblazers. On this team he shared playing time with Chris Dudley in order to protect his often-injured feet. By midseason Sabonis had developed into one of the NBA's most effective all-around centers and, when he was moved into the Blazers' starting lineup, he helped Portland win eighteen of its last twenty-one games and led the team in scoring and rebounding in the play-offs. He led the Blazers in rebounding, blocks, and double-doubles in 1996-1997; ranked ninth in the league in rebounding in 1997-1998; and was second on the club in rebounding, shot-blocking, and double-doubles in 1998-1999, when he played in all fifty games. In 1999 he was voted the international player who has had the most impact during the NBA's modern-era by users of NBA.com. He was the team's leading rebounder in 1999-2000, when the Blazers reached the Western Conference Finals.

Sabonis led the Soviet National Team to a gold medal at the 1988 Olympic Games in Seoul. Following the breakup of the Soviet Union, he helped Lithuania to a bronze medal at the 1992 Olympics in Barcelona and a second-place finish in the 1995 European Championships in Greece. In more than a decade spent as a professional player with club teams in the former Soviet Union and then in the Spanish League, Sabonis won five league championships and was named European Player of the Year four times by various publications.

Rik Smits

Rik Smits was born in Eindhoven, Holland, and was selected second in the draft by the Indiana Pacers in 1988, where he acquired the nickname "The Dunking Dutchman" and was named to the 1989 NBA All-Rookie First Team. Smits finished the 1996-1997 season with 9,909 career points, which is second in Pacers' NBA history and fourth on the all-time franchise list.

Detlef Schrempf

Detlef Schrempf was born in Leverkusen, Germany, and was once described by Spike Lee as a "brilliant white sax player jamming a set with the brothers, with great talent, but not wanting to intrude."[18] He went to high school and college in Washington State and was drafted in 1985 by the Dallas Mavericks. He was traded to the Indiana Pacers in November 1993, and later became a member of the Seattle Sonics before finally being traded to the Portland Trail Blazers. The Detlef Schrempf Foundation was formed in 1996 by Schrempf and his wife, Mari. The foundation is focused mostly on providing charity to children and families in the Northwest region of the United States.[19]

Hakeem Olajuwon

Hakeem Olajuwom was born in Lagos, Nigeria. Although he was known as one of the best goalkeeper prospects in Nigeria, his talent also made him one of the NBA's premier centers. He joined the University of Houston Cougars when he was seventeen, a team that he led to the NCAA Final Four two times. He was selected first in the draft by Houston, despite Michael Jordan and Charles Barkley being selected that same year. Olajuwon would lead the Houston Rockets to two championships in 1994 and 1995. Loyal to all of his fans, he wouldn't let his sneaker company charge more than $35 for shoes that bore his name.

Dikembe Mutombo

Dikembe Mutombo was born in Kinshasa, Zaire, under the full name Dikembe Mutombo Mpolondo Mukamba Jean Jacque Wamutombo, and can speak English, French, Spanish, Portugese, and five African dialects. Dikembe arrived in the United States on a USAID scholarship to attend Georgetown University. As a premed student, he dreamed of becoming a doctor and returning to the Congo to practice medicine. In his second year at Georgetown, coach John

Thompson convinced the 7'2" Mutombo to join the university's basketball team. After joining the team, Dikembe redirected his medical ambitions and graduated from Georgetown with dual degrees in linguistics and diplomacy. In 1997 Dikembe created the Dikembe Mutombo Foundation. Its mission is to improve the health, education, and quality of life for the people in his homeland. Dikembe would later earn the nation's highest honor for volunteer service, the President's Volunteer Service Award.

Vlade Divac

Vlade Divac, whose favorite movies are *American Beauty* and *American Pie*,[20] was born in Yugoslavia, and was so famous there that his wedding was nationally televised.[21] He was selected by the Los Angeles Lakers in the first round (twenty-sixth pick overall) of the 1989 NBA Draft. In order to make room for Shaquille O'Neal, both in the middle of the court and under the salary cap, Divac was traded to the Charlotte Hornets for the draft rights to Kobe Bryant in 1996. Before wearing a Charlotte uniform, Divac competed for Yugoslavia at the 1996 Olympics in Atlanta and helped his team win a silver medal. On January 22, 1999, Divac signed as a free agent with the Sacramento Kings and went on to average a double-double for the third time in his career and the first time since 1994-1995, averaging 14.3 points, 10.0 rebounds, and a career-high 4.3 assists per game. Although he never played in college, Divac played professionally for five seasons in his home country before joining the Lakers. In 1988 he won an Olympic silver medal for Yugoslavia and competed against the Boston Celtics in the McDonald's Open.

Steve Nash

Steve Nash was born in the unlikely place of Victoria, British Columbia, and is the first foreign-born point guard in the NBA.[22] He was the West Coast Conference Player of the Year at Santa Clara in 1995 and 1996, and was a first-round draft pick of the Phoenix Suns. The Suns traded Nash to Dallas in 1998 and he stepped in as the Mavericks' starting point guard, leading the team in assists in 1998-1999. A standout on the Canadian National Team, he played at the World

Championships held in Toronto in 1994, and in the Pre-Olympic Qualifying Tournament in San Juan in 1999.

On his official Web site, Steve had this to say about basketball in the NBA and around the world:

> The world has taken notice of the NBA and the incredible skills and talent of it's [sic] players. In the last 15 years, the popularity of the sport has grown worldwide[.] So have international programs, coaching and competition level. Therefore, the talent of international players, particularly in Europe, has increased significantly. Many European players join club teams at a young age, and are playing against men who are professional in their own right. I think that Europeans pride themselves on skill development more than athletic ability. That's why we're seeing so many skilled players from Europe who are ready to make an impact very quickly after their arrival in the NBA.[23]

Nash was the first Canadian to be named to the All-Star team when he was chosen in 2002. He had this to say about it.

> I feel really good about it. It's really good for all my family and friends back home. I think it's good for all Canadians. Hopefully, there's some sweetness in it for all the fans back in B.C. There were a lot of fans that supported the Grizzlies and followed that team. So hopefully there's a little pride and joy in it for them too.[24]

IMPACT ON LEAGUE

Though the game of basketball played overseas is certainly recognizable as the same game played in the United States, there are many differences in the way the game is played, and the more international players in the NBA, the more they effect the way the game is played in America. For example, FIBA does not allow play to be as physical as in the NBA, which can be a difficult adjustment for some foreign players to make.[25] Because of this, international players are more accustomed to playing as a team rather than man-to-man defense, making them less likely to drive and more likely to shoot. The Sacramento Kings and Dallas Mavericks, two of the league's highest-scoring teams, both like to play a fast-running game, which may have developed because they are both teams with a number of foreign players. International players feature the skip pass and a more perimeter-oriented game. Of course, there has also been an American influence on the international game, which has resulted in better ballhandling, improved perimeter defense, and the development of an inside game.[26]

International players have also joined together to help further peace and understanding around the world through basketball. Working along with the United Nations and led by Toni Kukoc and Vlade Divac, Basketball Without Borders was launched in 2001 when players aged twelve to fourteen from Bosnia and Herzegovina, Croatia, the former Yugoslav Republic of Macedonia, Slovenia, and the Federal Republic of Yugoslavia attended a basketball camp in Italy. In addition to working on basketball skills, the participants are also taught about leadership, conflict resolution, and the dangers of drugs.[27]

FUTURE PROSPECTS

Advances in television and computer technology have played a key role in bringing American basketball to the rest of the world. During the 1999-2000 season, games were broadcast to 750 million households in 205 countries in forty-two languages. The Web site <www.nba.com> receives about 35 percent of its hits from outside the United States. With these advances, the future of basketball promises to be even brighter as its appeal continues to grow around the world.

There have also been rumblings about the NBA expanding into Mexico in the near future, by perhaps moving an existing franchise there or starting a new one, which would bring the total in the league to an even thirty. David Stern said in an interview that "it serves to improve our league to have many athletes outside the U.S. competing for spots in the league. They enhance the quality of play and the ability to market the NBA around the world." At the 2002 All-Star Weekend Stern also said he might start pursuing opportunities in Europe and China, despite having made previous promises to overseas officials that he would not try and expand into their markets.[28]

In July 2002, Yao Ming was selected first in the draft by the Houston Rockets, marking the first time that an international player who has not played college basketball in America was chosen as the number-one draft pick.[29]

NOTES

1. Boyer, Mary Schmitt. "The International Player: A Growing Influence." In *The Official NBA Encyclopedia,* pp. 296-299. New York: Doubleday, 2000.

2. Ibid.

3. Barker, Barbara. "Global Warming." *Newsday,* April 11, 2002.

4. Heisler, Mark. "New World Order." *Los Angeles Times,* May 22, 2002.

5. Boyer, Mary Schmitt. "The International Player."

6. Ibid.

7. Reheuser, Rob. "Around the World: NBA Goes Global." In *The Official NBA Encyclopedia,* pp. 302-305. New York: Doubleday, 2000.

8. Hubbard, Jan. "The Dream Team: A Global Explosion." In *The Official NBA Encyclopedia,* pp. 290-293. New York: Doubleday, 2000.

9. Phelps, Digger. *Basketball for Dummies.* Foster City, CA: IDG, 2000.

10. <www.fiba.com>.

11. Frazier, Walt and Alex Sachare. *The Complete Idiot's Guide to Basketball.* New York: Alpha Books, 1998.

12. Boyer, Mary Schmitt. "The International Player."

13. Ibid.

14. Phelps, Digger. *Basketball for Dummies.*

15. Heisler, Mark. "New World Order."

16. Barker, Barbara. "Global Warming."

17. Dolin, Nick. *Basketball Stars.* New York: Black Dog and Leventhal, 1997.

18. Lee, Spike. *Best Seat in the House.* New York: Crown Publishers, 1997.

19. <www.detlef.com>.

20. <www.nba.com/playerfile/vlade_divac/bio.html>.

21. Barker, Barbara. "Global Warming."

22. "Cloud over Wang Going to the NBA." *Shanghai Star,* March 22, 2001 <app1.chinadaily.com.cn/star/2001/0322/sp28-1.html>.

23. <www.upperdeck.com/athletes/stevenash/fanclub_quotes.asp>.

24. Ibid.

25. Nance, Roscoe. "Foreign-born players make impact." *USA TODAY,* July 2, 1999.

26. Phelps, Digger. *Basketball for Dummies.*

27. <www.un.org/works/peace/peace1.html>.

28. Barker, "Global Warming."

29. Thomsen, Ian. "FIBA Not Thrilled About NBA's Plan." *Sports Illustrated,* February 25, 2002.

PART III:
THE PROFESSIONAL GAME

Chapter 11

Elgin Baylor: The First Modern Professional Basketball Player

James Fisher

Basketball is the only major professional sport that as a matter of course combines grace, speed, and power. It was not always this way, but when Elgin Baylor entered professional basketball in 1958, everything changed.

Imagine a player who possessed Michael Jordan's leaping ability, Julius Erving's grace and body control, Charles Barkley's strength, Larry Bird's court savvy, and Wilt Chamberlain's ability to dominate a game. Unimaginable, most modern basketball fans would say. In an age when 17 points per game can bring players multimillion-dollar commercial endorsements and international recognition, few can picture a player like Elgin Baylor, an irresistible force at 6'5" and 225 pounds, who single-handedly changed the way that professional basketball was played. A game that was once slow (and often unabashed thuggery), transformed into a game of beauty. Where method and strength were once premiums, athleticism and free-flowing style dominated the game.

Besides Jordan and Dr. J, think of other dazzling, acrobatic performers, such as Dominique Wilkins, David Thompson, Earl Monroe, and Connie Hawkins. All these players made names for themselves in part because of their astonishing athleticism. They all have Elgin Baylor to thank for blazing a trail—a twisted, winding, gravity-defying trail—through the often wooden play that had been professional basketball. *Boston Globe* sportswriter Bob Ryan, recognizing the way the sky-jumper changed the game, said, "Baylor invented modern basketball." He took a horizontal and vertical game and with his remarkable leaping ability and creativity, made basketball a diagonal game.[1]

In addition to his innovative style of play, Baylor was the first modern player because he understood that something else was germane to playing. He understood that pro basketball could not long exist without administration. It had to be a business as well as a game. He understood that professional basketball was also a battle between labor and management, and he became the leader of the new players' union.

Later, Baylor went on to become one of the first black coaches. After his coaching career ended, he then joined the ranks of senior management of the Los Angeles Clippers. In so doing, he was the first major player to make professional basketball his life's work, a path that many have since followed.

Elgin Baylor and the rest of the stars of professional basketball's golden age are often unheralded today due to the very infancy of a technology that is now taken for granted in its ubiquity: television. What is now a $2 billion-a-year revenue stream for the NBA brought the league only $39,000 a year for televising thirteen games, a paltry sum even in the 1950s.

A revealing fact is that many owners initially feared television broadcasts. They worried that televised games would keep fans at home. The rare game that was shown appeared locally. Until the 1970s, few games were shown nationally. Without a doubt, much of the best basketball ever played was lost due to the lack of interest in promoting professional basketball—both on the part of the league and broadcasters.[2] Fortunately, however, a few regular season, some championship, and most All-Star games were broadcast in some markets and copies of varying qualities still exist. But for Baylor, most of his moves left posterity so far behind that, like those who tried to guard him, we would never see him until he was past us.

Baylor has received little credit over the years for doing things that no one had done before. His style of play routinely bewildered his opponents, but most commentators then and now have not credited him with changing the way basketball was played. Usually one of two big men, Bill Russell or Wilt Chamberlain, was considered basketball's best all-time player (before Michael Jordan emerged decades later).[3]

Joining the NBA's Boston Celtics in 1956 after a stellar career at the University of San Francisco and winning an Olympic gold medal, Russell changed the game by proving that defense wins games. His size (6'11") and athletic ability threatened to make layups and short-range jumpers obsolete. Although a terror on defense and the boards, Russell was not the seminal player he is so often considered to be. Coaches had always longed for players who could dominate the defensive end of the court and yank down every rebound. Russell was simply the best defensively—before or since.

Chamberlain was Russell's alter ego. No one—no, not even MJ—has or will come close to being the offensive force that Wilt was. Even as a rookie in 1960, he was utterly unstoppable with the ball, as even Russell admitted. Consequently, many players and sportswriters felt that Chamberlain forever changed the face of basketball. His matchless strength, on his agile 7'1" frame, was unprecedented.[4]

Although they dominated the game on either end of the court, that does not mean that either Russell or Chamberlain redefined the way basketball was played. No one since has equaled either man, but Russell was not the first center to specialize in defense, and Wilt was not basketball's original scoring machine. To see what changed in professional basketball with the arrival of Elgin Baylor, we must look at basketball in its "pioneer" days: the years following World War II.

Basketball games in the pre-Baylor era were long, nasty, brutish, and low-scoring. Teams kept designated hackers on their benches to beat on—literally—opposing stars. Fisticuffs were not uncommon and some early players looked as if they belonged on an offensive line instead of a front line. Fans got into the act as well.

The Fort Wayne, Indiana, Zollner (now Detroit) Pistons home court earned the nickname "Tub of Blood" for the assaults visiting players endured at the hands of the home team's fans. Perhaps because players were dodging debris and ducking fists and women's handbags, plays often took minutes to unfold, usually culminating in a two-handed set shot, hook shot, or uninspiring layup. In fact, many early professionals lamented the advent of the twenty-four-second shot clock in 1954; it killed elaborately orchestrated plays.

Clearly, the goal was ball control. One game in 1951 went to three overtimes, and whoever controlled each overtime tip-off held the ball for five minutes, waiting for the last shot. Recalled one participant: "The fans booed the shit out of us." The final score? 75-73. Not surprisingly, teams did not begin flirting with 80 points per game until the mid-1950s. But it would get worse before it got better.

On March 20, 1954, during one of the few nationally televised games of the 1950s and 1960s, the New York Knicks and Boston Celtics traded fouls and foul shots during one of the most grotesque games in NBA history. The fourth quarter alone took forty-five minutes, but the television audience never saw the thrilling conclusion. Disgusted network programmers cut to alternative programming.[5]

The postwar era's star was George Mikan, center for the Minneapolis Lakers, who played from 1947-1954 and 1955-1956. Mikan represented the pinnacle of early professional basketball style. All professional leagues valued size, strength, and a methodical style of play.

At 6'10", Mikan was basketball's first great "big man" and a real bruiser. Taller and stronger than his opponents, Mikan physically dominated the game. Early in his career, before the introduction of foul limits, opponents would literally hang and pound on his huge frame in an effort to negate his advantages. Big and slow, Mikan excelled in the plodding half-court game that had dominated play since the inception of basketball.

Another favorite method to counter Mikan and the advantages of other talented players was to stall. Professional basketball games in the 1940s and 1950s were rarely shootouts, but against Mikan, teams slowed the pace even more. The worst seemed to come in 1950 when the Fort Wayne Pistons and Mikan's Lakers set the record for the least points scored in a game in the modern era: 37! Combined!

Obviously rules had to be changed. The stalling, fouling, and all-around uninspiring play was costing the league fans. Mikan was basketball's first marquee name, but no one wanted to see how long a team could play keep away or how many times a player could be deliberately fouled without a fight erupting. The mid-1950s became the age of rule changes aimed at opening up the style and pace of games.

With the changes came the origins of modern professional basketball. The lane was widened from six to twelve feet to keep centers from clogging lanes to the basket and monopolizing rebounds. Goaltending was banned. The twenty-four-second clock was introduced in 1954, as were limits on personal and team fouls.[6]

But rule changes themselves do not make for exciting basketball. Although the pace of games quickened and scoring increased, the league lacked a star that could fully benefit from the new regulations. In Seattle, Washington, however, a collegiate star was about to bring professional basketball the fast-paced, innovative style it wanted and needed to put fans in the seats.

Elgin Gay Baylor was born on September 16, 1934. He grew up in Washington, DC, and learned basketball on the playground, playing countless hours. Baylor doubtless acquired his midair improvisations during pickup games where his self-described "spontaneous" reactions to defenders was never discouraged. Here he was again a pioneer. The vast majority of his predecessors and contemporaries learned a more methodical and physical game at YMCAs, sporting clubs, schools, armories, or in the military. Although Julius Erving is generally credited with bringing wide-open, often acrobatic playground basketball to professional basketball and making it acceptable, Baylor was in fact the first.

Although a talented high school basketball player, all major colleges overlooked Baylor. Big-time college scouts simply did not bother recruiting at black high schools. Already physically powerful, Baylor landed a football scholarship at the College of Idaho for the 1954-1955 academic year and walked on to the basketball program. He immediately outran the talent at the small Caldwell, Idaho, school, putting in just over 31 points per game and hauling down better than 20 rebounds as a freshman. He transferred to Seattle University for his two remaining eligible years, posting similar numbers and carrying his team to a second-place finish in the NCAA Finals in 1958.[7]

Predictably, Baylor was the first player chosen in that year's NBA collegiate draft. The hapless Minneapolis Lakers, who after the retirement of star center George Mikan in 1954, could not win a game, picked him. Losing games, fans, and money, owner Bob Short was ready to sell the team. They had gone 19-53, had no dependable home court, and were broke.

Short placed all his hope in signing the collegiate star. He later recalled, "If he had turned me down . . . I'd have been out of business. The team would have gone bankrupt."[8] Because of the business circumstances of the team and his phenomenal skills, Baylor became the first true franchise player.[9]

He did not disappoint. Baylor scored 24.9 points and collected 15 rebounds per game as a rookie and led the Minneapolis Lakers to a second-place finish in the Western Division and to the NBA Finals, where the Celtics swept them. Throughout his fourteen-year career, Baylor (when healthy) never averaged less than 24 points or 10 rebounds per game. He set scoring records in 1959 and 1960 (later broken by Wilt Chamberlain). Baylor's 61 points against the Boston Celtics in the 1962 NBA Finals is still a play-off record for a regulation game.

Baylor was capable of achievements that seem otherworldly today. During the 1961-1962 season, Baylor played in only forty-eight games—all on weekends—after being called to active military duty. He never once practiced with his team, before the season or during. Still, he averaged 38.3 points (the second most in NBA history), 18.6 rebounds, and 4.6 assists per game. Not bad for a part-time job.

For his career, Baylor scored over 60 points in regular season games three times (third best behind Chamberlain and Jordan), over 50 points seventeen times (third all-time), over 40 points eighty-seven times (third again), en route to a 27.4 points-per-game career scoring average (third, one last time). He remains the Lakers all-time scoring and rebounding leader with 23,149 points and 11,463 rebounds, second most for all forwards in the history of the league. The Laker standout was elected to the Naismith Memorial Basketball Hall of Fame in 1976 and selected to the NBA's Thirty-Fifth and Fiftieth Anniversary All-Time teams.[10]

Baylor's Lakers never won an NBA title, finishing runner-up to the Boston Celtics six times. He retired nine games into the 1971-1972 season. Having been plagued by debilitating knee trouble over the past season and a half, Baylor, in a characteristically selfless move, stepped down rather than take up valuable a roster space. In what must have been heart-wrenching agony, the Lakers, with Baylor watching, finally won an NBA title.

Had Baylor played twenty years later, he probably would have been the original "human highlight film." Imagine crossing Julius Erving with Karl Malone or Charles Barkley with some Wilt Chamberlain thrown in. Baylor was the NBA's first modern superstar, if we consider the modern superstar one capable of spectacular moves, undeniable scoring, and an all-around talent. Baylor propelled an earthbound game skyward.

Chick Hearn, former CBS radio and Los Angeles Laker play-by-play announcer, saw them all: Baylor, Chamberlain, Erving, Magic Johnson, Jordan. He called Baylor the "pioneer for the kind of athletic player we see today. . . . A lot of moves people say were invented by Michael Jordan or Julius Erving, I saw Elgin Baylor do first." Pat

Williams, a longtime NBA executive with several teams, called Baylor "mesmerizing." The Laker forward had the kind of creativity and talent "that no one had before him." Opponents admitted that playing against Baylor was "one of those men-against-boys situations." Bob Petit, one the NBA's best all-around players ever, called him "probably the greatest offensive talent in the history of basketball," a sentiment shared by the best defensive player ever, Bill Russell. Chick Hearn was willing to go further: Elgin Baylor "may have been the greatest player ever."[11]

What made Baylor great and thus the original NBA superstar? His leaping ability, body control, and athleticism were unparalleled. Wrote one reporter, "He never broke the law of gravity but he's awfully slow about obeying it." NBA and ABA center Zelmo Beaty could not help but observe that Baylor "was the first NBA player with hangtime." Chamberlain, Baylor's teammate at the end of the forward's career and never one to be unduly impressed, marveled that he "would go up into the air [and] stay there until everyone else came down." All-Star forward Chet Walker claimed that Baylor would hang in the air, push lesser leapers aside, and then look to shoot or pass. The old coach's adage of never leaving your feet until you know what you are going to do with the ball did not apply to Baylor. He seemed unbound by the regular laws of physics. Several opponents insisted that he could leave the floor totally out of control and gain his balance in midair, so impressive was his body control.[12]

Baylor's aerial suspension and body control only represented part of his threat, however. No one understood how to drive like he did and he made his leaping part of the drive. As a consequence, no one could stop him. Once Baylor burst toward the basket, he was undeniable. Wilt once called Baylor "the best I ever saw" at penetrating and innovating in traffic. His former collegiate and Laker coach John Castellani said, "Elgin has more moves than a clock." In his first game against Baylor in 1963-1964, future All-Star Chet Walker recalled, "Elg went around, over, and through me. I was bounced off picks, left in my tracks, and had my head spun around." As though a consistent medium-range jumper, an unbelievably strong and quick first step, spinning reverse layups, bank shots at bizarre angles with reverse spin on the ball, and changing hands in midair were not enough weapons, Baylor had a facial tick that appeared only on the court and left defenders wondering whether it was an involuntary twitch or an actual head fake. Dave DeBusschere of the New York Knicks, widely considered one of the top defensive forwards in the history of professional basketball, was still befuddled in 1971 after eight years of guarding Baylor. "Every time I think I've got him figured out, he comes up with some tricky new move." Even as Baylor's career and his knees were near their end, DeBusschere claimed that no one could yet stop him. One could only hope to slow him down, or tire him out.[13]

Yet Baylor was more than a scoring machine or a human highlight film. He was the pioneer of the modern superstar for a second reason: he could beat you so many ways. Modern superstars—Dr. J, Magic, Bird, MJ—did more than awe opponents and crowds with razzle-dazzle; they also got rebounds and handed out assists. Baylor anticipated the modern superstar who is a complete player. Observing a young Elgin Baylor, *New York Post* writer Leonard Koppett explained, "He is, merely, the best basketball player in the world because he does everything so well." With career averages 27.4 points, 13.5 rebounds, and 4.1 assists per game Baylor put up numbers that only one other forward comes close to matching—Bob Petit.[14]

Even when Baylor was breaking league records, he did it as a team player. On November 15, 1960, against the New York Knicks, he broke his own record of 64 points in a single game, pouring in 71 markers. Each of those points, teammates and opponents agreed, came within the natural flow of the game. There was no effort to set records, just flawless execution. He also pulled down 25 rebounds that night.

New York guard Richie Guerin was on the court that night and next season when Chamberlain would score his 100 points against the hapless Knicks. Of the two, Guerin thought Baylor's the more impressive performance. Unlike the game against Wilt, there was no crowd chanting that Baylor get the ball, and until the end, Baylor's teammates did not work to get him the new record. Baylor and his Lakers were just playing another game.[15] In Baylor, one witnessed unparalleled athleticism devoid of the showmanship and freewheeling individualism that was already beginning to affect professional basketball (and in many ways, plagues the game today). He was always part of his team.

So why is Elgin Baylor not immediately recognized today as the original high-flying acrobatic act? Part of the reason is Baylor's personality. Wilt Chamberlain, a garrulous, fast-talking guy who loved to be the center of attention, called Baylor "a garrulous, fast-talking guy who loves to be the center of attention." As such, fans, teammates, and sports writers loved him. But Baylor was not one to promote himself. He shunned controversy in favor of his image as a "decent, traditional, clean-cut" athlete.[16] In part, this was due the nature of professional basketball at the time, before the era of "hot dogging" and "showboating," when players were not coddled, when civility and decorum in public were requisite.[17]

It was also the era of baseball. Until the 1980s, to the print and broadcast world, the NBA was bush-league sports. *Sports Illustrated* did not cover the NBA in the early 1960s. The issues following Baylor's 71-point outburst make no mention of the record or the game. Instead its editors gave space to Navy's new halfback, chess, amateur tennis, ski chalets, and antique aircraft.

Thus, the players of basketball's golden age, arguably the years of the greatest talent in basketball, received no national attention. Not until the mid-1970s did networks broadcast Sunday games of the week, leaving professional basketball as mere filler material between baseball and football seasons, often taking a backseat to boxing as well. Even the NBA Finals did not break prime time until the early 1980s, being instead broadcast by tape delay after the evening news. As a result, few games attracted even a lone cameraman. Wilt's 100-point night, for example, is forever lost to the memory of those in attendance and a few still photographs.[18] With little publicity outside the hometown faithful, superstars such as Elgin Baylor never received the opportunity to peddle cereal and hot dogs and sneakers, and thus they remained outside of the public eye.

An equally important reason that Baylor kept a low profile certainly concerned race relations in America in the 1960s, the prime of his career. Although black professional basketball teams had been around since the 1920s, and the Harlem Globetrotters had gained international fame in the 1940s, the first black player was not drafted by an NBA squad until 1950. By the time Baylor entered the NBA in 1958, the United States Supreme Court decision, *Brown* v. *Board of Education,* banning segregation in public schools, was only four years old. The Montgomery, Alabama, boycott took place less than two years before. The Civil Rights Act of 1964 was still six years away. Obviously, discrimination remained common and professional basketball players had to navigate the racist waters running rampant in the United States.

Despite Jackie Robinson's entry into baseball, racism continued to plague professional sports, but perhaps not as badly as in society as a whole. Pro basketball had had its beginnings in the Northeast and Midwest, while Baylor played most of his career on the West Coast, a more tolerant region than the South. Still, racism in the more liberal regions was frequent and flagrant enough.

Black players faced Jim Crow laws nationwide in restaurants and hotels. St. Louis Hawks guard Lenny Wilkins was warned not to appear too friendly with white women, and Bill Russell's house in a Boston suburb was vandalized with fecal matter and racial slurs when rumors spread that he was planning to move to a more prestigious neighborhood in the same city. Even a star such as Elgin Baylor had to maintain a quiet demeanor or risk reprisals.

As the head coach of the New Orleans Jazz during the late 1970s, after his retirement from the Lakers and enshrinement into the Hall of Fame, whites hostile to the preponderance of blacks on the team frequently muttered, "We're not going to make this an all-nigger team."[19] So whether by his own doing, the NBA's lack of status as a major sport, or racism, Elgin Baylor was not constantly in the public eye.

For a final, less glorious, but no less important reason, Baylor must be reckoned the league's first modern player. He understood that professional basketball was much more than grown men playing a game. He was head of the fledgling players union, and with teammate Jerry West, threatened to organize a boycott of the 1964 All-Star game in protest of the lack of player remuneration for the event. He later coached the New Orleans Jazz and joined the front office of the Los Angeles Clippers, where he is currently Vice President of Basketball Operations.

Professional basketball had seen nothing like Elgin Baylor before 1958. He brought a style of play to the game that has endured to this day and will likely never be replaced, as long as the laws of gravity apply. And who would want to go back to two-handed set shots? Baylor also brought an understanding deeper than most players and blazed another trail into management that many have since followed. Contemporary opponents could never stay in front of him. It is only fitting that the Ervings, Jordans, and their successors can only follow Baylor's lead.

NOTES

1. Quoted in Ken Shouler, *The Experts Pick Basketball's Best 50 Players in the Last 50 Years* (White Plains, NY: All Sport Books, 1996), p. 86.

2. John Fortunato, *The Ultimate Assist: The Relationship and Broadcast Strategies of the NBA and Television Networks* (Cresskill, NJ: Hampton Press, 2001).

3. For some examples, see Neil D. Isaacs, *Vintage NBA: The Pioneer Era, 1946-56* (Indianapolis: Masters Press, 1996), p. xvi.

4. The best short comparison and evaluation of Russell and Chamberlain is in Shouler, pp. 162-184. These pages also provide players', coaches', and writers' opinions on why each center changed the way basketball was played. For other opinions naming Russell or Chamberlain, see Terry Pluto, *Tall Tales: The Glory Years of the NBA, in the Words of the Men Who Played, Coached, and Built Pro Basketball* (New York: Simon and Schuster, 1992), p. 128.

5. Isaacs, *Vintage NBA,* passim; "History of the NBA," *Professional Sports Team Histories: Basketball,* Michael L. La Blanc, ed. (Detroit: Gale Research, 1994), p. 10.

6. Glenn Dickey, *The History of Professional Basketball Since 1896* (New York: Stein and Day, 1982), pp. 48-49, 61-66; Robert W. Peterson, *Cages to Jump Shots: Pro Basketball's Early Years* (New York: Oxford University Press, 1990), pp. 180-181; "History of the NBA," pp. 9-10.

7. Arthur Ashe Jr., *A Hard Road to Glory: African-American Athletes Since 1946* (New York: Warner Books, 1988), pp. 61, 291; Pluto, *Tall Tales,* p. 172.

8. *Modern Encyclopedia of Basketball,* revised edition, Zander Hollander, ed. (New York: Four Winds Press, 1973), p. 334.

9. Baylor did not solve all the Lakers' problems. They played in three different arenas during the season, confusing both fans and players. During the 1959-1960 season, they even added a fourth venue: the Los Angeles Sports Arena. In the 1960-1961 season, owner Short moved the team there permanently.

10. Ashe, *Hard Road,* p. 291.

11. Pluto, *Tall Tales,* pp. 171, 172; Bill Russell with William McSweeny, *Go Up for Glory* (New York: Coward-McCann, 1966), p. 171; Bob Petit with Bob Wolff, *Bob Petit: The Drive Within Me* (Englewood Cliffs, NJ: Prentice-Hall, 1966), p. 131.

12. Pluto, *Tall Tales,* pp. 171, 176; Wilt Chamberlain and David Shaw, *Wilt: Just Like Any Other 7-Foot Black Millionaire Who Lives Next Door* (New York: Macmillan, 1973), p. 212; Chet Walker with Chris Messenger, *Long Time Coming: A Black Athlete's Coming of Age in America* (New York: Grove Press, 1995), p. 135.

13. Chamberlain, *Wilt,* p. 212; Walker, *Long Time Coming,* pp. 129, 135; Dave DeBusschere, *The Open Man: A Championship Diary,* Paul D. Zimmerman and Dick Schapp, eds. (New York: Random House, 1970), p. 231.

14. Quoted in Shouler, *Basketball's Best,* p. 86.

15. Pluto, *Tall Tales,* pp. 174-175.

16. Chamberlain, *Wilt,* pp. 210, 214.

17. Walker, *Long Time Coming,* p. 133. Dunking was discouraged as hot dogging and not an especially skillful move.

18. Fortunato, *Ultimate Assist,* Chapter 1.

19. Lenny Wilkens, *The Lenny Wilkens Story,* introduction by Father Thomas Mannion (New York: Paul Eriksson, 1974), pp. 4-6; Pluto, *Tall Tales,* p. 337; quoted in Ashe, *A Hard Road to Glory,* p. 69.

Chapter 12

Chocolate Thunder and Short Shorts: The NBA in the 1970s

David Friedman

INTRODUCTION: THE SPORT OF THE 1970S

The 1969-1970 NBA season did not mark the end of the 1960s in a merely chronological sense; the league was in a state of transition on a number of levels. Bill Russell, the cornerstone of the Boston Celtics' dynasty, retired in 1969 after claiming his eleventh championship in thirteen seasons. Six of the titles came at the expense of the Los Angeles Lakers, who featured the superstar duo of forward Elgin Baylor and guard Jerry West.

The 1969 loss was particularly galling for the Lakers. That season Baylor and West were joined by Wilt Chamberlain, who was already the league's all-time leading scorer and had been the driving force on the 1967 champion Philadelphia 76ers, who set the mark for best regular season record (68-13). A Lakers championship seemed to be a foregone conclusion. Prior to the game seven showdown in Los Angeles, Lakers' owner Jack Kent Cooke hired the USC marching band and had hundreds of balloons placed in the rafters of the Forum. The band would perform amid descending balloons after the Lakers won the game. Player-coach Russell and his veteran teammates drew great inspiration from the Lakers' blatant disrespect and won, 108-106.[1] West performed so valiantly in defeat that he became the only player from the losing team to win the Finals MVP.

Russell's retirement appeared to open the door for the Lakers to finally win the title in 1970, but they still had to deal with several worthy challengers. Young guns such as Milwaukee Bucks rookie Lew Alcindor (soon to be known as Kareem Abdul-Jabbar), the New York

Knicks' Willis Reed, and the Baltimore Bullets' Wes Unseld eagerly awaited the opportunity to prove themselves in championship play.

While the league's greatest players battled to claim the ultimate prize, the NBA found itself in bitter competition with the upstart American Basketball Association. The NBA and the ABA fought to sign players, to attract fans, and to win court cases that would change the shape of sports (not just basketball) forever. Lucrative television deals vaulted the National Football League (NFL) to prominence in the 1960s and pro basketball seemed ready to enjoy the same good fortune in the 1970s. Pro basketball was promoted as the "Sport of the Seventies."[2]

The NBA in the 1970s was not short on action (see Tables 12.1 and 12.2). Eight different franchises won championships. Showmen such as Earl "the Pearl" Monroe, Connie Hawkins, "Pistol" Pete Maravich, Julius "Dr. J" Erving, George "Iceman" Gervin and many others performed dazzling acts of wizardry. Darryl "Chocolate Thunder" Dawkins dismayed purists by entering the NBA straight from high school, gained notoriety by shattering two backboards, and amused fans by naming his sensational dunks. (He also frustrated his coaches by his frequent indifference to rebounding and defense.) By the end of the decade the groundbreaking court cases were resolved, the leagues had merged, and the NBA was about to enter into a golden age—although no one would have predicted that at the time, considering the league's declining television ratings and problematic public image. The NBA went through some rough patches during the 1970s but it was seldom dull—on court or in court. Our story begins with a

TABLE 12.1. The 1970s by the Numbers: Team Leaders

Wins		Division Titles		Championships	
Milwaukee Bucks	492	Balt./Wash. Bullets	6	Indiana Pacers	3
Los Angeles Lakers	485	Boston Celtics	5	Boston Celtics	2
Balt./Wash. Bullets	483	Denver Nuggets*	5	New York Knicks	2
Boston Celtics	477	Los Angeles Lakers	5	New York Nets	2
Denver Nuggets	469	Milwaukee Bucks	5		

Note: Chart includes ABA wins, division titles, and championships.
*Includes 1975-76, when the Denver Nuggets had the best record among the seven ABA teams that completed the season in a one-division league.

TABLE 12.2. The 1970s by the Numbers: Individual Leaders

Points	Points	PPG	Rebounds	Rebs.	RPG	Assists	Assists	APG
Kareem Abdul-Jabbar	22,141	28.6	Elvin Hayes	11,565	14.2	Norm Van Lier	5,217	7.0
Elvin Hayes	18,922	23.2	Kareem Abdul-Jabbar	11,460	14.8	John Havlicek	4,185	5.8
Rick Barry	18,389	24.4	Wes Unseld	10,511	13.9	Rick Barry	4,093	5.4
Dan Issel	17,714	23.9	Artis Gilmore	10,353	15.5	Walt Frazier	4,092	6.1
Julius Erving	16,763	26.2	Dave Cowens	9,636	14.6	Kevin Porter	4,077	8.2
John Havlicek	15,747	21.9	Paul Silas	8,737	10.8	Nate Archibald	4,077	7.6
Pete Maravich	15,359	25.0	Sam Lacey	8,120	11.2	Dave Bing	4,012	6.0
Spencer Haywood	15,053	23.0	Spencer Haywood	7,724	11.8	Louie Dampier	3,975	4.9
Artis Gilmore	14,708	22.1	Bob Lanier	7,690	11.9	Jo Jo White	3,819	5.1
Gail Goodrich	14,692	20.2	Dan Issel	7,690	10.4	Gail Goodrich	3,769	5.2

Notes: Chart includes ABA statistics for Barry, Issel, Erving, Haywood, Gilmore, and Dampier. Tied players listed in order of per game averages.

Hall of Fame player who played in both rival leagues but whose greatest challenge was a lengthy legal battle with the NBA.

THE HAWK SOARS INTO THE NBA;
WILLIS REED LIMPS INTO IMMORTALITY

Connie Hawkins, an immensely talented freshman at the University of Iowa, was falsely implicated in the 1961 college basketball point-shaving scandal. Although he was never charged with or convicted of any crimes, his college career ended in disgrace and the NBA blackballed him from the league. In 1961-1962, Hawkins won the MVP as a nineteen-year-old rookie in the new American Basketball League.[3] Unfortunately, the ABL folded early in its second season.[4] He then traveled the world for four years with the Harlem Globetrotters, but he did not enjoy all the clowning around that was part of the job description.[5] Connie Hawkins wanted to play serious basketball against the best players in the world.

When the American Basketball Association was founded in 1967-1968 as an American Football League-type rival for the NBA, it was eager to attract name talent. The ABA welcomed many players unfairly shunned by the NBA, including Hawkins, Roger Brown, and Doug Moe. By this time Hawkins was already pursuing legal action against the NBA. When he signed to play with the ABA's Pittsburgh Pipers his representatives inserted clauses in his contract that enabled him to become a free agent at the conclusion of his two-year deal or in the event that he was traded. This was very unusual, because up until that time pro basketball teams retained the option to re-sign or trade players as they saw fit. Hawkins needed these provisions because a key element in winning or successfully settling his lawsuit with the NBA would be his prompt availability to play in the league.[6] Hawkins finished first in the ABA in scoring (26.8 points per game), won the MVP, and led the Pipers to the championship.[7] A knee injury cut short his second season with the Pipers.

Meanwhile, Hawkins' case against the NBA picked up steam. Shockingly, it soon became apparent that the NBA had never thoroughly investigated his guilt or innocence before blackballing him; in essence, he was banned on the basis of his name being mentioned in a newspaper article about the scandal![8] The NBA did not want to publicly admit this but it also realized that taking the case to trial would be a losing proposition. In the summer of 1969 the NBA reached an out-of-court settlement with Hawkins worth over $1.2 million. This total included damages (for lost wages), a five-year, no-cut contract with the Phoenix Suns (who owned Hawkins' rights after losing the coin toss for Alcindor[9]), deferred compensation, and payment of legal fees.[10] Hawkins immediately transformed the Suns, a 16-66 expansion team the previous year, into a contending team. Despite still being slowed by his injured knee, he averaged 24.6 points per game, ranking sixth in the league in scoring. Hawkins earned a spot on the All-NBA First Team.

While Hawkins made the most of his opportunity to play in the NBA, several of the league's elite teams eagerly awaited the start of the Play-offs. For the first time since 1949-1950 the Celtics did not qualify for postseason play; the two-time defending champions fell to 34-48 without Russell. Chamberlain sustained a devastating knee injury early in the season, further raising the championship hopes of the other contenders. Chamberlain contradicted the pessimistic evaluations of his doctors and vowed to return before the end of the season. Meanwhile, the New York Knicks roared out of the gates, winning their first five games, losing one, and then setting a league record with an eighteen-game winning streak.[11] They finished the season with a league-best 60-22 record. Rookie Alcindor carried the second-year Milwaukee Bucks to a 56-26 record and a second-place finish behind the Knicks in the Eastern Division. In the West, a talented Atlanta Hawks team led by Lou Hudson finished first with a 48-34 record. Baylor and West guided the Lakers to second place with 46 wins; Chamberlain kept his word and returned to the lineup with three games left in the season.

The Lakers faced Hawkins and the Suns in the Western Division Semifinals. The Suns shocked the Lakers by taking a three-to-one lead in the series, but the Lakers regrouped behind Chamberlain's rebounding and West's scoring to win the series in seven. Hawkins averaged 25.4 points, 13.9 rebounds, and 5.9 assists per game.

Atlanta defeated Chicago four to one in the other Western Division Semifinals, while Milwaukee advanced to the Eastern Division Finals by knocking off Philadelphia four to one. The Knicks won a thrilling seven-game series against the Bullets, their archrivals. The Knicks took the first two games, including a double overtime affair in game one, but the Bullets evened the series after four games. After that the teams traded wins, with New York advancing after a 127-114 game seven win at home. Considering that the series went the distance, it is interesting that the game scores were not particularly close, including a 21-point Knicks' win in game five and a 14-point Bullets' win in game three. Both Conference Finals proved to be anticlimactic: the Lakers swept the Hawks, while the Knicks dispatched the Bucks four games to one.

The balanced and deep Knicks were favored to defeat the Lakers in the Finals. They did not disappoint in the first game, winning 124-112 behind Reed's 37 points, 16 rebounds, and 5 assists. Chamberlain tallied 17 points and 24 rebounds, while West scored 33 points and Baylor contributed 21 points and 20 rebounds.[12] The Lakers bounced back to win game two, with Reed scoring 29 points and Chamberlain 19. Game three featured one of the most famous shots in NBA history. The Lakers trailed 102-100 with three seconds left. Chamberlain inbounded to West, who took a few dribbles and nailed a shot from three-quarters court. The shot was amazing not just because of the situation and distance but the way that West released the ball, followed through, and casually walked to the sidelines as if nothing remarkable had happened. Meanwhile, stunned Knicks forward Dave DeBusschere fell to the ground under his own basket. Unfortunately for West and the Lakers, the NBA did not adopt the three-point shot for another decade and the Knicks recovered to win in overtime, 111-108. Baylor had a triple double (13 points, 12 rebounds, 11 assists), West scored 34 points, and Chamberlain added 21 points with 26 rebounds. Reed dominated with 38 points and 17 rebounds.[13] In game four the Lakers evened the series behind West's 37 points, 18 assists, and 5 rebounds.

The momentum seemed to turn in the Lakers' favor early in game five when Reed tore a muscle in his right thigh while driving around Chamberlain. The Lakers led 25-15 at that point. With Reed out, Chamberlain possessed a decisive advantage over anyone the Knicks used against him in the post, but the Lakers tried so hard to force the ball in to him that they got out of rhythm and turned the ball over repeatedly. The Knicks stormed back to win 107-100. The Lakers finished with 30 turnovers; West did not make a field goal in the second half and Chamberlain managed only 4 second-half points. Back home in L.A. for game six the Lakers made the appropriate adjustments and destroyed the Knicks 135-113. Reed was unable to play and Chamberlain rang up 45 points and 27 rebounds.[14]

Game seven has become an integral part of the lore not just of pro basketball but of all American sports. Reed took painkilling injections in his injured leg and limped out onto the court. He managed only 4 points and 3 rebounds but his inspired teammates rolled to a 113-99 victory. Walt Frazier was magnificent for the Knicks with 36 points, 19 assists, and 7 rebounds. Like Reed, West took painkilling injections before the game, as he had suffered injuries to both of his hands earlier in the series.[15] He still managed to score 28 points, while Baylor added 19 and Chamberlain had 24 rebounds to go along with his 21 points.[16] Reed, who already had won the regular season and All-Star MVPs in 1970, was selected as Finals MVP; he became the first player to win all three awards in the same season,[17] a feat later matched by Michael Jordan (1996 and 1998) and Shaquille O'Neal (2000).

Although Chamberlain posted good numbers in the decisive game, it is somewhat puzzling that the Lakers did not do a better job of exploiting the fact that Reed was basically playing on one leg. A possible answer may be found in Chamberlain's frequent lament: "Nobody roots for Goliath."[18] He felt that his achievements were dismissed because of his size and he took great pride in accomplishing things that did not depend on physical dominance, such as becoming the only center to lead the league in assists (702 in 1968). He did not want to be perceived as the bad guy and consequently he did not look at a limping Willis Reed like a shark would look at blood on the water.

Chamberlain certainly did not react the way that Michael Jordan did during a similar situation in a December 31, 2001, game versus the Nets:

> He [Jordan] had been astounded, earlier in the season, when the New Jersey Nets' Kenyon Martin, in the midst of trying to guard him, jocularly confessed that he was playing with a back injury that hampered his movement. Jordan went on to score 45. Why, why, why had Martin been so naïve to tell him that? he asked later. Didn't Martin know he was a predator who "went for the kill" against weakened quarry? It illustrated, he said, why you never let on about the severity of an injury.[19]

Jordan's heroics that night were not in game seven of the NBA Finals or against a Hall of Fame player such as Reed, but the point is that Jordan eagerly pounces on any weakness that he detects in his opponents; given the same set of circumstances that Chamberlain faced, it is easy to picture Jordan going right at the hobbling Reed (in a similar vein, Russell once commented that he would have taken it as an insult if someone had played against him on one good leg). Of course, a major difference between Jordan and Chamberlain is that Jordan can bring the ball up the court and free himself for the shot, while Chamberlain depended upon his teammates to feed him the ball in the post; perhaps in game seven the Lakers were not effective or persistent enough in isolating Chamberlain versus Reed.

It should be emphasized that this comparison between two of the greatest players ever is not meant to suggest in any way that Chamberlain was not a winner; after all, he was the dominant player on the 1967 76ers and the 1972 Lakers, each of whom won the championship and posted the best regular season records in league history at the time. Chamberlain could not have had the individual and team success that he did without possessing tremendous drive. The fact that he was even playing in the 1970 championship series only months after suffering a serious knee injury testifies to his desire and intensity.

As the years passed, a certain mythology arose that the 1970 Finals matched a team of stars (the Lakers) versus a well-balanced team that emphasized passing and defense (the Knicks). DeBusschere commented: "The feeling that we were a team heightened most at the finals because they set Chamberlain, Baylor and West—best center, best forward, best guard—against a team of just guys. We weren't supposed to have a chance."[20] Calling the Knicks a "team of just guys" is a bit disingenuous considering that the Knicks had a Hall of Fame coach (Red Holzman) and four Hall of Fame players on their roster: Reed, DeBusschere, Frazier, and forward Bill Bradley. What's more, none of the Knicks' stars were older than thirty, while Baylor (thirty-five), Chamberlain (thirty-three), and West (thirty-one) were all past their thirtieth birthdays. It is true that by the conclusion of the 1970 play-offs West (3,708 points, 30.9 points per game) Baylor (3,623 points, 27.0 points per game), and Chamberlain (2,990 points, 25.8 points per game) were the three leading scorers in NBA play-off history. That is impressive and unprecedented, but it also reflects the fact that all three players were past their primes. Baylor's chronically bad knees would soon force him to retire and, as noted above, Chamberlain had not completely recovered from his early season knee injury. West still had plenty of great games left, but his body was also battered and bruised from so many years of battling deep into the play-offs. The Knicks were hardly an underdog team without a chance; there is a reason that they had homecourt advantage for game seven. None of these facts diminish Reed's courage, Frazier's clutch game-seven performance, and the overall greatness of the 1970 New York Knicks. Quite the opposite: the 1970 Knicks should be remembered as a great team, not as an underdog.

SPENCER HAYWOOD JUMPS LEAGUES; THE BUCKS BLANK THE BULLETS

The economics of pro basketball exploded in the 1970s. The average player salary rose from $35,000 in 1970 to $180,000 a decade later, and franchise values went up more than 600 percent in the same period.[21] The major cause of the skyrocketing salaries was the competition between the NBA and the ABA for star players. The ABA opened a new front in this war with the signing of Spencer Haywood, the nineteen-year-old star of the 1968 U.S. Olympic gold medalists. Haywood had played only one year of junior college ball and one year at the University of Detroit before he joined the ABA's Denver Rockets for the 1969-1970 season. At this time, NBA teams abided by the "four-year rule," which stipulated that a player could not be drafted or signed to an NBA contract until his college class graduated; that is why Chamberlain played a year with the Harlem Globetrotters after he left Kansas before his senior year. The ABA subsequently signed numerous underclassmen, most notably Ralph Simpson (1970), Julius Erving (1971), and George McGinnis (1971), each of whom became All-Stars.[22]

Haywood enjoyed a spectacular rookie season, leading the ABA in scoring (30.0 points per game) and rebounding (19.5 rebounds per game). He won the Rookie of the Year, the regular season MVP, and the All-Star MVP and averaged 36.7 points per game and 19.8 rebounds per game in the play-offs.[23]

Not surprisingly, Haywood's success caused him to take a second look at his contract. Little did he know that his case would eventually reach the U.S. Supreme Court and forever change American sports. When Haywood signed with the Rockets his contract was announced as a six-year, $1.9 million deal.[24] In fact, the vast majority of the value of his contract ($1.5 million) would be paid to Haywood at the rate of $75,000 a year for twenty years after Haywood turned forty.[25] The ABA devised this type of deferred compensation arrangement (known as the Dolgoff Plan) in order to be able to offer huge contracts to players. It involved paying a portion of a player's salary into a mutual fund or other growth fund for a ten-year period. Payments to the player commenced after waiting for an additional ten years and typically lasted for twenty years.[26] It was not clear whether Haywood would receive the $1.5 million if, for any reason, he did not play the full six years for the Rockets or if the ABA folded at some point in the future. Haywood was unable to reach an agreement with the Rockets to restructure his contract, so he jumped leagues and signed a six-year, $1.5 million deal with the Seattle Supersonics.[27] This contract paid Haywood $100,000 a year for fifteen years—all cash, no deferred compensation and no Dolgoff Plan[28] Agent Ron Grinker later observed, "The ABA paid in paper money, but the NBA responded to that by paying in real dollars, and it nearly bankrupted both leagues."[29]

Haywood's case involved a tangled web of legal issues: the Denver Rockets accused attorney Al Ross of convincing Haywood to breach his contract with them, while Haywood and Ross responded that the Rockets had signed Haywood when he was still a minor and did not have proper legal representation; the NBA objected to Seattle signing Haywood before his college class had graduated; the ABA wanted Haywood to be forbidden from playing for Seattle and compelled to fulfill the terms of his Rockets' contract; the NBA Buffalo Braves felt that they should have the rights to draft Haywood and attempt to sign him before any other NBA club dealt with him.[30]

The NBA's four-year rule was declared illegal by the courts and Haywood was permitted to play with the Supersonics until the remaining legal issues were resolved.[31] The legal wrangling wiped out most of Haywood's 1970-1971 season and he played in only thirty-three games for the Supersonics, posting very respectable averages of 20.6 points and 12.0 rebounds. Haywood's case was eventually settled out of court, with the end result that he was allowed to remain with the Supersonics permanently.

The overturning of the four-year rule had a lasting impact on collegiate and professional sports.[32] In 1971 the NBA instituted a "hardship" rule that allowed underclassmen to be drafted as long as they proved that they suffered from financial hardship. Needless to say, such declarations were a mere formality, as noted by *Sport* writer Jackie Lapin: "almost anyone who has been any good at the game in the past decade would qualify—with the probable exception of Bill Bradley, the banker's son."[33]

The competition between the leagues for players also extended into a battle for markets. In 1970-1971 the NBA expanded into Buffalo, Cleveland, and Portland, in no small part to keep the ABA out of those cities.[34] After the addition of those teams the NBA reorganized the Eastern and Western Divisions into conferences with two divisions each; also, Atlanta switched to the Eastern Conference and Milwaukee moved to the Western Conference. The defending champion Knicks won the Atlantic Division of the Eastern Conference with a 52-30 record, while the 42-40 Bullets took the Eastern Conference's Central Division. The Lakers acquired high-scoring guard Gail Goodrich in the off-season but lost Elgin Baylor to a season-ending knee injury after only two games. They still finished first in the Western Conference's Pacific Division with a 48-34 record.

The Bucks pulled off the biggest off-season trade in the league, shoring up their backcourt with Oscar Robertson, nine-time member of the All-NBA First Team. Robertson teamed with second-year players Alcindor and Bob Dandridge to turn the Bucks into a dominant team. Milwaukee went a league-best 66-16, broke the Knicks' one-year-old record by winning twenty straight games, and easily captured the Midwest Division by fifteen games over Chicago. Alcindor won the scoring title (31.7 points per game), ranked fourth in rebounding (16.0 rebounds per game) and was selected regular season MVP.

The only blemish on the Bucks' season was a 1-4 record versus the defending champion Knicks.[35] A championship showdown between the teams seemed to be inevitable but Reed was hampered by a knee injury and the Bullets defeated the Knicks 93-91 in game seven of the Eastern Conference Finals. Milwaukee overwhelmed the Lakers four to one in the Western Conference Finals, winning game five 116-98; Baylor and West both missed the 1970-1971 play-offs due to injuries.[36] In the Finals, Unseld, the Bullets' valiant but undersized (6'7") center, proved to be no match for Alcindor and the Bucks notched the first Finals sweep since 1959.

MR. CLUTCH FINALLY GETS A CHAMPIONSHIP RING

The 1971-1972 NBA season saw numerous changes. The San Diego Rockets moved to Houston and the San Francisco Warriors became known as the Golden State Warriors. Lew Alcindor publicly adopted his Muslim name, Kareem Abdul-Jabbar.[37] In March, Charlie Scott clinched the ABA scoring title, claimed a breach of contract by the Virginia Squires, and subsequently jumped to the NBA. The Celtics owned his NBA draft rights, but allowed the Phoenix Suns to sign him in exchange for future considerations. The next season, those considerations came in the form of rebounder deluxe Paul Silas,[38] who would make significant contributions to Celtics' championship teams in 1974 and 1976. The Lakers changed coaches for the fourth time in six seasons, replacing Joe Mullaney with former Celtics' All-Star Bill Sharman.

Many observers scoffed at the idea that any coach could get the aging Lakers over the hump after so many years of near misses. Sharman embraced the challenge and pioneered many innovations that are widely used today, including game-day shootarounds and the use of game film to discern opponents' tendencies.[39] Sharman faced a delicate situation early in the season when Baylor struggled to regain his form after missing all but two games the previous season due to a knee injury. The Lakers started the season with six wins in the first nine games but it was clear that they played better with rookie Jim McMillian on the court than with Baylor, who could not keep up with the fast-breaking style that Sharman was teaching the team. Sharman told Baylor that he valued his contributions to the team, but that it was in the best interests of the squad that he come off the bench. It was an awkward message to deliver to one of the game's all-time greats. Baylor chose to retire rather than continue playing so far below his accustomed level.[40]

After Baylor retired, Sharman named Chamberlain team captain. On October 31, 1971, the Lakers held a ceremony to honor Baylor; that night the Lakers also began a thirty-three-game winning streak, shattering the record of 20 set just the year before by the Bucks.[41]

Ironically, the defending champion Bucks ended the streak with a 120-104 decision in early January.[42]

The Lakers finished the season with a best-ever 69-13 record (since broken by the 1995-1996 Bulls and tied by the 1996-1997 Bulls), winning the Pacific Division by eighteen games. Goodrich led the team in scoring (25.9 points per game), with West just behind him (25.8 points per game). McMillian chipped in with 18.8 points per game and 6.5 rebounds per game. Chamberlain averaged 14.8 points per game while leading the league in field goal percentage (64.9 percent) and rebounding (19.2 rebounds per game). Abdul-Jabbar repeated as scoring champion (34.8 points per game) and MVP, again leading Milwaukee (63-19) to the Midwest Division title. In the Eastern Conference, veteran John Havlicek teamed with youngsters Dave Cowens and Jo Jo White to guide the Celtics to the Atlantic Division title with fifty-six wins. The Knicks fell to second place (48-34), mainly because Reed played in only eleven games due to injuries. Early in the season the Knicks traded Mike Riordan and Dave Stallworth to the Bullets for Earl Monroe, but he was plagued by nagging injuries and struggled to adjust to his new surroundings, averaging only 11.9 points per game after scoring over 20 points per game in each of his first four seasons.[43] The Bullets did not seem to benefit immediately from the deal either, falling to 38-44, although they did repeat as Central Division champions.

In his first full NBA season Haywood ranked fourth in scoring (26.2 points per game) and was selected to the All-NBA First Team. Seattle's 47-35 record was the best in the franchise's brief history but not good enough to make the play-offs in the tough Western Conference. Similarly, Hawkins (21.0 points per game) and the Suns missed the play-offs despite a 49-33 record that would have been second only to the Celtics in the Eastern Conference. The first round of the play-offs went according to form, with each of the division champions advancing. In the Western Conference Finals the Bucks seized the home court advantage with a stunning 93-72 win in Los Angeles, but the Lakers rallied to win in six games. The experienced Knicks triumphed over the up-and-coming Celtics four to one in the Eastern Conference Finals.

The Knicks trounced the Lakers 114-92 in Los Angeles in game one of the Finals, but the Lakers won the next four games to claim the title. Jerry West, known as "Mr. Clutch" for his many game-winning shots over the years, finally had his first championship ring. Ironically, he was hampered by injuries throughout the 1972 play-offs and he shot only 37.6 percent from the field, by far his worst postseason performance ever. West recalled the 1972 play-offs with mixed feelings: "I played terrible basketball in the Finals and we won. And that didn't seem to be justice for me personally, because I had contributed so much in other years when we lost. And now, when we won, I was just another piece of the machinery. It was particularly frustrating because I was playing so poorly that the team overcame me. Maybe that's what the team is all about."[44]

Chamberlain was without question the hero of the Lakers' play-off run. He played the fifth game of the Finals with a hairline fracture in his right hand and a sprained left hand.[45] He came up with a huge performance in that game with 24 points and 29 rebounds, winning the Finals MVP. Interestingly, he did not receive the lasting acclaim for playing injured that Reed did after his performance two years earlier, even though Chamberlain posted much better numbers than Reed had.

Chamberlain bristled at the suggestion that the Lakers won the title because he had somehow changed his game. "I have been shooting less for years now. I led the league in assists years ago. Where have you been?" He elaborated, "When I did not have shooters on my side and it was my job to shoot, I shot. Now we have shooters, so I don't have to shoot. The things I have been doing, I have been doing a long time—playing defense, blocking shots, rebounding, passing off . . ."[46] Sharman had nothing but praise for his center: "He's always had a bad rap. Whatever they ask of him, he's done. He's just doing more things better now that he is not mainly a scorer. He must block a zillion shots a game. And he scares guys out of other shots or makes them take bad shots. And when he gets the rebound, he gets rid of it fast to get our fast break going."[47] Looking back on the 1972 season, one writer commented, "Wilt was the biggest thing in basketball last season, and not just because of his physical size. Though he gives away a few inches to Jabbar, he remains the most awesome specimen in the sport."[48]

THE ROLLS ROYCE BACKCOURT
DRIVES OFF WITH THE TITLE

The Celtics were the class of the league in the 1972-1973 season, racing to a 68-14 record, only one game off the Lakers' mark set the year before. Cowens was selected MVP, Silas added rebounding and toughness, and Havlicek had yet another outstanding season. The Bullets (52-30) won their third-straight Central Division title behind the 21.2 points per game and 14.5 rebounds per game of Elvin Hayes, acquired in the off-season from the Rockets. The Philadelphia 76ers represented the opposite end of the spectrum. They hit rock bottom in 1972-1973 after a steady free fall since Chamberlain led the team to the 1967 championship. Sixers star Billy Cunningham signed a deal to play with the ABA Carolina Cougars, and although he later decided that he wanted to remain with the Sixers, a court ruling forced him to honor the contract with the Cougars.[49] Without the "Kangaroo Kid" the 76ers collapsed to a 9-73 record, worst in NBA history; Cunningham won the ABA MVP that season. Although the Sixers got the short end of the stick, the NBA did get a superstar forward to replace Cunningham: Rick Barry was compelled by court order to return to the Warriors after playing out his contract with the ABA's New York Nets.[50]

Rick Barry's arrival in Golden State brought his career full circle. In 1965-1966 he was the Rookie of the Year for the then San Francisco Warriors and the next year he won the scoring title (2,775 points, 35.6 points per game) while leading the Warriors to the NBA Finals. After that season he became the first big NBA star to jump to the ABA, signing with the Oakland Oaks, but a court ruling stated that he either had to play out his option year with the Warriors or sit out a season before joining the Oaks. Barry chose to sit out. The next year Barry won the ABA scoring title (34.0 points per game), becoming the first and only player to capture scoring crowns in both leagues. The Oaks won the championship, but Barry missed a sizeable portion of the regular season and all of the play-offs due to injury. The Oaks moved to Washington, DC, for the 1969-1970 season and Barry signed with the NBA Warriors, contending that his deal with the Oaks included an escape clause if the team left the Bay area. Again the courts ruled against Barry and he averaged 27.7 points per game for the Washington Capitols. In the off-season the Capitols became the Virginia Squires, but Barry complained so vociferously about this move that the team dealt him to the Nets. Barry enjoyed two successful seasons with the Nets and decided that he wanted to remain with the team, but there was the issue of the contract that he had signed with the Warriors in the wake of the Oaks' move to Washington. The courts ruled that he could not remain with the Nets after his contract with the club expired in 1972, so after five eventful years Barry ended up right back where his career began. He held the dubious distinction of being the one player in this time period who repeatedly lost his court cases, in contrast to Hawkins, Haywood, and others who eventually ended up with the teams for which they wanted to play.[51] Nevertheless, Barry's legal travails opened the way for numerous other players to jump leagues, including Zelmo Beaty, Joe Caldwell, and Cunningham.[52]

In his return to the Bay Area, Barry averaged 22.3 points per game, made the All-NBA Second Team, and led the Warriors to a 47-35 record, good enough for second place in the Pacific Division. The Lakers and Bucks again stood at the top of the Western Conference, winning the Pacific and Midwest Divisions respectively with identical 60-22 records. The Chicago Bulls, a tough, defensive-minded team paced by high-scoring forwards Bob Love (23.1 points per game) and Chet Walker (19.9 points per game) grabbed the other play-off spot, winning fifty-one games and finishing second in the Midwest Division.

One of the biggest stories of the season turned out to be one of the smallest players in the league. Coach Bob Cousy of the Kansas City-Omaha Kings (formerly the Cincinnati Royals) knew that his squad did not have the horses to make the play-offs, so he granted tremendous freedom to third-year guard Nate "Tiny" Archibald, who measured 6'1", 160 pounds. Archibald became the only player to ever lead the league in scoring (34.0 points per game) and assists (11.4 assists per game) in the same season. He joined West on the All-NBA First Team. The Kings finished last in the Midwest Division with a 36-46 record but attracted many fans to watch Archibald perform.

"Pistol" Pete Maravich of the Atlanta Hawks was another flashy guard who fans flocked to see. He joined the Hawks in 1970-1971 after setting the all-time NCAA Division I career scoring record by averaging an astounding 44.2 points per game. He averaged 23.2 points per game in his rookie year and 19.3 points per game in an injury-marred second season, but the Hawks, which had seemed to be a team on the rise, slumped in the standings. Maravich's fancy ballhandling and passing skills caused many critics to label him a "showboat" and "hot dog."[53]

Some of the criticisms of Maravich were muted, at least temporarily, by his performance in the 1972-1973 season, when he ranked fifth in scoring (26.1 points per game) and sixth in assists (6.9 assists per game) and made the All-NBA Second Team.[54] Maravich knew that he was ahead of his time: "You're going to see forwards and centers throwing the ball behind their backs, just like I do. The time will come before we know it."[55] In fact, he was literally a decade ahead of his time, because Magic Johnson later became a beloved superstar doing similar things. Johnson came along at the right time and had teammates who caught his passes instead of fumbling them out of bounds.

Maravich's competitive fires burned as fiercely as those of the other greats of the game and he was not satisfied with individual statistics or achievements: "I'm not pleased with anything I've done so far. . . . All I want to do is win the title and I'll quit. A title would be the highest level you can attain. They'll say 'He was a hot dog—but he was a champion.'"[56] He also understood that fans paid good money to watch professional athletes and deserved to be entertained: "[Fans] . . . should get total satisfaction from watching a game."[57] Although some of Maravich's success in 1972-1973 came from increasing maturity, George Vecsey noted, "There is more evidence that he was finally playing with teammates who could cope with his ability."[58] Johnson later assessed Maravich's impact on basketball history: "Maravich was unbelievable. He was ahead of his time with the things he did."[59] Isiah Thomas concurs: "The best showman of all time? I'd have to say Pistol Pete."[60]

Maravich's Hawks played the powerful Celtics to a standstill after four games in the Eastern Conference Semifinals, but the Celtics won the next two to close out the series. Maravich averaged 26.2 points per game and 6.7 assists per game in the play-offs. The Knicks obliterated the Bullets in the other Eastern Conference series, taking the first three games en route to a four to one decision. In the Western Conference, Barry and the Warriors pulled off one of the biggest upsets in NBA play-off history, defeating the Bucks in six games. The Bulls extended the defending-champion Lakers to the limit, losing

95-92 in game seven. The Lakers overpowered the Warriors four to one in the Western Conference Finals, while the Knicks savored a gritty seven-game triumph over the Celtics in the Eastern Conference Finals; Havlicek was severely hampered in the latter part of the series with a painful shoulder injury.

By this time the Knicks were peaking and their "Rolls Royce" backcourt of Frazier and Monroe was in full flower. "There's never been two players together that were so good in the same backcourt. They were the best ever," raved teammate DeBusschere.[61] The Lakers narrowly took game one of the NBA Finals, but the Knicks reeled off four consecutive wins to claim their second title in four years. Reed's numbers were up and down throughout the season and the play-offs due to his injuries, but he was again selected as the Finals MVP. A dissenting vote on the Finals MVP later came from Frazier: "They (the media) always jerked me around. When I didn't get the MVP that year (1970) they told me it was because they judged by the season; and when I didn't get it in 1973 they said it was because they judged by the series . . ."[62]

CELTIC PRIDE REBORN

Wilt Chamberlain jumped to the ABA to be a player coach for the San Diego Conquistadors in the 1973-1974 season, but the Lakers successfully sought an injunction that kept him from playing for San Diego for one year. This was the same option clause that forced Barry to sit out a year before joining the Oaks and that Hawkins' representatives removed from his Pipers contract so that he could join the NBA as soon as his case was resolved. The option existed only from the point of view of the team, which could choose to sign a player to a new contract when the original one expired or else restrain the player from signing with another team for a year; the player's "option" consisted of re-signing with the same team on their terms or losing a year's worth of earnings. This was a convenient way for the owners to restrict player movement and contain salaries, but the cases of Barry, Haywood, and others were the first steps in eliminating this clause from standard player contracts.

The Lakers' championship hopes were dealt a second blow by injuries that limited West to thirty-one regular season games and a fourteen-minute cameo appearance in one play-off game before he retired. The Lakers acquired Hawkins from the Suns but he was no longer a star player. They also dealt McMillian to the Buffalo Braves for journeyman center Elmore Smith, who led the league in blocked shots with a 4.85 per game average in the first year that the NBA recorded this statistic; Portland's aptly named Larry Steele averaged 2.68 steals per game as the NBA's first official leader in that category. The 47-35 Lakers won their fourth consecutive Pacific Division title but were no longer a legitimate title contender.

Robertson struggled with age and injuries in his last season but he, Jabbar, and Dandridge combined to lead the Bucks to their fourth straight Midwest Division crown with a league-best 59-23 record. The Bulls and a fine Detroit Pistons team led by center Bob Lanier (22.5 points per game, 13.3 rebounds per game, and 3.05 blocked shots per game) rounded out the play-off field in the Western Conference.

Similarly, the Eastern Conference play-offs featured three established play-off teams and one newcomer. The Celtics won the Atlantic Division for the third straight year, this time with a conference-best 56 victories, while the 47-35 Capital (formerly Baltimore) Bullets took their fourth Central Division title in a row. The veteran Knicks (49-33) and young Buffalo Braves (42-40) were the other participants in the Eastern Conference play-offs. Buffalo featured Bob McAdoo, a center who won the first of three straight scoring titles (30.6 points per game) while leading the league in field goal percentage (54.7), ranking third in rebounding (15.1 rebounds per game), and third in blocked shots (3.32 blocks per game). His shooting prowess was remarkable considering that many of his attempts were long jump shots, while his rebounding and shot blocking were impressive because he was undersized (6'9", 215 pounds) for a center. No less an authority than Bill Russell offered this high praise: "He's the greatest shooter of all time, period. Forget that bit about 'greatest shooting big man.'"[63]

McAdoo scored 31.7 points per game versus Boston in the play-offs, but the Celtics won the series four games to two. The Knicks and Bullets squared off for the sixth year in a row and the Knicks won for the fifth time, taking game seven 91-81 in New York. The Bucks annihilated the Lakers in five games, while Chicago and Detroit slugged it out for seven games before the Bulls advanced after a 96-94 triumph at home. The Celtics avenged the previous year's loss to the

Knicks with a five-game victory in the Eastern Conference Finals, while the Bucks swept the Bulls in the Western Conference Finals.

The Finals proved to be a seesaw affair. Milwaukee won a dramatic 102-101 double-overtime game six in Boston and seemed to have matters in control heading home for game seven. Instead the Celtics blew the Bucks out, 102-87. Cowens scored 28 points and grabbed 14 rebounds. During an eighteen-minute stretch Jabbar went 0-3 from the field, due mainly to Cowens' physical, aggressive defense, the Celtics' double teaming in the post, and tremendous defensive pressure on the Bucks' ballhandlers. "Their team concept of pressure was more than we could handle. With all the adjustments we tried, we just couldn't cope with it. Boston is a great team with no weaknesses. At least I haven't been able to find any," commented Bucks' Coach Larry Costello.[64] Havlicek averaged 27.1 points per game during the postseason and won the Finals MVP.

ENTER THE HIGH SCHOOLERS:
MOSES FROM VIRGINIA
AND CHOCOLATE THUNDER FROM LOVETRON

Once the Haywood case made the four-year rule passé, it was only a matter of time until players would be signed straight out of high school. In 1974, the ABA Utah Stars selected Moses Malone of Petersburg, Virginia, in the third round of the draft. His high school team had won fifty straight games and two consecutive state championships, attracting the attention of more than 200 colleges—despite the fact that Malone's grade point average was not high enough to be eligible for an NCAA scholarship, until he suddenly became an "A" student during his last semester. The miraculous grade increases and the tons of money being offered under the table led ACC Commissioner Bob James to call Malone's situation "the worst recruiting mess I've ever seen."[65] Even though Malone's body had not yet filled out and matured, he averaged 17.7 points per game and 12.9 rebounds per game in two ABA seasons, making the All-Star team as a rookie. After the NBA-ABA merger, Portland selected him in the ABA dispersal draft but traded him to the Braves for a first-round pick. He played briefly for the Braves before Houston acquired him for two first-round picks. Two years later he won the first of his three regular season MVPs and the first of his six rebounding crowns en route to a Hall of Fame career.

Malone's success did not go unnoticed. The 76ers looked far and wide for a dominant big man as part of their rebuilding process after the disastrous 1972-1973 season. Darryl Dawkins, a 6'10" senior center at Maynard Evans High School in Orlando, Florida, impressed Sixers' Coach Gene Shue with his play in the 1975 state finals. Once the Sixers' brass decided to select Dawkins it became imperative to keep word of their young prospect from other teams. They convinced Dawkins to not play in postseason tournaments so scouts from other NBA organizations would not find out about him. The Sixers accomplished this by hiring Dawkins' high school coach to be Philadelphia's Florida scout, his first job being to "baby-sit" Dawkins and keep him hidden until the NBA draft. The plan worked, and the 76ers made Dawkins the first high school player ever chosen in the first round of the NBA draft. He signed a $1.5 million, seven-year deal with the Sixers.[66]

Dawkins enjoyed a long NBA career and played in the NBA Finals three times as a Sixer but he never made the All-Star team and, unlike Malone, did not become a dominant NBA center. He is best known for shattering two backboards and the creative nicknames he invented to describe himself (Chocolate Thunder, Master of Disaster, Sir Slam) and his spectacular dunks (Gorilla, Yo Mama, In Your Face Disgrace, Left-Handed Spine Chiller Supreme, Hammer of Thor, etc.).[67] Borrowing lingo from Parliament-Funkadelic, he spoke of his "interplanetary funkmanship" and claimed to be from the planet "Lovetron." His backboard-shattering dunk over the Kings' Bill Robinzine inspired this momentous sobriquet from Dawkins: "Chocolate Thunder Flying, Robinzine Crying, Teeth Shaking, Glass Breaking, Rump Roasting, Bun Toasting, Wham, Bam, Glass Breaker I Am Jam."[68] Ironically, the careers of the two trendsetting big men intersected when Malone replaced Dawkins as the Sixers' starting center in 1982-1983 and led the team to the championship, winning the regular season and Finals MVPs in the process.

Another player made the jump straight from high school to the NBA in 1975. Bill Willoughby, a second-round pick of the Hawks that year, played eight NBA seasons but never averaged even 10 points per game.[69] It took twenty years until Kevin Garnett became the next player to make the leap directly to the NBA from high school, but the signings of Malone, Dawkins, and Willoughby paved the way for this to happen and also made it seem less shocking when increasing numbers of players invoked the hardship rule to leave college for the pros after only one or two seasons.

RICK BARRY IS SUPERMAN

Although the drafting of Malone attracted headlines, the story of the 1974-1975 season was unquestionably the stunning individual brilliance of Rick Barry. The cover of the April issue of *Sport* declared, "Rick Barry is Superman." His coach Al Attles said, "Right now I'm telling you he could be the best who ever played. He brings something new each night."[70] Opposing coaches were no less effusive. "Right now he is playing as well as anyone who has ever played this game," Pistons Coach Ray Scott raved.[71] After Barry went over, around, and through Knicks' forward Hawthorne Wingo to the tune of 44 points and 4 assists in an early season Warriors' victory, Wingo stated simply, "On every play, no matter who scores, he handles the ball at least one time. He makes them happen."[72] Barry led the league in free throw percentage (90.4 percent) and steals (2.85 steals per game), ranked second in scoring (30.6 points per game), and finished sixth in assists (6.2 assists per game), a remarkable statistic for a high-scoring forward. Golden State won the Pacific Division with a 48-34 record, best in the Western Conference.

Interestingly, Barry did not win the MVP. The award instead went to McAdoo, who also had an outstanding season, leading the league in scoring (34.5 points per game), while ranking fourth in rebounding (14.1 rebounds per game), fifth in field goal percentage (51.2 percent), and sixth in blocked shots (2.12 blocked shots per game). Although McAdoo was clearly a worthy recipient of the honor, Barry did not finish a close second but rather a distant fourth in the balloting. This can be explained in large part because the MVP voting was done by the league's players at this time and it is no secret that Barry, who did not hesitate to criticize teammates, opponents, referees, or anyone else, was not particularly popular. Since 1980-1981, the official NBA MVP voting has been conducted among media members instead of the players.

The Boston Celtics and Washington (previously Capital) Bullets paced the Eastern Conference with sixty wins each. Both teams padded their victory totals at the expense of the expansion New Orleans Jazz, the newest member of the Eastern Conference's Central Division. The Jazz attempted to fill the stands by acquiring Maravich—who played collegiately at Louisiana State—from the Hawks. Maravich averaged 21.5 points per game and 6.2 assists per game (fifth in the league) but the Jazz finished with the worst record in the league (23-59).

The NBA expanded the play-offs by one round, adding one more team from each conference to postseason play. New York and Detroit, owners of identical 40-42 records, were the first beneficiaries of the change. The Rockets eliminated the Knicks in three games, while the Sonics made the most of the franchise's first postseason appearance, beating the Pistons by the same score.

Boston easily shot down the Rockets four to one in one Eastern Conference Semifinal, but McAdoo and the Braves took the Bullets to the limit before Washington won a game seven rout at home, 115-96. In the West, the Bulls defeated Archibald and the improving Kings four games to two, while the Warriors knocked off the Sonics by the same margin. The Bullets beat the Celtics in the first two games of the Eastern Conference Finals and eventually closed out the series in six games, while Barry and the Warriors narrowly escaped the clutches of a determined Bulls team with an 83-79 game-seven win.

The Bullets were heavy favorites over Golden State in the Finals but the Warriors produced one of the most stunning upsets in play-off history, sweeping Washington. Due to scheduling conflicts, the Bullets played game one at home and then the next two on the road, instead of starting the series with two games in Washington; after Golden State won the first game the Bullets were already behind the eight ball, heading west for two games.[73] The Bullets were also without the services of ABA free-agent guard Jimmy Jones, a key contributor who injured his knee in the Boston series and was unable to play in the Finals. Several other factors contributed to the unlikely Golden State triumph: undersized rookie Jackson Keith (later known as Jamaal) Wilkes did a remarkable defensive job against perennial All-Star Hayes, holding him to 29 points in the first three games,[74] the unheralded Clifford Ray provided steady play at center and an attitude of togetherness permeated the entire roster; whenever the Warriors' starters faltered, the reserves came in and outperformed their opposing counterparts. However, none of this would have been enough without the heroics of Rick Barry, who averaged 28.2 points per game and 6.1 assists per game in the play-offs and was awarded the Finals MVP.

Such a perfect ending would be hard to top and the thirty-one-year-old Barry actually considered retirement: "It had been the perfect season, perfect in its drama, perfect in its outcome, and one of the first thoughts that went through my head was *I want to quit, I want this to be my last memory of my last game, I don't ever want to play another basketball game because it would have to be anti-climactic*."[75] Barry eventually decided to continue his career, playing for several more years, but never duplicating the individual or team success of that magical 1974-1975 season.

THE GREATEST GAME EVER PLAYED

The NBA-ABA rivalry heated up during the 1975 off-season. The Kentucky Colonels, a powerful squad coached by Hubie Brown and built around the talents of Artis Gilmore, Dan Issel, and Louie Dampier, won the 1975 ABA championship. Knicks' legend DeBusschere, newly selected as the ABA commissioner, promptly challenged the NBA to permit the Warriors to play the Colonels in a best-of-three series, but the established league refused.[76] Meanwhile, the Knicks signed ABA co-MVP McGinnis to a contract, blatantly disregarding the fact that the Sixers' owned his NBA draft rights. NBA Commissioner Larry O'Brien voided the Knicks' deal with the superstar forward, fined the team, and took away a draft choice.[77] McGinnis signed with the Sixers shortly thereafter.

The ABA scored a major victory when the Denver Nuggets agreed to terms with David Thompson and Marvin Webster, the first and third picks in the 1975 NBA draft.[78] Thompson went on to capture ABA Rookie of the Year honors; Alvan Adams, the NBA Rookie of the Year, began his acceptance speech humorously by thanking Thompson for not signing with an NBA team. Of course, this was no laughing matter for NBA owners; top-level talent was signing with the ABA regularly and the competition between the leagues for these players continued to push salaries higher.

The Lakers pulled off the blockbuster deal of the summer, acquiring Jabbar from the Bucks in exchange for Junior Bridgeman, Dave

Meyers, Elmore Smith, and Brian Winters. In his first year with the Lakers, Jabbar won his only rebounding crown (16.9 rebounds per game) and the fourth of his record six regular season MVPs. The Lakers improved by ten wins, but their 40-42 record did not qualify them for postseason play. Meanwhile, the Bucks matched their 1974-1975 win total (38) but incredibly moved from last place to first as the other three teams in the Midwest Division plummeted in the standings. Barry's Warriors, no longer upstarts, won the Pacific Division with the best record in the league, 59-23. Seattle, Phoenix, and Detroit claimed the other Western Conference play-off spots.

Boston finished with the best record in the East for the fifth straight season, 54-28. The surprising 49-33 Cleveland Cavaliers earned the franchise's first play-off appearance, winning the Central Division by one game over the Bullets. Seven Cavs averaged at least 10 points per game, led by center Jim Chones (15.8 points per game) and small forward Campy Russell (15.0 points per game). McAdoo won his third straight scoring title (31.1 points per game) for the 46-36 Braves, while McGinnis (23.0 points per game) and guard Doug Collins (20.8 points per game) led the Sixers to an identical record. The two evenly matched Atlantic Division rivals faced off in the first round, with the Braves winning game three 124-123 in overtime at Philadelphia. In the Eastern Conference Semifinals, Boston knocked off Buffalo in six games, while the Cavaliers won an action-packed seven-game series versus the Bullets. Unfortunately for the Cavs, Chones broke his foot and was not available for the Eastern Finals versus the Celtics, who defeated the Cavs in six games to earn their second NBA Finals berth in three years.

The Bucks had the worst record of the five Western play-off teams and did not receive a bye even though they won the Midwest Division. The Pistons beat them in three games, taking the final contest 107-104 in Milwaukee. Detroit took home court advantage from the Warriors with a 123-111 game-two win but Golden State closed out the series in six games, winning the last one 118-116 in overtime. Phoenix beat Seattle in six games but entered the Western Finals as decided underdogs. Their prospects looked even grimmer after the Warriors blew them out 128-103 in game one, but the resilient Suns seized home court advantage with a 108-101 win in game two. The teams traded wins after that, culminating in a 94-86 Suns victory in game seven at Golden State.

Boston-Phoenix looked like a decisive mismatch on paper. Paul Westphal, the Suns' leading scorer (20.5 points per game), had been a bench player with the Celtics until they traded him and two draft picks to Phoenix for Charlie Scott. Center Alvan Adams, Rookie of the Year and the Suns' second leading scorer (19.0 points per game), did not figure to have an easy series against a team that placed its entire starting frontcourt—Cowens, Havlicek, and Silas—on the 1976 All-Defensive First Team. However, Phoenix proved to be surprisingly tough, bouncing back after two losses in Boston to tie the series after four games.

The pivotal game-five encounter became a triple overtime thriller that is still considered by many to be the greatest basketball game ever played, filled with exciting plays, comebacks, and numerous twists and turns. At the end of the second overtime the Suns trailed by one and were set to inbound the ball from their own backcourt with one second left. Westphal, showing the strategic wiles that later made him a successful Suns coach, urged Coach John MacLeod to call a time-out, even though Phoenix had used up all of their time-outs. The Suns were assessed a technical foul and Jo Jo White made the free throw. Westphal knew that after the stoppage of play for the free throw the Suns would be allowed to advance the ball to half-court for the inbounds play as if a legitimate time-out had been called (a rule later changed as a result of this game). Gar Heard made a sensational shot to send the game into a third overtime.[79] In the third extra period, the clock struck midnight for the Cinderella Suns, as Celtics' reserve Glenn McDonald made several clutch plays to seal a 128-126 win for Boston; he was only in the game because Silas had fouled out.[80]

The Celtics wrapped up the title in game six. White scored 15 points and led Boston with 21.7 points per game in the series, earning the Finals MVP.[81] Cowens and Silas combined for 31 points and 30 rebounds in game six, while Scott totaled 25 points, 11 rebounds, 5 assists, and 3 steals. Scott, a much-maligned player during his stints with Phoenix and Virginia, also scored 31 points with 8 assists and 2 steals in the final play-off game versus the Braves and put up 20 points in the last game against the Cavs.[82]

ONE BIG, HAPPY LEAGUE

In May 1971, the NBA and ABA agreed in principle to a merger,[83] but the NBA Players' Association objected to the proposal on the grounds that it would drive salaries down by reducing the competition for players' services; they contended that a merger of the leagues violated the Sherman Antitrust Act[84] and had previously filed a legal action that became known as the Oscar Robertson lawsuit (Robertson was the president of the Player's Association at the time). The players sought not only to prevent a merger but also to strike down the onerous option clause that bound a player to a team for an additional season after his contract expired. A U.S. Senate Antitrust Subcommittee approved the merger but stipulated that the option clause was illegal and could not be part of player contracts in the combined league.[85] The NBA refused to accept this and merger negotiations broke down.

The ABA never achieved financial stability, largely because of its failure to obtain a national-network TV contract. Years of struggling against the NBA took their toll, and by the end of the 1975-1976 season the ABA was on the brink of financial collapse. Meanwhile, the NBA settled the Robertson suit in February 1976, agreeing to eliminate the option clause and pay $4.3 million to 479 players.[86] This removed the last legal hurdle to a merger between the leagues, and in the summer of 1976 the NBA and ABA agreed to terms: four ABA teams (Denver Nuggets, Indiana Pacers, New York Nets, and San Antonio Spurs) would pay $3.2 million each to join the NBA for the 1976-1977 season. In addition, the ABA teams would not receive any money from the league's television contracts for three seasons and the Nets would pay $4.8 million to the Knicks for the right to operate in their territory.[87] The owners of the remaining ABA teams received financial compensation and their players were distributed to the pre-merger NBA teams in a dispersal draft. Dan and Ozzie Silna, two brothers who owned the ABA's St. Louis Spirits, opted to receive a share of NBA television revenue in perpetuity in lieu of a lump-sum buyout; to this day the NBA continues to pay millions of dollars to the Silnas, beneficiaries of perhaps the greatest deal in the history of sports.[88]

The merger brought a wealth of talented ABA players into the combined league. The most prominent of these players was undoubtedly Julius "Dr. J" Erving, the three-time ABA MVP who eventually became the only player to win MVPs in both leagues; but the contributions of numerous others should not be overlooked. In 1976-1977, the first season after the merger, four of the league's top ten scorers were former ABA players. Don Buse of the Indiana Pacers led the league in assists and steals. Gilmore and Malone each ranked in the top five in rebounding and Gilmore and Caldwell Jones each finished in the top five in blocked shots. Five of the ten starters in the NBA Finals had played in the ABA. Ten of the twenty-four All-Stars had played in the ABA and, except for Barry, each of those players began their careers in the upstart league. Erving scored 30 points with 12 rebounds in the midseason classic (30 points, 12 rebounds) and became one of the few All-Star MVPs selected from the losing team.[89]

The Nets, who won the last ABA title thanks to a superhuman performance by Erving (averages of 37.7 points, 14.2 rebounds, 6.0 assists, 3.0 steals and 2.2 blocks in the Finals), traded for Archibald and looked forward with confidence to their first season in the NBA.[90] However, Erving wanted the team to honor a previous commitment to renegotiate his contract in the event of a merger and he sat out the preseason when the Nets failed to do so. Owner Roy Boe was strapped for cash between the merger fee and the additional money owed to the Knicks. He felt that the only way to satisfy Erving and solve the team's financial problems was to sell Erving to another team. Boe offered Erving to the Knicks in lieu of the indemnity payment but they turned him down. Instead, the 76ers purchased Erving from the Nets and signed him to a six-year contract for a total cost of $6 million. Pat Williams, then the 76er's general manager, offers a priceless account of the Erving deal. When he informed the Sixers' owner that it would be possible to buy the great Dr. J from the Nets, Fitz Eugene Dixon, who had only recently acquired the team and had not followed the sport very closely, replied, "Now, tell me, Pat—who exactly is this Erving fellow?"[91] Williams described him as "the Babe Ruth of basketball," whereupon Dixon agreed to the unprecedented expenditure by saying, "Fine and dandy."[92]

Erving joined a talented roster that included McGinnis, Collins, and Lloyd Free, who later legally changed his first name to "World" because he was—at least in his own estimation—"All-World." The Sixers finished 50-32, winning the Atlantic Division with the best record in the Eastern Conference. Erving and McGinnis shared the offensive load, averaging 21.6 and 21.4 points per game, respectively.

Both players were selected to the All-NBA Second Team. The Rockets captured the Central Division with a 49-33 record, while the Bullets, Celtics, Spurs, and Cavaliers earned the remaining play-off berths; in the wake of the merger the NBA expanded the play-offs by one team per conference. Maravich's Jazz still languished near the bottom of the East, but he had his finest NBA season, leading the league in scoring (31.1 points per game) and scoring 68 points in one game, at the time a record for a guard. Meanwhile, without Erving and with Archibald missing most of the season due to injuries, the Nets limped to a 22-60 record, worst in the league.

Jabbar led the Lakers to the Pacific Division title with the best record in the league, 53-29. He ranked among the leaders in scoring (26.2 points per game, third), rebounding (13.3 rebounds per game, second), field goal percentage (57.9 percent, first) and blocked shots (3.18 blocks per game, second). Jabbar was an easy choice for MVP and All-NBA First Team. The Nuggets, ABA Finalists the year before, won the Midwest Division with a 50-32 record. Thompson followed up his ABA Rookie of the Year honors by finishing fourth in the league in scoring (25.9 points per game) and making the All-NBA First Team. The 49-33 Portland Trail Blazers made the play-offs for the first time in franchise history, mainly because star center Bill Walton was healthy enough to play in 65 games. Portland was 44-21 in those games, but only 5-12 with Walton out of the lineup.[93] Walton averaged 18.6 points per game while leading the league in rebounding (14.4 rebounds per game) and blocked shots (3.25 blocks per game); he made the All-NBA Second Team. The Blazers also benefited greatly from the acquisition of power forward Maurice Lucas, an ABA veteran who led the team in scoring (20.2 points per game) and greatly helped Walton on the boards (11.4 rebounds per game, ninth in the league). The other play-off qualifiers in the West included the Warriors, Bulls, and Pistons.

The early play-off rounds went according to form, although the Sixers and Lakers were extended to seventh games in the Conference Semifinals by Boston and Golden State, respectively. Houston eliminated Washington in six games in the other Eastern Conference Semifinal, while the Blazers pulled off a mild upset, knocking off Denver, also in six games. The Blazers were playing better and better as the play-offs progressed and they swept the Lakers in the Western Finals, even though Jabbar outscored Walton (121-77).[94] Philadelphia eliminated Houston in six games in the Eastern Finals.

The Sixers jumped on the Blazers from the opening tip of game one of the Finals, Erving scoring on a sensational dunk after the center jump. He finished with 33 points and Collins scored 30 in a 107-101 victory.[95] The Sixers won game two, 107-89. Near the end of that game Dawkins and Portland forward Bobby Gross got in an altercation after a rebound. Dawkins fired a wild punch, but Gross ducked and Collins took the brunt of the blow; he later needed four stitches to close the wound. Then Maurice Lucas clocked Dawkins from behind. Dawkins and Lucas were both ejected and fined $2,500. The series shifted to Portland for games three and four, and between the fight and the change of scenery the momentum had clearly shifted as well. Portland won game three 129-107 and took game four 130-98. McGinnis was mired in a 16-48 shooting slump through the first four games. "I feel like a blind man searching for a men's room," he lamented.[96] Although he did not complain about it much at the time, in the 1977 Houston and Portland play-off series McGinnis received pregame injections of Xylocaine and cortisone to ease the pain of a severely pulled groin muscle. "I had no feeling in my left leg from the hip to just below the knee,"[97] he recalled later.

Once Portland evened the series it seemed as though all the wind had been taken out of the Sixers' sails. The Blazers won game five 110-104 in Philadelphia and clinched the title in game six, 109-107, after several Sixers missed opportunities to send the game into overtime. Erving had a marvelous series, averaging 30.3 points per game, but he could not rescue the Sixers from their bad defense and the poor shooting of McGinnis. Walton clinched the Finals MVP with 20 points, 23 rebounds, 8 blocks, and 7 assists in the final game.

THE DYNASTY THAT NEVER WAS:
THE OPERA ISN'T OVER UNTIL THE FAT LADY SINGS

The 1976-1977 season was a breakthrough for Walton and the Blazers. Injuries cost Walton forty-seven games in his rookie season and thirty-one games in his second year, but he missed "only" seventeen games during Portland's title run. During his outstanding college career at UCLA he had experienced some knee troubles but it later became clear that Walton had congenital structural problems with his feet. Altering his movements to accommodate his foot injuries led to the knee ailments.[98] Dr. James Nicholas, a New York physician whose clients included Jets quarterback Joe Namath, once examined Walton and told him simply, "You don't belong in this league, young man."[99]

During the brief stretch that Walton was relatively healthy he was a dominant player and his Blazers looked like a dynasty in the making. By the 1978 All-Star Break, Portland was 40-8 and had won forty-four straight home games. They pushed their record to 50-10 after a 113-92 win over the 76ers on February 28, but Walton badly sprained his left ankle in that game and missed the rest of the regular season. Portland went 8-14 the rest of the way without Walton, but still finished with the best record in the league. Walton's impact was so profound that he won the MVP even though he only appeared in fifty-eight of eighty-two games. Denver again won the Midwest Division, this time with 48 wins, while Phoenix, Seattle, Los Angeles, and Milwaukee completed the play-off field in the Western Conference.

The 1977-1978 season concluded with the closest, most exciting contest for the scoring title in league history. Maravich seemed to be heading for his second straight scoring crown until he was slowed by injuries, culminating in a blown-out knee that ended his season before he played enough games or scored enough points to qualify for the title. From then on it was a race between ABA standouts George Gervin and David Thompson. They dueled until the last day of the regular season, April 9, 1978. That afternoon Thompson seemed to clinch the scoring title with a stunning 73 point outburst (tied for third best in NBA history) in a 139-137 loss to the Pistons. He scored a record 32 points in the first quarter, breaking Chamberlain's mark for points in one period (31), which had been set in his famous 100-point game. Thompson scored 53 points in the first half. Overall, he shot a blistering 28-38 from the field and 17-20 from the free throw line. Gervin's Spurs faced the Jazz in the Superdome that evening. The Iceman broke Thompson's hours-old record by scoring 33 points in the second quarter. He also had 53 points by halftime. Gervin knew that he needed 59 points to pass Thompson and he finished the game with 63. Amazingly, he played only thirty-three minutes (Thompson logged 43) as the Spurs lost 153-132. Gervin launched 49 shots, making 23, and he matched Thompson by converting 17-20 free throws.[100] Less than two weeks later, Thompson became the highest-paid player in NBA history, signing a five-year, $750,000-per-year contract with the Nuggets. This surpassed the salaries of Jabbar ($650,000 per year) and Maravich ($600,000 per year).[101] Thompson later won the 1979 All-Star MVP (becoming the only player to win All-Star MVPs in the ABA and the NBA), but a drug problem soon diminished his production considerably. His career ended prematurely after he sustained leg injuries falling down a staircase while partying at New York's Studio 54.[102]

Gervin led the Spurs to the Central Division title with a 52-30 record. Sixers' Coach Gene Shue, already on thin ice after his team's collapse in the 1977 Finals, was fired after Philadelphia stumbled to a 2-4 start. New Coach Billy Cunningham, only recently retired as a player after a severe knee injury, rallied the Sixers, who won their second straight division title with a conference-best 55-27 record. The other Eastern Conference play-off teams included the Bullets, Cavaliers, Knicks, and Hawks, none of whom won more than forty-four games. Erving (20.6 points per game), McGinnis (20.3 points per game), and Collins (19.7 points per game) seemed to be poised to make a return trip to the Finals. The Sixers easily swept the Knicks in the Eastern Semifinal but had to wait a week while San Antonio and Washington slugged it out in the other Eastern Semifinal. The underdog Bullets eventually prevailed in six games. Bob Dandridge, who won a title playing alongside Jabbar and Robertson with the 1970-1971 Bucks, joined Washington as a free agent before the 1977-1978 season and proved to be a key addition, particularly in the play-offs. The Bullets were devastated during the regular season by injuries, hence their mediocre record, but their strong frontline, anchored by Hayes, Unseld, Dandridge, and Mitch Kupchak, peaked during the postseason. They took the Sixers' homecourt advantage with a 122-117 game one win and closed out the series in six games.

In the West, Walton got an extra week of rest because Portland earned a first round bye. Then the Blazers faced Seattle in the Western Semifinals. The Sonics started the season 5-17 but closed with a strong 42-18 mark after Coach Bob Hopkins was replaced by Lenny Wilkens.[103] Seattle was an excellent defensive team whose offense was built around the talents of guards Gus Williams, Fred Brown, and Dennis Johnson. The Sonics knocked off Jabbar and the Lakers in the first round but Portland beat Seattle three out of four times in the regular season. The big question was whether Walton could perform effectively after being out of action for nearly two months. In game one he scored 17 points and grabbed 16 rebounds in thirty-four minutes, but Seattle won, 104-95. Although Walton's statistics were not bad, he limped noticeably throughout the game and could not walk without pain the next day, spending most of the time in the whirlpool. Two days later he practiced but did not run. His availability for the second game was questionable at best. Early in his career Walton refused to take painkilling injections,[104] but this time he relented. Walton scored 10 points with six rebounds in fifteen first-half minutes. He did not play in the second half but the Blazers hung on to win, 96-93. When Walton's foot was x-rayed the next day a fracture was found in the tarsal navicular bone below his left ankle. Blazers' team doctor Robert Cook denied that the injections contributed in any way to the fracture, stating that the painkilling drugs were administered in a part of his foot "completely separated from the area of the break."[105] In the other Western Semifinal the Nuggets took a three-games-to-one lead over the Bucks, but Milwaukee won two straight before losing game seven 116-110 in Denver. The Sonics took the home-court advantage in the Western Finals with a 121-111 win in Denver and eventually won the series in six games.

It is unlikely that too many preseason prognosticators selected Washington and Seattle for the 1978 Finals. Washington was built around its veteran frontcourt, while Seattle's strength was its young guards. These differences lent some intrigue to the matchup. Due to scheduling problems, Seattle faced the same disadvantage that the Bullets had dealt with in the 1975 Finals: playing game one at home and then going on the road for the next two. Seattle was not fazed by this, winning the first game 106-102 and taking a three-games-to-two lead in the series. The Bullets faced the prospect of their third final-round loss without a single championship but Washington Coach Dick Motta picked an appropriate slogan for his scrappy team: "The opera isn't over until the fat lady sings."[106] The Bullets blew Seattle out 117-82 in game six and the series came down to a seventh game in Seattle. Johnson, who played valiantly in the postseason, went 0-14 from the field and his backcourt mate Williams shot 4-12. The Bullets became only the third NBA team to win a game seven in the Finals on the road.[107] Unseld was awarded the Finals MVP for his rebounding, passing, and bone-crushing picks.

SONIC BOOM

The 1978 off-season featured plenty of action. Free agent Rick Barry left the Warriors for Houston, but some of the impact of this move was lessened when the Warriors were awarded point guard John Lucas as compensation. Philadelphia traded McGinnis to Denver for Bobby Jones—perhaps the best defensive forward in the league—and guard Ralph Simpson, a former ABA All-Star. Pat Williams later wrote about how the Sixers' perceived McGinnis at the time:

> For the third year in a row, George—a productive player in regular season—had let us down in the play-offs. In a strange way, it boiled down to the fact that George was not all that enamored with the game of basketball. He had great agility, strength, and skills and the game had been good to him—but he wasn't intense in his approach to the game. He didn't have a good work ethic, and he hardly ever touched a basketball in the off-season. George's mind was just not in the game.[108]

Undoubtedly, the strangest transaction occurred when Buffalo owner John Brown and Boston owner Irv Levin swapped franchises. Levin wanted to relocate to the West Coast and knew that he could not transplant the storied Celtics. Instead, after completing the deal with Brown he moved the Braves to San Diego and renamed them the Clippers. Brown and Levin also traded some players in the process but Boston's Red Auerbach wisely refused to give up the rights to Boston's top draft pick, a junior eligible by the name of Larry Bird.[109] Meanwhile, Walton's sad saga continued. After doctors informed Walton that he would have to miss the entire season due to his foot injury, he blasted the medical treatment that he received from the Blazers and announced that he would not return to the team when his contract expired; in 1979, Walton signed with the Clippers but he played only fourteen games in the 1979-1980 season due to his continuing injury problems.

Although the Bullets and Sonics were surprising visitors to the Finals in 1978, they were favorites in 1979. Washington marched to a league-best 54-28 record, and the Sonics nipped right at their heels at 52-30.[110] Portland dropped to fourth place in the Pacific Division without Walton, barely nabbing the last play-off spot with forty-seven wins. The surprising Kansas City Kings won the Midwest Division at 48-34, one game better than the Nuggets. The Kings featured star guards Otis Birdsong and Phil Ford. Birdsong led the team with 21.7 points per game, while Ford scored 15.9 points per game, ranked fourth in the league with 8.6 assists per game, and finished fifth in steals (2.2 steals per game). Ford won Rookie of the Year and All-NBA Second Team honors. The Suns and the Lakers earned the other two play-off spots in the West.

Gervin and the Spurs (48 wins) narrowly beat the Rockets (47) and Hawks (46) for their second consecutive Central Division title. The Atlantic Division was not nearly as close. The Sixers had become more defensive-minded and team-oriented but a midseason injury to Doug Collins (19.5 points per game) left the team seriously bereft of scoring. Erving raised his average to 23.1 points per game but he also battled lingering injuries. With Collins out, the Sixers could have used World B. Free, who had been dealt to the Clippers for a first-round pick just before the start of the season. Free, who always complained about his lack of playing time while he was with the talent-laden Sixers, finished second in the league in scoring (28.8 points per game) to Gervin (29.6 points per game). Philadelphia slumped to forty-seven wins and did not have the best record in the conference for the first time since Erving joined the team. The Nets, led by guard "Super" John Williamson (22.2 points per game) and second-year forward Bernard King (21.6 points per game), snared the last Eastern play-off berth with 37 wins.

Both Eastern Conference Semifinals featured great drama. The Bullets took a three-to-one lead against the Hawks but stumbled badly in the next two contests and barely survived game seven at home, 100-94. In the other bracket, Gervin's Spurs won the first two against Erving's Sixers and led three to one after a 115-112 win in Philadelphia in game four. The Sixers responded by blowing out the Spurs in San Antonio in game five and narrowly winning game six at home, 92-90. The series shifted back to Texas for game seven and the Spurs outlasted the Sixers, 111-108. In the Eastern Finals the Bullets jumped to a three-to-one lead versus the Spurs only to again end up in a do-or-die seventh game. This time Washington escaped by two points, 107-105.

The Western Conference Semifinals were not nearly as close. The Sonics eliminated the Lakers four to one, although two of the games went to overtime. Phoenix wiped out Kansas City by the same margin. The Seattle-Phoenix encounter was much more competitive, although it did not start that way when the Sonics comfortably won the first two games at home. The Suns tied the series by taking games three and four in Phoenix and then grabbed the lead by winning game five in Seattle. The Sonics narrowly avoided elimination with a 106-105 victory in Phoenix and closed out the Suns with a 114-110 win in Seattle.

The Bullets stormed to an 18-point lead against the Sonics in game one of the Finals, but Seattle came all the way back only to lose when Dennis Johnson fouled Larry Wright during a shot attempt as time expired. The Sonics derived a great amount of confidence from their ability to come back from such a deficit against the defending champions.[111] Seattle promptly stole home-court advantage with a 92-83 win in game two and then took the lead in the series after a 105-95 victory in game three. The next two games were close, but Seattle won both of them to claim the title in five games. Versatile guard Johnson avenged his horrible game-seven performance from the previous year, winning Finals MVP honors. The Sonics are one of the few teams in NBA history to win a championship without the services of at least one player from the 1996 50 Greatest Players in NBA History list.

Speaking of great players, the Pro Basketball Writers' Association of America selected Jabbar as the Player of the Decade for the 1970s, the Knicks' Red Holzman as Coach of the Decade and the following quintet as the Team of the Decade: Jabbar at center, Erving and Havlicek at forward, and Frazier and West at guard.[112]

EPILOGUE: ROONE'S REVENGE

The NBA went through a dizzying roller-coaster ride in the 1970s. The decade began with the retirement of the greatest winner in the history of the sport, lawsuits seemingly flying in all directions, and a costly rivalry with the ABA. Teams such as the Knicks, Lakers, and Bucks quickly stepped to the forefront, as a veritable galaxy of stars battled for individual honors and championship glory. By 1976, the resolution of various legal issues paved the way for a merger between the leagues. NBA attendance climbed to a record 8.8 million in 1975-1976.[113] It nearly reached 10 million in the first season after the merger.[114] Pro basketball seemed to be living up to its billing as the "Sport of the Seventies." The era of good feelings after the merger was short-lived, however. Although the NBA and CBS agreed to a four-year, $74-million contract in 1978, each party soon became disenchanted with the other. In his classic book *The Breaks of the Game,* Pulitzer Prize-winner David Halberstam explained the conflict: "CBS privately charged the owners with expanding too fast, out of greediness; the owners in turn thought that CBS had been too greedy, too concerned with ratings, to give their game a fair chance at developing its true constituency."[115] CBS sought to boost sagging ratings by only televising the games of select marquee teams. Halberstam noted, "there were in effect *two* leagues—one consisting of the twenty two NBA member teams, the other a six or seven team league covered by CBS."[116]

Some of the seeds of future trouble were sown when the NBA's television contract with ABC expired in 1973. Many of the NBA owners at the time were new to the scene and had not been around for the previous decade when Roone Arledge, ABC's sports impresario, had overseen telecasts that effectively and enthusiastically presented the NBA to a growing national TV audience. These owners did not appreciate what Arledge had done for the league. All they cared about were the larger broadcast deals that the National Football League and Major League Baseball enjoyed; the NBA owners decided to claim what they felt was their fair share of the TV dollar. Although ABC had an option to renew its TV deal with the NBA, the NBA owners demanded that ABC split the contract with CBS and agree to televise Saturday-afternoon games in October and November, knowing that ABC would not be able to comply without abandoning its coverage of college football. When ABC refused these terms, CBS ended up with the whole NBA TV package. Arledge took the NBA owners to court, but lost the case.[117]

As Red Auerbach and a few wise NBA executives predicted, Arledge did not take this setback lying down. He launched a full-fledged programming assault against CBS' NBA games. ABC promoted its Saturday college football games to an unprecedented degree, capturing the lion's share of ratings and Madison Avenue advertising dollars. The NBA and CBS soon conceded defeat and abandoned Saturday telecasts. Arledge attacked the NBA's Sunday games with a new program called *Superstars*—which pitted athletes from various sports against one another—and a Sunday version of *Wide World of Sports,* his wildly successful Saturday program.[118] Halberstam notes, "In the first year of the CBS contract the ratings plummeted from 10 to 8.1; soon the decline became steady and very serious. Along Madison Avenue it was known as Roone's Revenge."[119] The NBA's television troubles reached an infamous nadir when CBS chose to broadcast the 1980 Finals on tape delay at 11:30 at night, an unthinkable indignity for the Super Bowl or World Series. One of the unsavory undertones of CBS' progressive neglect of the NBA was the perception of many observers that CBS did not want to showcase pro basketball because the vast majority of the league's players were blacks.[120]

Another serious problem for the NBA as the decade closed was an escalation of on-court violence. The conclusion of game two of the 1977 Finals was marred by an ugly brawl involving the 76ers' Dawkins and the Blazers' Lucas. Early in the 1977-1978 season Jabbar broke his right hand while punching Bucks' center Kent Benson in retalia-tion for an earlier blow that had gone unnoticed by the officials. Adrian Dantley, at the time a young player with the Pacers, was sus-pended for three days after following Dave Meyers of the Bucks to the locker room and attempting to fight him.

Unfortunately, the worst was yet to come. In a December 1977 game, an altercation broke out between Lakers' forward Kermit Washington and Rockets' center Kevin Kunnert. Rockets' All-Star forward Rudy Tomjanovich came over to attempt to break up the fight and ended up in intensive care after Washington wheeled around and connected with a thundering punch that basically shattered Tomjano-vich's face. Tomjanovich missed the rest of the season and Washing-ton was suspended for sixty days by the league.[121]

In the wake of these and other incidents the NBA formed a com-mittee of league executives, referees, and players to look into ways to limit flagrant fouls and fighting. Over time, the NBA developed a number of ways to regulate on-court violence: the addition of a third official so that "cheap shots" do not go unnoticed and lead to fights, automatic ejection for any player who throws a punch (even if it does not connect), a flagrant, foul point system that culminates in fines and suspensions, and a rule that any players who leave the bench area dur-ing a fight are automatically suspended.[122]

While declining ratings and escalating violence were serious causes for concern, two cornerstones of the NBA's dramatic recovery in the 1980s arrived in the fall of 1979: Magic Johnson and Larry Bird. Their rivalry for individual and team supremacy would push the league to new heights. The spirit of the ABA also played a major part in the 1980s renaissance as well: players such as Erving (1981 MVP), Malone (1979, 1982, and 1983 MVP), Gervin, and other ABA veterans were among the most successful and popular stars in the league; in addition, the adoption of the ABA's three-point-shot rule and All-Star Game Slam Dunk Contest added excitement and attracted fans.

NOTES

1. Merv Harris, *The Lonely Heroes: Professional Basketball's Great Centers* (New York: The Viking Press, 1975), p. 36.

2. Joe Gilmartin, "NBA Preview," *Street and Smith's College, Pro and Prep Basketball Yearbook,* 1976-77, p. 148.

3. David Wolf, *Foul! The Connie Hawkins Story* (New York: Warner Paperback Library, 1973), p. 161.

4. Ibid., p. 164.

5. Ibid., p. 189.

6. Ibid., pp. 206-207.

7. Ibid., pp. 236-237.

8. Ibid., p. 315.

9. Ibid., p. 335.

10. Ibid., p. 344.

11. Roland Lazenby, *The NBA Finals: A Fifty-Year Celebration* (Indianapolis: Masters Press, 1996), p. 144.

12. Ibid., pp. 146-147.

13. Ibid., pp. 147-148.

14. Ibid., pp. 148-149.

15. Ibid., pp. 149-150.

16. Gene Brown (editor), *The Complete Book of Basketball: A New York Times Scrapbook History* (New York: Arno Press, 1980), p. 169.

17. Lazenby, *The NBA Finals,* p. 144.

18. Harris, *The Lonely Heroes,* p. 40.

19. Michael Leahy, "For Jordan, Insatiable Drive Yields Heavy Toll," *Washington Post,* March 3, 2002, p. A01.

20. Lewis Cole, *Dream Team* (New York: William Morrow and Company, Inc., 1981), pp. 255-256.

21. Ibid., p. 131.

22. Jackie Lapin, "Phil Chenier is no Longer a Hardship Case," *Sport,* April 1975, p. 48.

23. Bill Libby and Spencer Haywood, *Stand Up for Something: The Spencer Haywood Story* (New York: Tempo Books, 1972), p. 85.

24. Ibid., pp. 71-72.

25. Terry Pluto, *Loose Balls: The Short, Wild Life of the American Basketball Association* (New York: Simon and Schuster, 1990), p. 185.

26. Ibid., pp. 177-179.

27. Ibid., p. 186.

28. Libby and Haywood, *Stand Up*, p. 157.

29. Pluto, *Loose Balls*, p. 178.

30. Libby and Haywood, *Stand Up*, pp. 95-96.

31. Ibid., p. 90.

32. Ibid., pp. 127-128.

33. Lapin, "Phil Chenier," p. 48.

34. David S. Neft and Richard M. Cohen, *The Sports Encyclopedia: Pro Basketball*, second edition (New York: St. Martin's Press, 1989), p. 246.

35. Ibid., p. 246.

36. Lazenby, *The NBA Finals*, p. 153.

37. Neft and Cohen, *Sports Encyclopedia*, p. 262.

38. Ibid., p. 279.

39. Lazenby, *The NBA Finals*, p. 156.

40. Ibid., p. 158.

41. Bill Libby, "Who Says Wilt's in His Second Childhood?" *Sport*, March 1972, p. 32.

42. Neft and Cohen, *Sports Encyclopedia*, p. 262.

43. Ibid., p. 262.

44. Lazenby, *The NBA Finals*, p. 161.

45. Harris, *The Lonely Heroes*, p. 44.

46. Libby, "Who Says," pp. 30-31.

47. Ibid., p. 32.

48. All-Pro Picks, *Street and Smith's College & Pro Basketball Yearbook*, 1972-73, p. 91.

49. Neft and Cohen, *Sports Encyclopedia*, p. 279.

50. Ibid., p. 288.

51. Libby and Haywood, *Stand Up*, pp. 97-98.

52. Ibid., pp. 103-105.

53. George Vecsey, "Pistol Pete Is the Player of the Future, Admits Pistol Pete," *Sport*, December 1973, p. 69.

54. Ibid., p. 69.

55. Ibid., p. 69.

56. Ibid., p. 73.

57. Ibid., p. 71.

58. Ibid., p. 69.

59. Alex Sachare, *100 Greatest Basketball Players of All Time* (New York: Byron Press Multimedia, 1997), p. 122.

60. Ibid., p. 122.

61. Ibid., p. 140.

62. Cole, *Dream Team*, p. 274.

63. Sachare, *100 Greatest*, p. 126.

64. Harris, *The Lonely Heroes,* p. 146.

65. Pluto, *Loose Balls,* p. 323.

66. Pat Williams (with James D. Denney), *Ahead of the Game: The Pat Williams Story* (Grand Rapids, MI: Fleming H. Revell, 1999), pp. 187-190.

67. Ibid., p. 214.

68. Pete Dexter, "Darryl Dawkins the Powerful," *Inside Sports,* April 30, 1980, p. 79.

69. Peter C. Bjarkman, *The Biographical History of Pro Basketball* (Lincolnwood [Chicago], IL: Masters Press, 2000), pp. 403-404.

70. Jerry Izenberg, "It's a Bird . . . It's a Plane . . . It's Rick Barry!" *Sport,* April 1975, p. 26.

71. Ibid., p. 26.

72. Ibid., p. 26.

73. Harris, *The Lonely Heroes,* pp. 137-138.

74. Lazenby, *The NBA Finals,* p. 176.

75. Rick Barry, "All the Fantasies Came True," *Sport,* November 1975, p. 67.

76. Neft and Cohen, *Sports Encyclopedia,* p. 320.

77. Williams (with Denney), *Ahead of the Game,* pp. 190-191.

78. Neft and Cohen, *Sports Encyclopedia,* p. 320.

79. Joe Gilmartin, *The Little Team That Could . . . and Darn Near Did!* (Phoenix: Phoenix Suns, 1976), p. 226.

80. Ibid., p. 227.

81. Lazenby, *The NBA Finals,* p. 181.

82. Gilmartin, *The Little Team,* p. 229.

83. Pluto, *Loose Balls,* p. 421.

84. Libby and Haywood, *Stand Up,* p. 109.

85. Pluto, *Loose Balls,* p. 424.

86. Ibid., pp. 427-428.

87. Ibid., p. 432.

88. Ibid., pp. 432-433.

89. Ibid., pp. 435-436.

90. Neft and Cohen, *Sports Encyclopedia,* p. 362.

91. Williams (with Denney), *Ahead of the Game,* p. 194.

92. Ibid., p. 194.

93. Lazenby, *The NBA Finals,* p. 185.

94. Ibid., p. 187.

95. Ibid., p. 187.

96. Ibid., p. 188.

97. Ralph Moore, "George McGinnis Is Discovering Defense in Denver," *Basketball Digest,* February 1979, p. 29.

98. David Halberstam, *The Breaks of the Game* (New York: Ballantine Books, 1983), pp. 323-324.

99. Ibid., p. 324.

100. Brown, *Complete Book of Basketball,* pp. 200-201.

101. Ibid., p. 201.

102. Sachare, *100 Greatest,* p. 182.

103. Lazenby, *The NBA Finals,* p. 191.

104. Halberstam, *Breaks,* p. 324.

105. John Papanek, "Off on a Wronged Foot," *Sports Illustrated,* August 21, 1978, p. 22.

106. Lazenby, *The NBA Finals,* p. 192.

107. Ibid., p. 194.

108. Williams (with Denney), *Ahead of the Game,* p. 206.

109. Neft and Cohen, *Sports Encyclopedia,* p. 386.

110. Lazenby, *The NBA Finals,* p. 197.

111. Ibid., p. 198.

112. NBA Briefs, *Basketball Pro-Style,* March-April 1980, p. 4.

113. Gilmartin, "NBA Preview," p. 148.

114. Joe Gilmartin, "Where Does the NBA go from Here?" *Street and Smith's College, Pro and Prep Basketball Yearbook,* 1977-78.

115. Halberstam, *Breaks,* p. 13.

116. Ibid., p. 16.

117. Ibid., pp. 245-246.

118. Ibid., pp. 247-248.

119. Ibid., p. 248.

120. Ibid., pp. 436-437.

121. Brown, *Complete Book of Basketball,* pp. 196-197.

122. Craig Carter and John Hareas (editors), *The Sporting News 2001-2002 Official NBA Guide* (St. Louis: The Sporting News, 2001), pp. 732-733; 738.

Chapter 13

Crashing the Boards:
The WNBA and the Evolution of an Image

Lisa A. Ennis

[E]very female athlete who stepped into the spotlight, sub-ject[ed] herself to the enduring stereotypes that dismiss women athletes as freakish trespassers in a male arena.[1]

The history of women's basketball is just a few months shorter than the history of men's basketball. Ever since Senda Berenson adapted Dr. James Naismith's original rules for her Smith College students in 1892 women have played the game.[2] The women's game, however, evolved very differently and much slower than the men's game. Women, after all, had hundreds of years of stereotypes and gender barriers to break through.

When Berenson adapted Naismith's game, she did so to conform to popular ideas about women. For instance, in order for women to avoid overexertion and the "vapors," she shortened the court by half, limited dribbling to just three bounces, and players were not allowed to run.[3] Women played the half-court game until 1971 when full-court play was introduced along with five-player teams and the thirty-second shot clock.[4]

The Women's Movement and the Equal Rights Amendment (ERA) brought changes and awareness for women in a variety of areas. Then, in 1972, President Nixon signed Title IX of the Educational Amendment of 1972, which stated in its preamble that "No person in the United States shall, on the basis of sex, be excluded from partici-pation in, be denied the benefits of, or be subject to discrimination un-der any educational programs or activity receiving federal financial assistance."[5]

Although Title IX had a huge impact on female collegiate sports by providing more opportunity and scholarships, the image problem surrounding the perceived physical limitations of women and societal restrictions of what was "ladylike" behavior still existed. The struggle to reconcile athletic, competitive women with the feminine caretaker expectations of society continued to plague women's sports, especially for professional athletes. The popularity of women's college basketball began to grow, but opportunities to play after graduation were limited at best.

There were plenty of good, even great, female basketball players with nowhere to go. Then, on December 9, 1978, the Women's Professional Basketball League (WBL) debuted. The league boasted some of the best women athletes in the world, such as Ann Meyers, Nancy Lieberman-Cline, and Lynette Woodard, but they were caught in a catch-22. As Sara Corbett explains, the players were "dismissed by accusations of not playing with the athleticism that the men did and simultaneously lambasted for appearing 'unfeminine.'"[6]

In an effort to market their league, the WBL presented "women's basketball, and particularly its players, as unintimidating, attractive, and irrefutably heterosexual. In other words, classically feminine," explained Sara Corbett in her book *Venus to the Hoop: A Gold Medal Year in Women's Basketball.*[7] Passive team names, such as the Fillies, Foxes, Does, Gems, Angels, Cornets, Rockettes, Hustle, Stars, and Dreams, were selected to emphasize the marketing strategy.

Sex appeal was also a large part of the WBL's marketing strategy. Many teams played exhibition games against the Playboy Bunnies, and the California Dreams were required to attend a five-week modeling course.[8] The league lasted only three years before going bankrupt. According to Mary Jo Festle, author of *Playing Nice: Politics and Apologies in Women's Sports,* the WBL failed because of the "apologetic stance they adopted, and the dilemmas management faced in appealing to sexist audiences."[9]

In her thesis, "The Rise and Fall of the First Professional Women's Basketball League," Amanda K. Long examines how popular female stereotypes affected one franchise in particular, the Panthers, as well as the league as a whole. In her research she interviewed four people from the Panther's franchise; a coach, a general manager, a player, and a sports writer.[10] One of the overriding themes in Long's thesis is that because of the perceived stereotypes surrounding women athletes the WBL suffered from a lack of support in a number of areas. Long found that "The lack of financial, fan and media support of this early league were often cited by the four participants as leading to the league[']s demise."[11]

Long goes on to explain that the lack of support contributed to the belief that compared to men, women were inferior athletes.[12] Lack of support, however, tends to indicate that the feminine stereotype still had a tight grip on the popular perception of women athletes. It is doubtful the WBL could have succeeded without changing the core belief that athletic women are unfeminine even unnatural. In their effort to manufacture femininity, however, they failed to retain the legitimacy of the game, in effect overcompensating for the perceived lack of femininity of their players.

Over the next few years several organizations tried starting a professional women's league. The Women's American Basketball Association (WABA), formed in 1984, lasted the longest—a mere one season—while the 1991 Liberty Basketball Association with its leotards, smaller ball, shorter court, and lowered basket lasted only one game.[13] As the popularity of college and Olympic women's basketball grew, fans, supporters, and players continued to fight for an American women's professional team. It was a colossal struggle of a few believers standing up to the Goliath of popular opinion. But in the meantime the only way for women players to make a decent living and prepare for the Olympics was to play on foreign teams.

Despite the lack of an American professional league, women's college basketball and Olympic play gained fans and popularity. So much so that by the mid-1990s two different groups, the American Basketball League (ABL) and the WNBA, had plans for forming a professional league. But the image problem was still hounding women's basketball. The best illustration of this is the 1996 USA Basketball women's national team.

In *Venus to the Hoop,* Sara Corbett chronicles the year leading up to the Dream Team's gold medal. Corbett explains that USA Basketball (USAB), the same organization that had created and marketed the men's 1992 Dream Team, was at a loss over how to successfully market the 1996 women's Dream Team. To illustrate her point, Corbett lists the various names considered for the team. USAB officials, most of whom were female, came up embarrassing names such as the Dreamettes, Fab Femmes, Golden Girls, and the awful Chicks

Who Set Picks.[14] Luckily for women players everywhere, the team's name was left at USA Basketball Women's National Team. The choice to keep gender out of the name, whether intentionally or not, provided the women's national team with a degree of legitimacy and respectability. In effect, USA Basketball had given the women's team a life of its own and set the team in a position equal to that of the men's national team.

Uniforms were also an issue. In the past, women athletes were forced into uniforms that sacrificed functionality for femininity. The USAB, however, designed a uniform to mirror that of the men's team. The 1996 women's team wore loose-fitting shorts and jerseys like the men's, except the women's were crimson instead of blue.[15] Although these minor changes may seem trivial to a casual observer, by leaving gender out of the name and the uniforms the USAB created an atmosphere of creditability never before experienced by women's basketball. This spirit of creditability spread, resulting in renewed life for the women's game. The 1996 team went on to win gold and was wildly popular; each of the team's six games attracted over 30,000 spectators.[16]

Riding the momentum of collegiate women's basketball and the 1996 Dream Team's popularity, two new leagues were formed in the late 1990s; the ABL and the WNBA. Many felt, given the popularity of the game, the skill and number of female players, and the inroads women had made into all areas of life, this was professional women's basketball's last chance. Given the number of high-caliber players; the response to the women's national team; the backing of the professional basketball premiere organization, the NBA; and the changing perceptions of women players due to the rise and popularity of both the college game and the Olympic team, if this mix of the right time with the right people and the right circumstances failed to create a successful professional women's league few held much hope that there would ever be a pro league for women.

Formed in the fall of 1996, the ABL was described as a "grassroots democratically run, feminist-inspired venture."[17] Players had stock options that made them part owners in the league, higher salaries, better benefits, and included seven members of the 1996 Dream Team. What the ABL did not know was that the NBA board of governors had approved a women's league concept on April 24, 1996.[18] Once the NBA announced its plans, sponsors and players began to back out of deals with the ABL. By all accounts the two leagues never considered a merger. WNBA president Val Ackerman stated, "We don't even think about a merger," while ABL founder and CEO Gary Cavalli called the WNBA "just an NBA subsidiary."[19]

One of the main points of turmoil was over sponsorship. The WNBA was able to use the marketing power of the NBA to secure television time on NBC, Lifetime, and ESPN, while the ABL games were often tape delayed on the Black Entertainment Television network and Fox Sports Net. Further, the WNBA's sponsor included Coca-Cola, Spalding, Nike, and Sears, while the only companies to stay with the ABL were Phoenix Home Mutual Life and Reebok.[20]

Despite the efforts to make the ABL financially viable, the league could not hold up against the power and financial infrastructure of the NBA. The ABL declared bankruptcy in the midst of its third season. ABL founder Cavalli explained, "It became clear that, although we had the best product, we could not find enough people willing to confront the NBA and give us the major sponsorships and TV contracts we needed."[21]

Even with the vast resources of the NBA, success was far from certain for the WNBA. All the money and sponsorships in the world would not make a difference if the game could not be sold to the public. One of the first decisions was to have the season take place in the summer, so it would not directly compete with the NBA.[22] Although some criticized the decision as a concession to the men, it made good marketing sense. Fall and winter are packed with major sporting events, whereas the summer was practically wide open. It also meant a more flexible television schedule and more consistent air times.[23] Most important, but not widely discussed among the media and observers, was that the WNBA never intended to compete with the men's teams for fans.

The WNBA creators wanted the new teams to reflect the men's teams and uniforms, and team names were part of that plan.[24] However, the "tradition of 'lady' hoopsters, which has women ballplayers seen as clearly inferior" was avoided, explained Linda Ford in her book *Lady Hoopsters: A History of Women's Basketball in America*.[25] The names would compliment one another, but there would be no "Lady Lakers" as female counterparts to the men's team.

The eight original teams, which were founded in geographic areas with strong NBA support, had names that reflected a connection to the men, but did not imply a position inferior to them. For example, the Houston team was named Comets to go with Rockets, while the Phoenix team became Mercury, which matched nicely with the Suns.

WNBA team colors also matched the corresponding NBA team colors. However, as Kelly Whiteside states in her book *WNBA: A Celebration Commemorating the Birth of a League,* every uniform "option was explored no matter how outlandish, including unitards, jumpers, and skirts. Even dresses (panty hose and pumps not included)."[26] Although Whiteside gives no indication of how seriously some of these options were considered, the fact that unitards, jumpers, and skirts were mentioned is an indication of the level of image awareness of the WNBA officials.

Luckily for WNBA players, these illogical uniform choices were scrapped and league officials did not put image ahead of common sense. It is highly unlikely that fans would have approved of such bizarre attire, particularly since the WNBA was being marketed as a serious basketball league, not some kind of circus sideshow. Whiteside does go on to note, "the designers regained their senses and settled on the tried and true" shorts and jerseys.[27]

With teams and uniforms in place, the league now had to market the sport and the women who played it to mainstream society. An immediate problem was how to balance fierce female competitors with the general public's idea of femininity. This dichotomy plagued earlier attempts at establishing a fan base for professional women's basketball. After the success of the 1996 Olympic team and the rising popularity of the women's collegiate game, the tide seemed to turn toward acceptance of a hardcore women's pro league. The first several years, however, had to be carefully orchestrated to build on the sport's newfound popularity.

Early WNBA executives included pioneers in women's basketball such as Val Ackerman and Carol Blazejowski, who were unwilling to sacrifice the legitimacy of the game but understood that in order to get fans to buy in they had to show a woman could be powerful and competitive, as well as feminine and gentle. As Sarah Banet-Weiser discusses in "Hoop Dreams: Professional Basketball and the Politics of Race and Gender," the WNBA situated itself "within a long and conflicted history about women and sport and has attempted to assuage sponsors and fans that their sport, although professional and athletic, was not overly 'masculine'."[28] To do this the WNBA focused on showcasing players that modeled "normative femininity, heterosexuality, maternity," and respectability.[29]

Luckily for the WNBA, the first three players to sign with the new league, Sheryl Swoopes, Rebecca Lobo, and Lisa Leslie, were ideal candidates to represent the fledgling league. These women were accomplished athletes, presented themselves well on camera, and had the innate charisma necessary to carry the WNBA in its infancy.

Sheryl Swoopes first won awards for her basketball play in high school. Her long list of accomplishments included being named a junior college All-American and 1991 Player of the Year when she averaged 21.5 points per game. Swoopes had an even more distinguished career after transferring to Texas Tech University. She led the Lady Raiders to the crowning glory of the 1993 NCAA championship, in addition to two Southwest Conference titles.

With no viable women's pro game in the United States, Swoopes had few alternatives. As did many of America's best women players, Swoopes played in several foreign leagues after college and then on the 1996 and 2000 Olympic Teams. In recognition of her growing popularity among female athletes, she was even honored by Nike with her own "Air Swoopes" basketball shoe.

Once drafted by the Houston Comets, Swoopes continued to dominate the floor.[30] Sheryl Swoopes also provided the league with something rarely before seen, a pregnant player. In fact an obviously pregnant Swoopes made the cover of the premiere issue of *Sports Illustrated: Women Sport*'s with the caption "A Star Is Born: Sheryl Swoopes and the WNBA Are Both Due in June."

Swoopes, back with her teammates only three weeks after giving birth to her son, Jordan, was featured in Whiteside's *WNBA: A Celebration.* The book provides fans with an inside look at the WNBA and the players, allowing the WNBA to showcase their players and league in a positive way. The first paragraph of the chapter titled "We Are Family" described Swoopes hearing her son cry over the roar of the crowd and running off to feed him at halftime. Two weeks later when she checked into her first game the crowd roared, "Welcome Back, Mom!"[31]

Although the chapter chronicles other players who were also mothers, as well as other familial relationships, Swoopes' very public pregnancy provided the WNBA with a priceless opportunity to spotlight an athlete/mother in a way never done before—and the fans cheered! As Whiteside states:

> When Swoopes was asked if she felt that the endless questions about motherhood were intrusive—after all, no one grills NBA players about fatherhood—she replied, "No, not at all. I think it's something we should talk more about," she said. "No one asks guys, because they figure they have a wife at home to do it. I play basketball. It's my career. There's a lot of women out there who juggle business and children. It's just as hard for them."[32]

Rebecca Lobo also proved to be an excellent spokesperson for the league. Lobo began playing basketball when she just five years old and showed an innate natural talent for the game. In third grade the precocious youngster even wrote the general manager of the Celtics to let him know she thought he was doing a good job and that she intended to be the first woman to play for the Celtics. Lobo won awards and accolades throughout high school and became a powerful force on the popular University of Connecticut Lady Huskies squad.

During the 1994-1995 season, Lobo and the Lady Huskies beat the favorites, the University of Tennessee Lady Vols, to rack up an undefeated season and national championship. She was named Final Four MVP. The combination of the victory over the heavily favored Tennessee team and an undefeated season thrust Lobo and the University of Connecticut into the national spotlight. Because of her outstanding play and personal charm, Lobo became a media darling and role model for young basketball players (male and female) all around the world.

In addition to having a reputation as a fierce competitor, Lobo also has a reputation as a nice person. She participates in supporting breast cancer research and awareness, and she also works with the Children's Miracle Network and the Pediatric AIDS Foundation. In 1997 *USA Today* named her to its Most Caring Athletes list.[33] Lobo's role as a spokesperson for the WNBA was a natural extension of her humanistic character. She always appeared confident and charming, whether speaking with pediatric children in the hospital or in front of MTV cameras.

If the WNBA was going for a feminine role model, however, they got the ideal person in Lisa Leslie. Leslie played only half a game in high school so other players could have the opportunity to score, averaged over 27 points a game, and earned All-American honors in 1992, 1993, and 1994. In college she was the first freshman to make the Women's College Basketball All-Pac-10, averaged 20.1 points per game, and was the only Pac-10 player named to the All-Pac-10 four times. In addition, she likes to wear makeup, dresses, pumps, and is a Wilhelmina model. Leslie even appeared on the cover of Vogue.[34]

As the league's primary spokesperson, Leslie appeared in numerous WNBA television and print ads. One of the most popular has Leslie eating breakfast at a diner counter. She is dressed in a suit, with makeup and perfect hair, but when the guy next to her inadvertently starts to dunk his doughnut in her coffee, Leslie whacks the doughnut away and says, "Nobody dunks in my house." The scene then switches to WNBA highlights of Leslie defending the goal.

Although the WNBA was careful to promote their players in a particularly feminine way, Sarah Banet-Weiser stresses in her article, "Hoop Dreams," that "players are not objectified in the way that women's bodies have been objectified traditionally."[35] Women basketball players have been granted a whole new existence in the sense that they can be both competitive and compassionate and are rewarded and idolized for both.

Here is the key: no one asked Lisa Leslie to be a model, no one asked Rebecca Lobo to be nice, and no one, at least in the WNBA, asked Sheryl Swoopes to get pregnant. They are all warriors on the court and play no mercy basketball, but off the court they are who they are—a model, an activist, and a mother. The WNBA highlighted its first three players for who they were, allowing the women to form their own images rather than attempt to fit them into someone else's stereotypes, as earlier women's basketball leagues had done. Along the way, the WNBA achieved balance and respectability. The result is a whole plethora of role models for young girls and boys. As the winter 1998 issue of *On the Issue* observes, "Playing like a girl is no longer an insult."[36]

Although no one doubts any longer the ability of women to play competitive basketball, the success of the WNBA is still not guaranteed. The league is still plagued by low television ratings, low attendance, and lack of corporate sponsors, which forces teams to fold and move in order to survive. Despite these problems the NBA and WNBA remain committed to the success of women's basketball. For instance, the young league worked through its greatest challenge to date by developing a new collective-bargaining agreement among rumors of player strikes and NBA Commissioner Stern's threat to call off the draft; the 1999 agreement expired September 15, 2002. The new four-year agreement, announced on April 25, 2003, provides players with the first free agency system in professional women's sports, a raise, and better individual endorsement contracts.

The league has also decide to change its business model. The original plan was organized so that the teams were located in an NBA city with an NBA staff. But both the Orlando Miracle and Miami Sol folded in 2002 and the Utah Starzz moved to San Antonio, Texas. These changes, along with Val Ackerman's dedication to the integrity of game, provide the WNBA with a solid foundation as it continues to grow. In an interview shortly after the signing of the new collective bargaining agreement, Ackerman was asked if she could raise the exposure of the WNBA without "sexing up the game."[37] Importantly, Ackerman responded "yes" and reinforced the role that Leslie and Swoopes have already played and the expectations she has for new players.[38] Focusing on the athletic performance and off-court personalities of the women of the WNBA will ensure the continued positive evolution of women sports and the image of the athletes.

NOTES

1. Sara Corbett, *Venus to the Hoop: A Gold-Medal Year in Women's Basketball* (New York: Doubleday, 1997), pp. 57-58.

2. Kelly Nelson, "Berenson Abbott, Senda," in Scribner's *Encyclopedia of American Lives: Sports* (New York: Charles Scribner's Sons, 2002), p. 73.

3. Ibid.

4. *WNBA Inaugural Program* (Sears, Roebuck and Co., 1997), pp. 6-7.

5. "Overview of Title IX," <http://bailiwick.lib.uiowa.edu/ge>.

6. Corbett, p. 40.

7. Ibid., p. 41.

8. Ibid.

9. Mary Jo Festle, *Playing Nice: Politics and Apologies in Women's Sports* (New York: Columbia University Press, 1996), p. 262.

10. Amanda K. Long, "The Rise and Fall of the First Professional Women's Basketball League," (Master's thesis, Springfield College, 1999), p. 10.

11. Ibid., p. 33.

12. Ibid.

13. Linda Ford, *Lady Hoopsters: A History of Women's Basketball in America* (Northampton, MA: Half Moon Books, 1999), p. 145.

14. Corbett, p. 58.

15. Ibid., p. 58.

16. Anngel Delaney, "A Whole New Ball Game," *On the Issue,* Winter 1998, p. 21.

17. Sara Gogol, "Big Business and Women's Pro Basketball," *Z Magazine,* June 1999, p. 55.

18. *WNBA Inaugural Program* (Sears, Roebuck and Co., 1997), pp. 6-7.

19. Terry Lefton, "Leagues of Their Own," *Sport,* October 1997, p. 38.

20. Sara Gogol, "The League That Was: The End of the ABL and the Future of Women's Professional Basketball, *Sojourner,* May 1999, p. 31.

21. Mariah Burton Nelson, "Why the ABL Threw in The Towel," *Ms.,* April/May 1999, p. 25.

22. Kelly Whiteside, *WNBA: A Celebration Commemorating the Birth of a League,* (New York: Harper Horizon, 1998), p. 56.

23. Ibid., p. 56.

24. Ibid., p. 61.

25. Ford, p. 148.

26. Whiteside, p. 61.

27. Ibid.

28. Sarah Banet-Weiser, "Hoop Dreams: Professional Basketball and the Politics of Race and Gender," *Journal of Sport & Social Issues,* November 1999, 403-404.

29. Ibid., pp. 403-404.

30. Janet Ingram, "Swoopes, Sheryl Denise," in *Scribner's Encyclopedia of American Lives: Sports* (New York: Charles Scribner's Sons, 2002), pp. 409-411.

31. Whiteside, p. 39.

32. Ibid., p. 40.

33. Di Su, "Lobo, Rebecca Rose," in *Scribner's Encyclopedia of American Lives: Sports* (New York: Charles Scribner's Sons, 2002), pp. 55-56.

34. Lisa Ennis, "Leslie, Lisa DeShaun," in *Scribner's Encyclopedia of American Lives: Sports* (New York: Charles Scribner's Sons, 2002), pp. 37-39.

35. Banet-Weiser, p. 416.

36. Delaney, p. 21.

37. Karen Benezra, "WNBA Challenge: Boost Ratings, Sponsor Activity," *Brandweek,* July 28, 2003, 8.

38. Ibid.

Chapter 14

Dr. J, Bird, Magic, Jordan, and the Detroit Bad Boys: The NBA in the 1980s

Lawrence E. Ziewacz

The Wednesday, March 28, 1979, edition of *The State News,* Michigan State University's official student newspaper, proclaimed headlines such as "Spartans Shoot to Kill" and "Magic's the Word, Not the Bird" as the paper boasted triumphantly of "the Spartans 75-64 victory over the previously undefeated Indiana State University to claim the NCAA title."[1]

The game featured Earvin "Magic" Johnson versus Larry "the Birdman" Bird. Both had performed brilliantly in the semifinals, as the Indiana State squad squeaked by DePaul 76-74, with Bird scoring 35 points on 16 of 19 shooting from the field, while adding 16 rebounds and 9 assists. For Michigan State, Johnson had a triple-double, 29 points, 10 rebounds, and 10 assists, as the Spartans pummeled the University of Pennsylvania Quakers 101-67.[2]

Many believed it was a "fan's dream to see the two best passers in college basketball . . . go head to head in the title game." However, in the individual dual, Johnson outperformed his rival, aided by a better supporting cast. Johnson had 24 points, 10 rebounds, and 5 assists, while Greg Kelser added 19 points, 8 rebounds, and 9 assists. Michigan State guard Terry Donnelly poured in 15 points, 13 coming in the second half. Meanwhile, Michigan State constantly double-teamed Bird. As a result, the star scored only 21 points on 7 of 21 shooting and was limited to a mere 2 assists. Poor shooting from the charity stripe also hampered the Sycamores, as they hit less than 50 percent of their free throws, 10 for 22.[3]

What made this particular finale to the college basketball season all the more intriguing was the anticipation of many fans that this head-to-head rivalry between the "Magic Man" and the "Birdman" was only a preview of many exciting confrontations to come on the courts of the National Basketball Association. This expectation would come to fruition when Bird became a Boston Celtic and Johnson left college after his sophomore year to join the Los Angeles Lakers. Over their careers, Magic would lead the Lakers to five NBA championships: 1980, 1982, 1985, 1986, and 1987, while Bird would take the Celtics to the NBA "promised land" in 1982, 1984, and 1986. In fact, Johnson's key role in leading the Lakers to five NBA championships during the 1980s convinced *Sport* magazine to name Johnson "The Sport Athlete of the Decade."[4]

For *Sport* magazine, the arrival of the two big men—both standing 6'9" tall and displaying phenomenal dribbling, passing, and shooting skills, which enabled them to completely dominate the game, signaled a revolutionary change in the NBA game. Bird and Johnson proved that center-dominated play was a thing of the past. According to one sports journalist, the traditional offensive of "picks, screens, and set plays became far less important. There was less play away from the ball . . . Thus, the five-man offensive show of 10 years ago gave way to one-man dribble penetration against the traps."[5]

In addition to big, strong players who displayed finesse skills, rule changes in the 1980s contributed to the demise of offense's run through the center position. One of the greatest innovations for professional basketball in the United States was the adoption of the 3-point shot. The 3-point line was drawn from a perimeter around the basket, which was 23 feet, 9 inches from the front of the basket and 22 feet in the corners. The 3-point field goal was implemented in the 1979-1980 season. The shot had been used in the short-lived American Basketball League, founded by Abe Saperstein in 1960, and the old American Basketball Association, which merged some of its teams into the NBA in 1976. Many observers felt that there had been reluctance to adopt the shot earlier in the NBA "because it was associated with failure and thought of as a gimmick."[6]

The theory behind the introduction of the 3-point play was to reduce the fierceness of the under-the-basket play, which often led to injuries and less aesthetic games. However, the main reason for its introduction was that television ratings had been declining for NBA games and the shot was popular with the fans.[7]

Initially, teams avoided the 3-point shot and utilized it only in desperation. In the first season of its introduction, an average of a fraction fewer than five 3-pointers a game were attempted. Players connected on a horrendous 24.5 percent. By the end of the 1980s, though, teams launched an average of 13.1 attempts and hit on 32.3 percent of those shots.[8]

However, as one NBA scholar has noted, 3-point statistics could be very "deceiving," since " a player got half again as many points for hitting a 3-pointer, his percentage was really the equivalent of a half-again figure." Seattle's Freddie Brown—who became known as "Downtown Freddie Brown," because of his 3-point shooting prowess—averaged a percentage of .443 for 3-point shooting on 39 of 88 shots in one season. Yet, as one scholar notes, "Brown averaged more points per attempt on his 3-pointers than did Cedric Maxwell, whose field goal percentage of .609 on regular shots led the league."[9]

Although the Boston Celtics anchored their offense with undersized center Dave Cowens and power forward Cedric Maxwell—both of whom preferred to play around the basket, coach Red Auerbach saw the advantages of the 3-pointer. With sharpshooting players such as Larry Bird and Chris Ford, the legendary coach integrated the three-pointer into the offense, thus freeing up the inside players.[10] Many other teams in the rough-and-tumble Eastern Conference attempted to follow the Celtic lead by balancing outside shooters with big-bodied centers and burly power forwards.

Other teams, particularly in the West, such as the Los Angeles Lakers, Phoenix Suns, Golden State Warriors, and Denver Nuggets, began crafting teams without huge size inside. These teams relied on athletes who were mobile, agile, and good outside shooters, which sped up the pace of the games and put a burden on teams that had lumbering frontline players. As defenses spread themselves to defend against the 3-pointer, it made them vulnerable to nimble penetrators, who could take it all the way to the "hole" or pull up and shoot the medium-range jumper or if double-teamed, fling it out to one of the gunners strategically set up outside the 3-point line to launch a "killer" three.[11]

The penultimate impact of the 3-pointer was the development of a hybrid team such as the Detroit Pistons, which won the NBA's 1988-

1989 championship by a "fusing of the two styles." According to one analyst, "The Bad Boys' extraphysical, Celtic-style starters would push the ball inside and beat you near death. Then their Laker-like reserves would come in, fly up and down the floor, and finish the job."[12]

Despite the introduction of the 3-point shot and the Bird-Magic rivalry, all was not well in the league in the early 1980s. According to one group of experts, "There was financial chaos, the result of fractious ownership, an unfocused league office and player salaries that had escalated. . . . Reckless expansion had diluted the talent, created too many unattractive matchups, and increased travel costs."[13] Adding to the plight, TV ratings had plummeted, partly because CBS showed only a few "contenders." Even Magic Johnson's heroic play in the NBA Finals (in the absence of Kareem Abdul-Jabbar), scoring 41 points and grabbing 15 rebounds, had been shown in many parts of the country on a tape-delay basis. As a matter of fact, many teams were in danger of financial collapse.[14]

In February 1984, however, the NBA's savior arrived on the scene. David Stern, a former New York lawyer, began a reign that continues to the present day. Under his leadership, average league attendance would increase by slightly over 50 percent during the 1980s, with a nearly 10 percent increase in the 1988-1989 season alone. Television revenue, explained an author from the venerable business magazine *Fortune* "doubled to 44 million per year, while the income from cable TV went from $5.5 million a year in 1984 to $25 million last year [1989]." In addition, NBA products sold for millions of dollars. Stern also played a critical role in making basketball a global game. In 1980 no foreign countries could view televised NBA games. By 1989, however, NBA games played on television in eighty countries.[15]

During the decade, Stern increased the number of teams allowed in the play-offs and expanded the number of franchises. Each franchise approved for addition to the NBA in 1987 brought in $180 million, which translated to an additional $5.6 million to the coffers of the existing NBA franchises. Yet in 1989 the expansion teams helped to boost NBA attendance by 22 percent. Surprisingly, the Charlotte Hornets led the league in attendance with 23,172 spectators per game.[16]

Stern also instituted the All-Star game weekend, which featured slam-dunking and became an "All-Star weekend extravaganza." (This was done while he was still the NBA's legal counsel.) The event was a huge success the year Stern replaced Larry O'Brien as the head of the

NBA. Yet again, Stern was not being an innovator, but a sharp entre-
preneur, since dunking was a legacy of the American Basketball Association's 1976 All-Star game in which Julius Erving won with a
"wild windmill" fling. With the merging of the leagues, such high flyers as Dr. J and David Thompson could provide the same electrifying
moments as they had in their old league, and Stern was clever enough
to incorporate this activity into the NBA for the financial benefits it
brought.[17]

An unsung hero in the drive to make the NBA more fan-friendly
and profitable is Larry Fleisher—even though the average fan has no
idea who he is. Fleisher became the general counsel for the player's
union in 1962. He endeared himself to the players by threatening a
wildcat strike of the 1964 All-Star game, which forced the NBA to
initiate a rudimentary pension plan. He initiated a successful attack in
1970 on the reserve clause, which bound a player forever to a single
team. This move eventually led to free agency. In 1983 Fleisher
helped negotiate a salary cap (desired by management), but also managed to have the owners agree "no team would spend less than $3.4
million annually on its payroll."[18]

Along with the salary cap, a key factor for the NBA to stay financially successful, the negotiations for a drug-testing policy was
equally important. The perception that many black NBA players were
using drugs and out of control was having an impact on league advertisers, who wanted to reduce the coverage of the NBA. As a result of
this situation, Stern and Fleisher hammered out a drug policy agreement that satisfied both their constituent groups. By stating that there
would be drug testing, the NBA indicated it was being "responsible."
According to the stipulations of the agreement, a player could come
forward and receive treatment and his salary. A second time, he
would receive treatment but no salary. However, if it happened a third
time, the player was banned for life.[19]

Although there was harmony in 1984 between Stern and Fleisher,
an all-out war occurred in 1988. The collective bargaining agreement
between the Players Association and the NBA owners had expired in
1987. Fleisher, on behalf of the Players Association, had filed a class
action lawsuit against the NBA management, but the case would not
be heard until some months in the future.

As a result, Fleisher convinced the union representatives to dis-
solve the union. Fleisher's reasoning was that without a union the

new agreement would not incorporate such objectionable items to the Union as "the draft, salary caps and the club's right of first refusal of free agents" could be incorporated into the new agreement. (The judge had ruled that the expired agreement remained official as long as "management 'reasonably believes' that those provisions, or close variations of them, will be incorporated in the next agreement.") Stern reacted by saying that Fleisher's action was "smart" and "an interesting strategem."[20]

On April 26, 1988, however, Fleisher and his union were able to announce a collective bargaining agreement. Teams could have only two picks in the players' draft. The agreement also stipulated that after a player's contract expired, the team had the opportunity to make a matching offer. This was amended by the fact that after the second contract expired, the player would be a free agent. Another important point that emerged was the use of a salary cap, whereby a team can pay a player what he desires, but there is a total sum, which each team cannot exceed. This means that teams with the largest pocketbooks would not be able to sign all the best players and practically ensure a total dominance. Certainly, these key provisions negotiated by Fleisher for his union helped to stabilize it and to avoid the totally ruinous free-agency spending that threatens other professional sports.[21]

Perhaps one of the most electrifying players of the old ABA, who made the transition to the NBA without skipping a beat and whose style of play would foreshadow that of Michael Jordan, was Julius "Dr. J" Erving. Erving was born and raised in Roosevelt, Long Island, and attended the University of Massachusetts, leaving school early so that he could pay for his mother's medical bills. Erving signed a $500,000 contract in 1972 with the ABA's Virginia Squires and "immediately caught everyone's attention by leaping over five guys for a dunk."[22]

Erving played two seasons with the Squires and then three seasons with the New York Nets, where his distinctive athletic moves led his team to two ABA titles. Erving's soaring acrobatics not only enthralled audiences but "opposing coaches used to admonish their players to keep their eyes off him," since he could "transfix you with the artistry of his game."[23]

One observer noted that when Erving elevated himself, he stayed there for a long period of time, "seemingly an irresistible force of nature as he improvised some acrobatic maneuver."[24]

Erving himself, commenting on his gravity-defying feats, noted that when he had a "Chance to power jump off both legs, I can twist, change directions and decide whether to dunk the ball or pass it to an open man. . . . In other words, I may be committed to the air, but I still have some control over it."[25]

In 1976, the two leagues merged and four ABA teams were brought into the NBA. However, because of the $8 million fee assessed to Nets owner Roy Boe, Erving was sold to the Philadelphia 76ers. He played in the NBA for eleven years, averaging 22 points per game during the regular season and leading his team to the Eastern Conference title three times in his first six years. Finally, in the 1982-1983 season, Erving led Philadelphia to the NBA championship.

In game four, with the Los Angeles Lakers leading 106-104, Erving scored 7 straight points in 98 seconds to lead the 76ers to a 115-108 sweep of the Lakers. The ability to completely take over a game with a mix of deft shooting and acrobatics typified Dr. J's impact on the professional game. Erving was elected to the NBA Hall of Fame in 1993, and in 1996 was selected as one of the 50 Greatest Players in NBA History.[26]

In 1984, the player who would be the link to the past and the harbinger of the future came into the league: Michael Jordan. Like Erving, Jordan possessed an "array of incredible moves and scintillating dunks" and caused Larry Bird to comment that Jordan really was "God disguised as Michael Jordan."[27]

Jordan made the winning shot in the 1982 NCAA finals as a freshman, was named the college player of the year in 1983 and 1984, and was the Bull's number-one draft pick. Jordan signed with Pro Serv, which helped him negotiate a lucrative contract with Nike to develop a special shoe in red and black, the Chicago Bulls' colors. The Jordan-endorsed sneaker earned Nike about $130 million dollars in the first year of its existence. As a result of the success with the Jordan brand, Nike became the major shoe provider for NBA players in the 1990s, partly because it was so generous with its products to all the players, not just the stars and megastars. In the 1980s, Nike's revenues eclipsed $3 billion. Before he even played in a Bulls' uniform, Jordan declared that he "worked for Nike."[28]

Soon, Jordan became an endorsement machine—earning income from Gatorade, Coca-Cola, Wheaties, Wilson, Ball Park franks, and Hanes underwear—eventually totaling almost $45 million from endorsements, according to one observer, making "the business of hawking products more lucrative than playing the game."[29]

The NBA was poised for growth. The league had exciting new players mixed with its established stars, and the technological and media revolution that took place allowed the game to acquire a global following. One important advance was the development of cable television and super stations, which featured more NBA games. At the same time, the development of technology featuring more cameras, better pictures, isolations, and replays gave the televised game new life and made it a more exciting product for broadcasters and advertisers. The soaring dunks and robust rejections could be isolated and frozen—better to feature the exploits of the individual stars. Even the fact that players suited up in shorts and jerseys close up to the audience gave basketball an "intimacy" that football and baseball could not replicate. Few sports gave fans a closer look at the action. Soon more players followed in Jordan's footsteps and played the endorsement game for all that it was worth. Even longtime rivals Larry Bird and Magic Johnson would team for a Converse commercial, featuring the two players back to back holding a Converse shoe much like one would a dueling pistol, with the caption, "Choose Your Weapon."[30]

However, such endorsement, of basketball shoes in particular, created problems as many youths—particularly black youths—committed "sneaker crimes," a definition later expanded to stealing not only sneakers but also articles of clothing endorsed by NBA players. Much of the violence associated with the sneaker crimes involved Nikes, since "an estimated 70 percent of all money spent on footwear by American boys between the ages of thirteen and eighteen was spent on the swoosh." Journalists from the *New York Post* and *Sports Illustrated* criticized the aggressive marketing of the expensive shoes to inner-city youth, calling it "murder" and stating that society was "slipping into economic and moral oblivion."[31]

In addition, the shoe companies themselves came under harsh attack for farming out their production to Asian factories, which paid their workers pennies on the dollar in comparison with American workers and did not face health or safety regulations. Nike, for example, had rid itself of its last domestic shoe factory in the late 1980s and moved most production to Asia. Yet with endorsements well in hand, many NBA stars could hold out in negotiations, since various companies paid them lucrative endorsements.[32]

Jordan won Rookie of the Year honors in 1985, averaged 25.1 points per game from 1984 to 1989, and was named the NBA's Most Valuable Player and the Defensive Player of the Year in 1988. However, Jordan did not earn the treasure he most coveted—the NBA championship trophy—until 1991. His impact on the NBA, both in terms of his stellar and spectacular play and his introduction of the NBA player as individual economic entity who could be marketed much like a NASCAR driver, created an indelible legacy, which helped create the modern NBA.[33]

The essential tale of the NBA in the 1980s, however, is how the "dynamic duo of Bird and Magic kept their college rivalry of 1979 rolling right through the 1980s, jockeying for NBA titles and MVP trophies."[34] Although most NBA scholars hold to this view, one analyst argues fairly convincingly that what really defined the rivalry was the sixth game of the 1980 NBA play-offs, with the Lakers leading the Philadelphia 76ers 3-2. This series included such hoop luminaries as Julius Erving, Darryl Dawkins, and free-shooting dervish, Lloyd Free. An injury to Jabbar meant a serious loss at the center position for the Lakers. With a brilliant bit of strategy, Coach Paul Westhead inserted Johnson at center. The tactic completely baffled Philadelphia, and the more agile and athletic Johnson responded to the challenge by scoring 42 points, garnering 15 rebounds, and dishing out 7 assists. Forevermore, the issue of size determining a player's position was no longer a factor, setting the stage for athletes of the future, such as Sean Elliott and Kobe Bryant, to fill such roles.[35]

Certainly the key to Johnson's success was his commitment to the team game—making sure everyone was involved and ensuring that the proper pass was made so that the most open player could take the highest percentage shot available. In addition, he was extremely competitive. Jabbar recalled in his autobiography that Johnson was "too competitive," since many practices ended up in "almost fisticuffs." The great center surmised that Johnson simply did not like "losing at anything." He also noted, however, that the game was affected by Johnson's intensity and thought that was "one of the reason's the NBA got to be so popular in the 1980s."[36]

Magic summed up how he viewed his play and that of Bird and how they were different than others in the following words: " Me and Larry are just different from everybody else. It's not like we're just two great scorers, because you can shut scorers down. We do so many other things. Even if one of us isn't scoring, we make our presence felt."[37]

Larry Bird possessed similar unselfish characteristics. Drafted by the Boston Celtics in 1979, he would remain with them through the 1991-1992 season. His NBA career was spectacular. He scored 40 points or more in 52 games and had four games in which he scored 50 or more points. He scored 2,000 points in four consecutive seasons and was also the first NBA player to shoot 50 percent from the floor and more than 90 percent from the free throw line. He is only one of five players in the NBA to have over 5,000 assists and score more than 29,000 points. His total statistics in the NBA are truly amazing: 21,791 points, 1,556 steals, 88.6 free throw percentage, 8,974 rebounds, 5,965 assists, and a 24.3 scoring average. He was selected to the NBA Hall of Fame in 1998 and was also named to the 50 Greatest Players in NBA History in 1996.[38]

Bird also realized that he and Magic dominated the game. Comparing his play with that of Johnson's, however, he said, "We both do the same things, but we're not the same type of player. The impact I have on the game is usually scoring but with him it's always his passing."[39]

Bird led his team to the NBA Championships in 1981, 1984, and 1986. He was named the Most Valuable Player in 1984 and 1986. Of course, Bird had a strong supporting cast, with Kevin McHale and Robert Parrish, the twin anchors underneath, and aided and abetted by other strong players such as Tiny Archibald, Danny Ainge, Cedric Maxwell, Bill Walton, and Dennis Johnson.[40] "Larry Legend," however, was the heart and soul of the Celtics. The others recognized his overall dominance and took their cues from his greatness.

In 1984, the Lakers would finally meet the Celtics in the NBA Finals—a dream match that fans had been waiting to see for four years. After six tense games, the series was even, with the final game taking place in Boston. Cedric Maxwell led four Celtics in double figures and to the championship in a thrilling 111-102 victory. Bird was named MVP after averaging 27.4 points and 14 rebounds in the series.[41]

In 1985, both teams again made it to the Finals. Again Boston hosted the Lakers for the crucial game, but this time the series stood at three to one in favor of the Lakers. In Boston, at the famed Garden, the Lakers rode Jabbar's 29 points, Johnson's leadership, and Bird's poor shooting (an uncharacteristic 12 for 29 from the field) to a 111-100 victory.[42]

In 1986, the Lakers fell to Houston 4-1 in the opening round of the NBA play-offs. They had to watch disconsolately as the Boston Celtics, with a marvelous 67-15 regular season record, beat Houston four games to two, winning the final game at the Garden. As one writer stated, "Boston had too much firepower, too much depth, and too much depth."[43]

Like all great teams, the Los Angeles squad retooled after their stunning loss to the Houston Rockets. The Lakers had learned something in their defeat by Houston. The Rockets had harassed Johnson in the backcourt and flanked Jabbar with the twin towers of Ralph Sampson and Hakeem Olajuwon, forcing the other perimeter players to provide the offense. They simply could not produce.[44]

A longtime student of the game, Lakers coach Pat Riley decided to balance the offense by allowing more players to have the "green light" to shoot. Although the focus was still on the inside-out game, it was not just Kareem and Magic providing the offensive punch. In spreading the offense around, it was theorized that there would be less double-teaming, thus forcing teams to play "honest," man-to-man defense.[45]

The task was daunting for the Lakers. The Celtics had visions of being the first team in eighteen seasons to win back-to-back championships. It would not happen. Instead, it would be the Lakers who would achieve that accomplishment.[46]

The Lakers sailed through the play-offs in 1987, losing only one game in the preliminaries. The Celtics, meanwhile, had to fight their way through a seven-game series with the strong, hungry Detroit Pistons. After a grueling series with the young Detroit team, the Celtics eventually dispatched the Pistons by 117-114 margin.[47]

The Lakers proved too much for the Celtics in the Finals and banished them from the NBA throne by winning in five games. The final game score was 106-93. Jabbar led the Lakers with 32 points, while Johnson tallied 16 points and an astounding 19 assists to earn the Most Valuable Player title. Johnson himself believed that this was the best team he had ever played on.[48]

The next season, the Lakers accomplished what had been the Celtics goal—a repeat of the championship.[49] What made the 1987-1988 championship an even more difficult task was that Laker coach

Pat Riley said that he would "guarantee" a repeat. Yet Riley was obviously cognizant of his talent. At forty-one, Kareem could still hold his own and could be deadly with his skyhook. No one could match up with Johnson and James Worthy streaking down the lane was a big target for Johnson's pinpoint passes. Byron Scott would regain his shooting eye, which had deserted him the previous season. Scott led the Lakers in scoring during the regular season, with 21.7 points average, thus providing the key outside shooting threat.[50]

The Lakers earned a 62-20 regular season record and, after sweeping San Antonio 3-0 in the first round of the play-offs, had to slug their way past both Utah and Dallas in seven games.[51]

Their opponents were not the same old Celtics team of old, relying on the deft shooting touch of Bird and the stifling team defense of McHale and Parrish. This year's opposition was the newly reborn Detroit Pistons. The cocky, aggressive Pistons were not awed by the Lakers "Showtime" aura. In fact, they met the Lakers with some "Motown" madness of their own, often using physical force to thwart the Lakers' finesse.

The Pistons jumped to a 3-2 game lead in the series. In the sixth game they led by 3 points, at 102-99, before rallying for a dramatic 103-102 victory. In the seventh game, the Lakers led by 25 points, 90-75 in the fourth quarter before fending off a furious Detroit rally, which fell just three points short, as the Lakers eked out a 108-105 victory to gain their coveted championship repeat.[52]

Yet, there would not be a three-peat for the Lakers. The brash and bold "Bad Boys" of the Detroit Pistons, a nickname earned through the black-and-blue physicality of their defensive efforts, prevailed in the final year of the 1980s.[53]

Chuck Daly, the coach of the Pistons, made a decision in 1986 to concentrate on defense and assembled such stalwarts as Bill Laimbeer, Rick Mahorn, and Dennis Rodman to anchor the defense. To bolster Detroit's offense, Daly acquired a trio of sharpshooting guards, Isiah Thomas, Joe Dumars, and Vinnie Johnson.[54]

Many regarded the Pistons' physical play as going far beyond the bounds of fair play. For example, on February 28, 1989, Mahorn threw an elbow at Cleveland Cavaliers star shooter Mark Price when both were coming down the floor trailing the play. Mahorn's elbow came out of nowhere and had nothing to do with the flow of the game. Price went down with a concussion. Doctors examining the star reported that if the blow had landed two inches higher, Price might have suffered brain damage. It was these kinds of cheap-shot plays that helped to create the "Bad Boys" image.[55]

Many have maintained that the Detroit Pistons' ascendancy reflected the "blue collar image" of Detroit itself. For the most part, this is simply fanciful thinking. The Pistons played in the Palace of Auburn Hills, a distant suburb of Detroit. The team's fans were mainly affluent suburbanites. The offense was not predicated on working the ball into the middle, but instead was basically a perimeter shooting set. The key mismatch Detroit maximized was center Bill Laimbeer's ability to hit long jump shots and 3-pointers. The rest of the offense was fueled by the shooting of the three guards, Isiah Thomas, Joe Dumars, and Vinnie "the Microwave" Johnson, so named because he was the sixth man off the bench who provided instant offense with his accurate and almost unstoppable shooting. No high school or college coach would usually base his offense on the outside shooting of three guards and a center. No, this was not the "lunch bucket brigade" that Detroit's supporters claimed . . . far from it.

However, the NBA banner might not have flown over the Palace had not a key trade been made. On February 15, the general manager traded forward Adrian Dantley to Dallas for Mark Aguirre. Dantley was a low-post specialist who could score but did not distribute the ball and hampered the Pistons' fast break. The trade proved to be a success and a key element in the Pistons' triumph.[56]

The Lakers team the Pistons faced was lacking its starting guards Magic Johnson and Byron Scott. Although the Lakers fought gamely, the Pistons' numbers overmatched them. The Pistons swept the first three games and beat the Lakers 105-97 in the clincher, despite trailing by 16 points in the first half. Coach Chuck Daly, in probably one of the greatest understatements of all times, commented that " 'I think our depth finally won out.' "[57]

The NBA had come a long way in the 1980s. According to veteran sportswriter Terry Pluto, the 1970s had been full of "greed, drugs, and the duel between the ABA and the NBA. The advent of players such as Bird, Johnson, and Jordan who captured the fans' imaginations and the leadership of NBA Commissioner David Stern and Players Association President Larry Fleisher" helped provide a "drug policy, a salary cap and a commitment on the part of the entire league—from the boardrooms to the locker rooms—to clean up the game and make it fan-friendly."[58]

The league had passed the point where there were worries about black-dominated teams, since by 1990 the NBA rosters would be dominated by black players. For better or for worse, the endorsement packaging of an athlete, as exhibited by Michael Jordan, would become a fundamental fact. Of course, Jordan would win six championship rings in the 1990s.

Perhaps one element of NBA play in the 1980s, which is its enduring legacy, is the intensity of the games. Eccentric Piston "Bad Boy" Dennis Rodman would agree with this assessment, asserting that indeed the 1980s were the best years, since they didn't give rookies "70 million dollar contracts before playing a minute in the league."[59] Certainly the 1980s will remain as a crucial decade in the history of the NBA and its development.

NOTES

1. *The State News,* March 28, 1979, p. 1.

2. Ibid.

3. Ibid.

4. "The Sport Athlete of the Decade," *Sport,* October 1989, p. 96.

5. Tom Kertes, "Basketball, '80's," *Sport,* October 1989, pp. 51-52.

6. Glenn Dickey, *The History of Professional Basketball Since 1896* (New York: Stein and Day, 1982), p. 189.

7. Ibid., p. 190.

8. Kertes, pp. 51-52.

9. Dickey, p. 191.

10. Ibid.

11. Kertes, p. 50.

12. Ibid.

13. Armen Keteyian, Harvey Araton, and Martin F. Dardis, *Money Players: Days and Nights Inside the New NBA* (New York: Pocket Books, 1997), p. 83.

14. Ibid., pp. 83-84.

15. Kertes, p. 64; "Full Court Success," *Fortune,* August 28,1989 (5): 123.

16. Francz Lidz, "The play-off Madness II," *Sports Illustrated,* April 22, 1985 (2): 18; Jack McCallum, "Twenty-Seven's a Crowd: The Last Things the NBA Needed Was Four New Franchises," *Sports Illustrated,* May 25, 1987: 92; Linda Deckard, "Expansion Teams Help NBA Post 22% Attendance Gain," *Amusement Business,* May 27, 1989, 101(21): 1.

17. David Halberstam, *Playing for Keeps: Michael Jordan and the World He Made* (New York: Random House, 1999), pp. 124-125; Nelson George, *Elevating*

the Game: Black Men and Basketball (New York: Harper Collins,1991), pp. 183-184.

18. Alexander Wolff, "NBA Players Counsel Larry Fleisher Wears a Second Hat As an Agent," *Sports Illustrated,* February 11, 1985, 208.

19. Halberstam, pp. 119-120.

20. Steve Wulf, "Disunion," *Sports Illustrated,* February 15, 1988: 40.

21. "Standing Tall," *The Economist* (US) May 7, 1988: 24.

22. Larry Schwartz, "Dr. J Operated Above the Rest," *Sports Century Biography,* <espn.go.com/classic/biography/s/Erving_Julius.html>. Fredrick McKissack Jr., *Black Hoops: The History of African Americans in Basketball* (New York: Scholastic Press), p. 114.

23. Schwartz, p. 1; Kareem Abdul-Jabbar with Mignon McCarthy, *Kareem* (New York: Random House, 1990), p. 82.

24. Schwartz, p. 1.

25. Ibid., pp. 1-2.

26. Schwartz, p. 3; McKissack, p. 114; David Walton and John Hareas, eds., *The Sporting News Official NBA Register: 2000-2001 Edition* (St. Louis, MO: The Sporting News, 2000), p. 359.

27. Larry Schwartz, "Michael Jordan Transcends Hoops," <espn.go.com/sportcentury/features/00016048.html>.

28. McKissack, p. 121; George, p. 234; Wetzel and Yeager, pp. 7, 27.

29. George, p. 235; Wetzel and Yeager, pp. 5-6.

30. Halberstam, p. 131; "Sport Athlete of the Decade," *Sport,* October 1989, p. 86.

31. George, p. 235; Wetzel and Yaeger, pp. 27-28.

32. Wetzel and Yaeger, pp. 28-29.

33. Ibid., p. 391.

34. Kertes, p. 51.

35. George, pp. 226-227.

36. Jabbar, p. 167.

37. Bill Gutman, *Magic: More Than a Legend* (New York: Harper, 1992), p. 142.

38. Walton and Hareas, *Sporting News,* p. 340.

39. Gutman, p. 143.

40. George, p. 224.

41. Roland Lazenby, *The Lakers: A Basketball Journey* (New York: St. Martins, 1993), p. 249.

42. Ibid., p. 255.

43. Lazenby, p. 256; "Houston Rockets History," <nba.com/rockets/history>.

44. Jabbar, p. 77.

45. Jabbar, p. 77; Lazenby, pp. 256-257.

46. Lazenby, p. 258.

47. Ibid., p. 259.

48. Ibid., pp. 262-263.

49. Jabbar, p. 38.

50. Lazenby, pp. 265-266.

51. Ibid., p. 266.

52. Ibid., pp. 268-269.

53. Steve Addy, *The Detroit Pistons: Four Decades of Motor City Memories* (USA: Sports Publishing, Inc., 1997), p. 166.

54.Terry Pluto, *Falling from Grace* (New York: Simon and Schuster, 1995), pp. 216-219.

55. Ibid., p. 224.

56. Addy, pp. 165-166.

57. Addy, pp. 165-166.

58. Pluto, p. 15.

59. Dennis Rodman with Tim Keown, *Bad As I Wanna Be* (New York: Delacorte Press, 1996), p. 88.

Chapter 15

The Jordan Era: The NBA in the 1990s

Doug Fox

The best way to appreciate greatness is to witness it firsthand.

To feel the butterflies in your stomach as time slows down. To notice your palms getting sweaty even as your body tingles with the nervous excitement of the moment.

To realize you are watching the greatest in their field not only in their finest hour but also their greatest minute and moment.

To see history unfold before your own two eyes—and *recognize* it as such!

It would be tantamount to being on hand at Wrigley Field to watch Babe Ruth call his shot in the fifth inning of Game Three of the 1932 World Series.

Like sharing the stands at Joe Robbie Stadium with John Candy, among others, and seeing Joe Montana run the two-minute offense to perfection in the fourth quarter of yet another Super Bowl (XXIII) victory.

Like sitting courtside at the Delta Center for Game Six of the 1998 NBA Finals as Michael Jordan drained what would become, for a couple of years anyway, the last shot of his career—giving the Bulls their sixth championship in eight seasons.[1]

Never mind that I was personally pulling for a seventh game in that exciting series between the Bulls and Utah Jazz, I will consider myself forever grateful that is exactly where I was when Jordan swished home the shot seen 'round the world.

But while most of the world relies on videotape and replays to relive that special moment in time—I can simply close my eyes, queue up my memory, and capture the greatness time and time again from my own personal perspective.

I can still hear the roar of the crowd turn to dumbfounded silence by the time the ball trickled out from the bottom of the net at the basket directly in front of the Jazz bench.

Bulls 87, Jazz 86.

It's a moment frozen in time and celluloid.

Look at all the pictures snapped from every imaginable angle and study the faces in the crowd. Some stunned. Some in shock. Some sorry. But none truly surprised at the outcome.

They, like I, innately knew the shot was good the second it left the coolest right hand the NBA has ever known.

They knew it from the pit in their stomach that developed while watching Utah defender Bryon Russell reach, backpedal, and slip.

But mostly they knew it, as we all did, because of who shot it.

Deity in Nikes.

As you would expect, postgame praise was effusive for Jordan, who totaled 45 points, but he will mostly be remembered for those final two.

"It was just an awesome thing," said Bulls coach Phil Jackson. "I think you have to say that Michael is the guy who comes through. He's the guy that always comes through in the clutch. He's a winner, and he's proven it so many times, over and over again. How many times does he have to show us that he's a real-life hero?"

"Let's face it," said Chicago guard Steve Kerr. "We all hopped on Michael's back. He just carried us. It was his game tonight. That guy was ridiculous. He is so good it's scary."

"He is that kind of player," said Utah center Antoine Carr of Jordan. "He is going to step up and do what he can. He stepped up again and did what he normally does."

There was no doubt in the mind of Utah coach Jerry Sloan as to how Jordan should be recalled in the annals of basketball lore:

> I think everybody knows how he should be remembered as the greatest player that has ever played. I don't know what else you can do. That's the great thing about him, and with all he's done for not only the league, but everybody that's a part of this league. And that's to be commended. We just have so many things that are sideshows to this game, that he hasn't allowed to happen, and I think that's the most important thing. Being as great as he is has allowed the game to be the important thing. And the other things came afterwards. And I think sometimes

we have a tendency to get those things in reverse. All the side-shows that go on outside are more important than the game. For-tunately with him it's never been that way. And I hope he continues to play.

Hinting strongly at a second retirement, which he would make offi-cial several months later, Jordan said he would trust his feelings and do what he felt was right.

Hopefully I've put enough memories out there for everybody to at least have some thoughts about what Michael Jordan did in his 13 years or 14 years or whatever it takes and put some com-parisons up there for kids to follow and compare themselves, and reach. And that's part of the challenge. And I have another life. And I know I have to get to it at some point in time. And hopefully the fans and the people understand that.

They do. The same way they did when he came back yet again—this time with the Washington Wizards.

But that's another decade.

THE RUNNING OF THE BULLS

Jordan's series-clinching shot, complete with his right hand mo-mentarily paused for effect in an extended follow, was clearly the de-fining moment of the 1990s—a decade dominated by the Bulls.

Chicago's previous nemesis, the Detroit Pistons of "Bad Boy" fame, claimed the first title in the decade, with the second of their back-to-back championships in 1989-1990 coming in their third con-secutive trip to the NBA Finals.

The Bulls ushered in a changing of the guard the following season, however, sweeping the demoralized Pistons in the 1991 Eastern Con-ference finals and earning a chance to match up against the seasoned Los Angeles Lakers, featuring Finals-tested stars Magic Johnson, James Worthy, and Byron Scott.

It was a dream Finals matchup for the NBA, pitting the marquee team of the 1980s—the Showtime-era Lakers claimed five champi-onships in that decade—against the up-and-coming Bulls, who, in addition to Jordan, also featured an emerging star in Scottie Pippen.

And it was no contest.

The Lakers claimed Game One, with Jordan missing a game-tying shot at the buzzer, but Chicago, and MJ in particular, was unstoppable the rest of the way. Chicago won the next four games—and, in truth, didn't stop winning championships until His Airness retired.

Twice.

In addition to the 1991 championship, Jordan led the Bulls to titles in 1992 (4-2 over Portland) and 1993 (4-2 over Phoenix) before stunning the sports world with a surprise off-season retirement following the murder of his father.

Jordan then revisited a childhood fantasy by making a foray into minor league baseball, generously allowing a two-year, mid-decade reign by the Houston Rockets and their MVP Hakeem Olajuwon. The Rockets rallied from a 3-2 deficit to defeat the New York Knicks in a grueling seven-game series in 1994.

With a faxed statement that simply read, "I'm back," Jordan returned to the NBA in mid-March 1995. His skills were a bit rusty, however, and he was unable to get the Bulls past Orlando, which not only featured young stars Shaquille O'Neal and Anfernee Hardaway, but also former Bull vet Horace Grant. The Magic ousted the Bulls 4-2 in the Eastern Conference semis. Historians and fans will note that proved to be the last play-off series Jordan's Bulls ever lost.

After knocking off Indiana 4-3 in the Eastern finals, Orlando was no match for the Rockets, who won the second of their back-to-back titles with a sweep of the Magic.

Rust was not a problem for Jordan in the 1995-1996 season. The revamped Bulls completely dominated the league from start to finish. Gone were key members of the Bulls' three-peat championship squad from two years earlier, including John Paxson, Bill Cartwright, and Grant, and in their place were Steve Kerr, Luc Longley, and the cross-dressing Dennis Rodman. Other key additions included lanky forward Toni Kukoc, from Europe, and Ron Harper. Led by Jordan and Pippen, the Bulls posted an NBA-record 72-10 regular season mark. The Bulls then went 15-3 overall in the play-offs, bumping off Seattle 4-2 in the Finals to regain the championship.

AN EMERGING THREAT

Until that time, the Bulls had faced four different opponents in each of their Finals forays. In succession, Chicago had knocked off the Los Angeles Lakers, Portland, Phoenix, and Seattle. Once vanquished, none of those teams would ever return to face the Bulls.

This trend was about to change.

After many years of finding themselves just a notch or two behind contenders in the Western Conference, the steady and predictable Utah Jazz finally seemed poised for a run at the title. The Jazz, behind power forward Karl Malone and point guard John Stockton, arguably two of the best players to ever play their respective positions, were no strangers to the play-offs, as Utah had appeared in the postseason every year since 1984.

At 6'9", 240 pounds, the sculpted Malone was a dominating presence inside and out. A punishing finisher around the basket, Malone had also developed a deadly midrange outside game, making him doubly difficult to defend. The crafty Stockton, in his thirteenth year during the 1996-1997 season, was already the NBA all-time career leader in both assists and steals. Together, the two future Hall-of-Famers were enough to make the Jazz play-off contenders year after year. They simply needed a stronger supporting cast, however, to make that final push. They gradually improved their roster with the development of draft picks such as second-rounders Bryon Russell and Shandon Anderson, and first-rounder Greg Ostertag. The key puzzle piece, however, fit into place when the team acquired shooting guard Jeff Hornacek from the Philadelphia 76ers. Now in his third full season in Utah, Hornacek, with his deadly outside shot and sharp passing skills, was the perfect complement to the Stockton-Malone tandem.

The Jazz had appeared in the Western Conference finals three times, and were one win away from the Finals in 1996 before dropping a 90-86 decision to Seattle in Game Seven. The Jazz had also come close the previous two years, losing a pair of series to eventual champion Houston. The Jazz, like the rest of the league at that time, simply had no answer for Olajuwon and his myriad "Dream-shake" offensive maneuvers.

But the 1996-1997 season proved different for the Jazz, who posted a 64-18 record for the best mark in the West. With homecourt advantage secured until the Finals, Utah personally eliminated Los Angeles from the postseason, bouncing the Clippers 3-0 in the first round and the Lakers 4-1 in the second.

Which brought up a Jazz-Rockets play-off matchup for the third time in four years. The Western Conference finals went according to form for the first five games, with each team holding serve on its home court. With Houston leading 90-77 midway through the fourth quarter, it appeared Game Six would follow suit, setting up a series-clinching seventh game at the Delta Center.

Stockton, however, had other ideas.

Stockton led a mini-rally, but the Jazz still trailed 98-91 inside of the two-minute mark. Stockton found Russell for a trey to trim the deficit to four. Stockton followed that up with a driving layup at the 1:22 mark, then picked up a steal on the other end, and ran that in to tie the game with 1:03 to play. Houston's Charles Barkley made a pair of free throws and Stockton tied the game again on a leaning jumper in the key. When Clyde Drexler could not convert for Houston, Utah had the ball out of bounds with two ticks on the clock.

By this point in his career, Stockton had also developed into the Jazz player elected to take that one shot at the end of a game with the outcome on the line. Though not quite on the level of Jordan—and really, who is?—Stockton was already accomplished in the clutch and could beat an opponent in any number of ways, whether it be by shot, a pass to an open teammate on offense, by drawing an offensive foul, or recording yet another steal on defense. Game Six against Houston that year was the perfect example. The smallest man on the court, Stockton was the biggest factor as he beat the Rockets every which way during those final minutes.

It was no surprise then that the Jazz put their fate—and the ball—in Stockton's hands. Stockton received the inbounds pass from Russell, and behind a Malone screen—albeit a moving one—he calmly launched a wide-open 3-pointer at the buzzer. It is interesting to listen to repeats of the NBC broadcast of that game. Right before Stockton released his shot, one announcer, who sounds an awful lot like Bill Walton, could be heard muttering, "Uh, oh." The shot ripped cord, sparking a mad on-court celebration that even involved the hard-nosed Sloan.

Stockton scored 13 of Utah's final 15 points. He also recorded assists on a pair of 3-pointers—giving him a hand in the Jazz's final 19 points.

"You see why John Stockton is one of the five best players I've ever played against," said Barkley. "That guy is as tough as nails. Karl Malone deserved to be the MVP, but he wouldn't be there without John Stockton."

The Jazz were finally going to the Finals.

THE 1997 FINALS

The Jazz arrived in Chicago unaccustomed, certainly, to the hoopla that would surround such a series. But the team, molded in the image of Sloan, would prove to be unintimidated playing on the world's stage. Whether or not that would be enough to contend with the four-time champion Bulls remained to be seen. To have a legitimate shot at dethroning the Bulls, the Jazz needed to win one of the first two games on the road at the United Center. Utah had the perfect opportunity to steal a game in the opener when Malone, who beat out Jordan in voting for league MVP honors, stepped to the line with 9 seconds remaining and the score knotted at 82.

He clanked both free throws.

Once again, basketball fans need only rewind the video highlights to picture what happened next. In a scene replayed time and time again, Jordan patiently wound the clock down while working against Russell—Utah's supposed stopper. Russell got greedy and made the mistake of reaching out and stabbing at the ball in an attempted steal. Jordan smoothly evaded him, shifted left, and stuck a jumper from the left wing to win the game 84-82.

The main block of press seating at the United Center is directly behind the basket in front of the Bulls' bench—the same basket where Jordan just put a game-ending dagger in another opponent. How many times had I watched games on TV and seen Jordan knock in the winning shot? How many times had I seen the late-night ESPN highlights, dissecting, analyzing, and breaking down every breath of yet another Jordan moment? It was unbelievably surreal, for the first time, to see it unfold before my very eyes. Suddenly I had empathy for the Cleveland Cavaliers and their endurance of not one, but two series-deciding Game Five buzzer-beaters. Craig Ehlo meet Bryon Russell. And the torch is passed.

The series had only begun.

The three days between the first and second games naturally focused on Jordan and Malone. The story lines were obvious and, in truth, too easy to determine by the events of the final 9 seconds. Much had already been written comparing the two superstars, starting back in the conference finals series when Malone was awarded the league's MVP ahead of Jordan. Malone missing those final free throws, followed by Jordan's heroics, only fueled the comparisons, fairly or not.

The press conferences the day after Game One offered an interesting contrast and insight between the two, which I will never forget. In a lighthearted and jovial session, Jordan discussed his shot and his penchant for hitting game-winners. It was all the more intriguing because he had a popular commercial out at the time that highlighted the 26 potential game-winning shots he had taken—and missed—which easily exceeded the number of game-winners he'd converted. Jordan's implication was clear: He did not fear failure, which, in turn, allowed him to succeed on a much greater scale. Miss or make, he was not afraid to let the outcome ride on his abilities.

Malone's press conference offered the polar opposite view. Malone said it was his fear of failure that had driven him to the weight room nearly every day since his rookie season. It was his fear of letting himself and his teammates down that provided the inspiration for his fanatical off-season training regimen. It was his fear of disappointing some fan in any city who might have bought a ticket to see him mixing it up out on the court, that had driven him to play through every injury, year in and year out—to the point where he had missed only five games over the course of thirteen years in the league, three of those by league suspension. His message was clear: His fear of failing himself and others had been the driving force behind his rise to stardom. Picked thirteenth by the Jazz in 1985, Malone remains the lowest-drafted player ever to win the NBA's Most Valuable Player award—and by the end of the decade he would do it twice.

One star driven to success by his fear of failure, the other by his disdain of it. An intriguing dichotomy.

The Bulls cruised to a 97-85 victory in Game Two before the series shifted to Salt Lake City—where the Jazz owned the best home record in the league—for the next three contests. The Jazz rolled to a 104-93 win in the third game before evening the series with a 78-73 victory in Game Four.

That game featured an exciting finish as well, as Stockton took the game over much as he did against Houston in Game Six of the Western finals. The Jazz were trailing 71-66 when Utah's Stock options rose. With time running down on the 24-second clock, Stockton threw in a 3-pointer from the parking lot with 2:23 to play that completely swung the momentum over to the Jazz.

"In reality, the play that hurt us the most was Stockton throwing in a 3-pointer from about 28 feet that got them back in the ballgame," Jackson said. "We had all the momentum and I don't know, three minutes, two minutes and a half to go in the ballgame. And he came up with a rather large shot."

Stockton said not much thought went into his decision to shoot.

"I just shot it. I don't know, you just play. I'm not a cerebral player. When I'm out on the floor, I just try to play and I'm very fortunate that it fell."

Then, as Jordan was maneuvering for a shot against Russell, Stockton anticipated MJ's spin perfectly from the backside and picked his pocket. Stockton raced down court, but Jordan caught him before he could make an uncontested layup. Jordan got a piece of the ball, but enough of Stockton to earn a foul. Stockton made one of the two free throws to cut Chicago's lead to 73-70.

"He picked me clean, I think," admitted Jordan. "I was more or less looking at Russell and I felt like I had him in an advantage situation. And I went to spin. He got the ball and knocked it away.

"I didn't think Stockton would gamble on that play," Jordan said. "In Chicago, it would be a foul. Here, it's a great play."

Stockton then pulled down a missed Pippen shot and Pippen fouled him. Stockton hit both free throws, inching the Jazz to within one point.

Then came one of those signature plays that stand out long after a series is over. The kind of play Jordan has so many of. Hauling in a missed Jordan jumper, Stockton saw a streaking Malone and instinctively let fly with an off-stride heave to the other end of the court that barely eluded Jordan's fingertips. The ball was cradled home by Malone for a layup and a one-point Jazz lead.

"I think if you could have suspended time right there as the ball was in the air, Jerry [Sloan] would have probably strangled me for throwing it," Stockton said. "But it got there and it was one of those 'No, no, no, no, yes!' type of deals."

"I'll remember that pass for the rest of my life," Malone said. "Of all the passes, that may be the biggest of his career. It had to be perfect to get over Michael.

"I never even thought about doing anything fancy or dunking the ball. All I remembered was the first thing I learned in high school: Put it on the square."

The Jazz were still ahead by one with 18 seconds to play and, in a scene eerily similar to Game One, Malone on the free throw line for a pair of tosses. Pippen, who had walked up to Malone before his crucial misses at the end of Game One and said, "The Mailman doesn't deliver on Sunday," again tried to rattle Malone from behind. But Stockton set an intervening pick, intercepting Pippen before he could reach Malone.

Malone hit both free throws to help seal the win and even the series at 2-2.

"I wanted that chance again," Malone said of the key free throws. "You call it redemption or whatever. I just wanted a chance again.

"I usually think of faraway places while at the line," he said, "but all I could think of is 650 million fans watching me."

"Karl Malone is not lunchmeat," Jordan told reporters following the game. "In Malone and John Stockton, we're talking about two of the top 50 players (ever) in the game."

Game Five

If Jordan had taught the Bulls one thing, it was that games are won in the fourth quarter, not the first.

The Jazz went for the quick Game Five knockout in the first half, but the Bulls, behind a monster effort from an ill Jordan, were the ones left standing at the end. Well, everyone except Jordan, who had to be helped off the court by Pippen after his 38-point effort.

With a chance to capture a 3-2 series lead before heading back to Chicago, the Jazz shot out of the gate and built a 16-point lead early in the second quarter. But on the verge of being blown out, the Bulls erased that deficit before the half.

"That's one of the scariest things you can have in basketball, especially in a game like this," said Sloan of his team's explosive start. "And Chicago knows it. Anybody that plays knows it. When you come out and try to blow a team away, which is what it looked like we were trying to do, are you going to have the energy to finish?"

A lack of energy did not deter Jordan, who was playing with a temperature of 100 degrees and suffering from food poisoning, from scoring 15 of his points in the final quarter. After the Bulls survived Utah's first flurry, the Jazz made another significant push late in the third and early in the fourth periods. Chris Morris' 3-pointer gave Utah a 77-69 lead with 10:19 to play.

It took the Bulls only 49 seconds to tie the score and 1:19 to grab the lead.

In the most important quarter in franchise history, the Jazz offense was anemic. Utah shot only 4 of 17 from the floor.

"We got tentative and stopped passing to the open people," said Utah reserve Greg Foster. "You can't get scared. You can't play not to win, and we did."

The key shot in Chicago's 90-88 victory was—stop me if you've heard this before—delivered by Jordan. After pulling in an offensive rebound and after Russell inexplicably left him to double-team Pippen, Jordan drained a 3-pointer from the top of the key with 25 seconds left to break the game's final tie.

After the game, which ended Utah's 23-game win streak at the Delta Center, everybody was talking about Jordan's amazing performance.

"In all my years playing with Michael, I've never seen him that sick," Pippen said. "He couldn't talk (before the game). I didn't think he could even put his uniform on."

"Before the game he was laying down in the locker room in the dark and everyone was concerned about his health," said teammate Jud Buechler. "The thing is, the rest of us were happy because the last time he was sick he scored about 40 points."

"I almost played myself into passing out," Jordan said. "I'm just glad we won because if we'd lost, it would have been very devastating."

One for the Thumb

Game Six of this series was reminiscent of Game One—a hotly contested affair that would be determined by yet another defining Jordan moment, this one for a different reason.

Once again the score was tied in the waning moments, the ball in Jordan's hands, the serve in his court. Similar to Game One, Jordan maneuvered against Russell looking for the win.

In a timeout immediately preceding the key segment, Jordan had called over to Kerr, warning him to look for the pass in case of a double-team. And that's exactly how it happened. After deciding so many games with career-defining shots, this time Jordan set up a fifth championship with a pass to Kerr, left open at the free throw line by a doubling Stockton. Kerr knocked down the shot with 5 seconds left on the clock.

The Jazz did have time for one last play, but Russell's inbounds pass was stolen by Pippen, who deflected a pass intended for Anderson. Pippen then dove for the loose ball, tipping it to Kukoc, who raced downcourt for an uncontested dunk at the buzzer, accounting for the final 90-86 margin and setting off delirium in the United Center.

"Tonight, Steve Kerr earned his wings, from my perspective," Jordan said. "'Cause I had faith in him. He believed in himself and I passed him the ball and he knocked the shot down."

It was an intriguing scene standing on the floor of the United Center, looking up as multicolored confetti rained down to the strains of "Sweet Home Chicago" blaring throughout the arena. Little did I know what was in store a year later.

THE 1998 PLAY-OFFS

The previous year's Finals had been a necessary learning experience for the Jazz, which paid further dividends during the following season. Utah and Chicago both finished the regular season with NBA-best records of 62-20, but the homecourt edge swung to Utah by virtue of a 2-0 mark against the Bulls. In the game in Salt Lake City, the Jazz rallied from a 24-point second-quarter deficit for a 101-93 victory. NBA followers all suspected a Bulls-Jazz rematch in the

Finals, but the two teams faced disparate paths to their return engagement.

Although it took the Jazz 82 games to ensure homecourt advantage throughout the play-offs for the first time in franchise history, it only took them one postseason contest to lose it.

Old nemesis Houston bounced the Jazz 103-90 in the first-round opener between Midwest Division rivals. Utah claimed the second game, but fell behind 2-1 with a loss in Game Three. Facing a pair of elimination games, the Jazz responded with two blowout victories.

The Jazz were also tested in the second round by San Antonio, bolstered by the addition of Rookie of the Year Tim Duncan. Utah won the series 4-1, but two Utah home wins weren't decided until the final seconds and the Spurs served early notice that they would contend the following season.

In the East, Chicago's first two rounds were fairly uneventful as the Bulls rolled over New Jersey 3-0 and Charlotte 4-1 to reach the Eastern Conference finals against Indiana. The Bulls-Pacers series would be anything but easy for the two-time defending champions, however.

Conference Finals

Utah's struggles in the opening two rounds had left the Jazz appearing somewhat vulnerable, and there were some doubts heading into the conference finals against the Los Angeles Lakers. As a result of their second-round series the previous year and some testy regular-season encounters in the 1997-1998 regular season, there were some definite hard feelings and hard talk between the two teams. The Lakers had been absolutely dominating in their second-round ouster of Seattle, steamrolling the Sonics with an average victory margin of 16.7 points in the final four games.

But something funny happened on the way to the Finals. The Jazz swept the Lakers, claiming the final two games in the Great Western Forum—a building that literally oozed NBA history.

On one wall of the house that Jack (that's Kent Cooke, not Nicholson) built, there were the Lakers' six NBA championship banners, won between 1972 and 1988.

On another wall, there were seven retired jerseys enclosed in glass frames, bearing the names of former Laker greats. From left to right, the names read Goodrich, Worthy, Johnson, Abdul-Jabbar, West, Chamberlain, and Baylor. No first names necessary.

And when the Jazz finished up their Western Conference finals sweep, they strolled off the court happy but, more important, composed and restrained. There was no mad celebration as there had been the previous year against Houston.

"Probably of all the things I'm most proud of, it's how we walked into the locker room," Malone said. "We were not surprised."

The Forum's visiting locker room . . . a place with quite a bit of history itself.

On May 5, 1969, Laker great Jerry West sat disconsolate in his own locker room on the other side of the wall, listening to the Boston Celtics whooping it up after beating LA in Game Seven of that year's Finals. West was just named MVP of the series—the only time the award has not been won by a member of the championship team—but it was no consolation.

When West, LA's general manager, visited the Laker locker room after Utah's sweep in 1998, he heard no such celebrating on the other side of the wall.

"We celebrate in our own way," noted Stockton in the cramped visitors locker room. "We're kind of a private team."

"Everybody is pleased in here, but we're not going to show it. We want to win the whole thing; that's where we're coming from."

Winning the Western Conference finals in front of a backlot of movie stars and accomplishing it in a building with so much history added no small amount of significance.

"There's banners up there and you see Magic (Johnson) out there (in the stands), but we're not playing those guys," Hornacek said.

Earvin "Magic" Johnson, co-owner and vice president of the team he personally guided to five NBA championships, was in the house for Game Four—and he was not very pleased with how the Lakers cleaned up after themselves.

"There's just something missing with this team," Johnson said. "I don't mind that we lost 4-0. I do mind that we didn't play with a sense of urgency. And then we played the same for [all] four games. You cannot play the same for four games against a team this smart. They will pick you apart. [The Jazz] are better, but not 4-0 better. We lost because we did not adjust. They made adjustments; we didn't."

Johnson, it turns out, was just warming up. Holding an impromptu press conference for a small group of reporters in the hallway outside the press room, an animated Magic could not hold back his emotions.

"I'm really upset at this. They go in and we let them lay it up. We go in and they foul us. That's the sign of a championship team. [The Jazz] play hard, they play together, they play smart. When we understand that, we will be champions."

Johnson continued his tirade, "Also we didn't show the class we're supposed to show. The talk about the referees, the fans, forget all that. Even before the series we were talking about them holding and grabbing. Hey, I held and grabbed, too. That's how you win. Nobody plays by the book and wins."

The Lakers would eventually learn all those lessons Johnson spoke about that day. But they would have to wait until 2000.

The Bulls, meanwhile, had already learned all the lessons they would ever need—and they needed all of them against the Pacers. The home team would go on to win every single game in this series, but there were three down-to-the-wire finishes—all Pacer victories. The Bulls held on for an 88-83 win in Game Seven, setting up a much-anticipated rematch with the Jazz.

THE LAST DANCE (1998 FINALS)

With mounting squabbles between himself and management, Phil Jackson had earlier dubbed Chicago's season, "The Last Dance." Pippen also complained about his contract throughout the season, and Jordan had gone on record as saying he would play for no other coach than Jackson and planned to retire if the Bulls let their coach walk away. Considering the team's brutal seven-game series with Indiana (while Utah had ten days off after sweeping the Lakers) and all the internal bickering—the Chicago dynasty appeared to be teetering.

Jordan as an underdog? Hard to believe, but momentarily true.

The Jazz and Bulls picked up where they left off the previous year. Déjà vu, but not over again. Once more, Game One of the Finals came down to a Jazz Dream Teamer at the free throw line with a chance to seal a victory. But unlike last year, when Malone failed to convert on his pair of charity tosses late in Game One, this time around Stockton did, paving the way for an 88-85 overtime victory for the Jazz.

Stockton had converted a running floater in the lane over Kerr with 9.3 seconds left in overtime, giving the Jazz what appeared to be a relatively safe 86-82 lead. But Kukoc rained in a 3-pointer with 5.4 seconds to trim Utah's lead to one. The Bulls immediately fouled Stockton on the inbounds pass. His two free throws provided the final margin.

"We came in great, gave a great effort and we had chances to win," Jordan said. "When you're on the road, if you have chances to win, that's all you can ask for. It's up to you next time to capitalize on it."

The Bulls would do just that in Game Two.

Chicago players claimed all along they were coming to Salt Lake City to earn a split—and that's what they earned with a 93-88 victory in the second game. Still, considering the fact that no NBA home team has ever swept the middle three contests since the league adopted the 2-3-2 Finals format, it seemed likely the series would return to Utah.

Considering the magnitude of the third game in a 1-1 series, it is difficult to comprehend Utah's performance in Game Three. The Bulls tattooed the Jazz 96-54 in a game that didn't even seem *that* close. The game set numerous Finals records for futility. To wit: Utah's 54 points were the lowest ever scored in a Finals contest—smashing the old mark by 17 points. The Jazz also set new marks for fewest field goals in a game (21) and points in a half (23). The Bulls set a new record for largest margin of victory in the Finals (42). And to top it all off, the Jazz set a new all-time standard for offensive incompetence, for the least amount of points in any NBA game since the advent of the 24-second clock.

The acerbic Sloan dissed the Jazz for their inability to adapt to Chicago's defense.

"You have to adjust," he said. "We didn't have time to call a practice to work on it."

Rodman on the Run

Everybody knows the early bird gets the worm, but what does the late "Worm" get?

Fined.

Frequently.

With Chicago—the city and the team—in high spirits following the unprecedented blowout, it seemed like a good time for another Rodman distraction. The year before, Rodman, tagged with the nickname "Worm" as a youth for the way he "squirmed like a worm" while playing arcade games, had been fined by the league for anti-Mormon comments made while the series was in Utah. He also jetted off to Las Vegas following team practice sessions on off-game days. This time around, instead of attending his team's practice session the morning after Game Three, Rodman called in sick—or something like that.

"I talked to Dennis," Jackson informed members of the media. "He did not speak back."

"He never tells me he's got a flat or, 'The dog ate my keys,'" Jackson said, having some fun at Rodman's expense. "I asked, 'Dennis, what do you want me to tell the press?' and he hung up on me."

Rodman hang-ups are something Jackson and the Bulls were well acquainted with.

"There would be no society if we were all like Dennis," Jackson said. "There would be no lines on freeways. He is not a normal member of society. That's why those that understand him love him, and those that don't despise him."

Jackson was asked if he sometimes felt like a kindergarten teacher when it comes to dealing with Rodman.

"No," he deadpanned, "it's a little more like being in special ed."

So, in the end, where was Rodman?

He turned up in Detroit with Hulk Hogan at a World Championship Wrestling event.

It's a good thing for the Bulls that he also turned up for Game Four in Chicago.

Games Four and Five

The fourth game of the Finals showed why the Bulls paid Rodman big bucks—and it was not because he returned a lot of it back to them in the form of fines. When he was so inclined, the multitattooed guy with Crayola-colored hair could flat out rebound, defend, and wreak havoc on the opposition.

In Game Four, he did all of the above and connected on some key free throws—going 5 of 6 from the line in the fourth quarter, including four in a row in the final 2:53—to keep the Bulls ahead. In the final period, he also pulled down four rebounds, two of them on the offensive end, while holding Malone to two points and three shots.

Go figure. Jordan certainly couldn't.

"I can never figure this guy out, I won't even start," Jordan said of Rodman following the game, an 86-82 Bulls victory. "One day he's wrestling, the next day he's defending. We have come to live with it and not really try to dissect this individual, but somehow he is always ready to play the game of basketball and especially when time is really of the essence. I know you guys were probably ready to write a bad article about him today, tomorrow. (Then) the guy steps up and makes four free throws in the closing minutes. What else can you say about him? He may go wrestle tomorrow. He may not show up for practice, I don't know. But he seems to excel in adversity. And we have to come to grips with that. It's amazing."

With a 3-1 series advantage and Game Five at home—where the Jazz were 0-5 over the past two Finals—the Bulls were looking to wrap things up without a return trip to Salt Lake City. That would not happen.

Coming off a Game Four effort for which he was widely criticized for passive play, Malone hoisted the Jazz on his massive shoulders throughout Game Five, scoring 39 points and dominating play on both ends of the court as the Jazz extended the series with an 83-81 victory. In addition to his scoring, Malone grabbed 10 rebounds and dished out 5 assists in a well-rounded effort. Malone rallied the Jazz from a 36-30 halftime deficit by scoring 17 points in the third quarter.

"I try to get ready to play the same all the time and unfortunately you don't have the games you want to have all the time," Malone said. "And that's the nature of the business. But it's just one game, you've got to take the good with the bad, and just take their doses and try not to listen to everything said about you—because you know it's not good. So you try not to read the paper."

Despite Malone's great game, the outcome still hinged on a final shot by Jordan.

Doesn't it always?

Trailing by two, the Bulls had an inbound opportunity with 1.1 seconds remaining. Jordan got off a 3-pointer, but the shot fell short.

"I was sitting there thinking about the whole thing, and at 1.1 I knew I wanted the ball, but no one knew what was going to happen,"

Jordan said of the final sequence. "That's part of my personality, that's the way things have always happened for me in my career. I was sure everybody was hoping it would end that way, except for Utah people, which at 1.1 seconds, everybody was kind of holding their breath—which is kind of cute."

Except for the Jazz and their fans, nobody had been expecting, or wanting, a return trip to Salt Lake City, whether it entailed one or two games.

"How long do *you* want to stay in Utah?" Pippen asked the assembled media. "I know no one wanted to make this trip, especially the players. I'm sure you guys don't want to make the trip, all of you guys who are not from Utah. But we have to do it. And it's very disappointing on our part that we have to do it. We wanted the season to end tonight."

TALE OF TWO CITIES

With their on-court rivalry heating up over the course of back-to-back Finals, it's interesting to take a look at the differences between the Bulls and Jazz—and their respective cities—circa 1998.

"One's a major city and one isn't," opined Jordan.

Speaking of air, the Jazz say Delta, while the Bulls say United.

The Bulls featured a "Worm" stiffing practice in the middle of the Finals and jetting to Detroit to don tights in a made-for-TV wrestling event. The Jazz featured a "Mailman," wearing leather while riding a Harley and practicing with his teammates before taking his wife to the hospital for a truly special delivery—the birth of their fourth child, Karlee.

The Bulls were a team without a true point guard. The Jazz were a team with, perhaps, the game's best-ever true point guard.

Chicago sits near a Great Lake. Salt Lake takes its name from a pretty great lake.

The Bulls ran the triangle offense. Many observers considered the Jazz's pick-and-roll-based offense square.

Chicago coach Jackson publicly feuded with management and terminated his tenure with the Bulls after the season. His Utah counterpart, Sloan, quietly signed a contract extension with the Jazz, which was not announced until after the Finals.

Jordan started the shaved-head look in the NBA. Malone, then a pitchman for Rogaine, tried to end it. (He failed.)

Chicago's best-known executive was Jerry Krause, a short little fat man loathed by the players and city alike. Utah's biggest exec was Frank Layden—well before he lost 100 pounds on a diet—who remained the toast of the team and the town despite stepping down as coach ten years earlier.

Chicago—a river runs through it. Utah resident Robert Redford made the movie of the same name.

Jackson hung six banners from the United Center rafters—one for each of his team's championships. Sloan hung one there—his retired jersey from his playing days as a Bull.

Jackson practices Zen Buddhism in Chicago. Sloan follows John Deere-ism in Salt Lake.

Rodman enjoys Hooters at all hours. The Jazz despise night owls.

The Bulls once fired Sloan. The Jazz hired him—and might never let him go.

There's no denying that the Bulls' way was not the Jazz way.

"Thank goodness," said both sides, finally sharing some rare common ground.

STORYBOOK FINISH

It was halftime of Game Six and the Bulls were on the ropes.

Chicago had led 17-8 in the first quarter when Pippen was forced out of the lineup with an injured back. The Jazz promptly outscored Chicago 41-28 the remainder of the half to take a 49-45 advantage.

As the Bulls filed into the locker room, one by one they peered into the trainers' room, where Pippen was receiving treatment, in an attempt to verify his playing status.

Jordan walked in behind them. Instead of looking in on Pippen, Jordan looked squarely at his teammates.

"Don't even look in there," Jordan said. "If he ain't goin' in, he ain't goin' in."

Pippen did return in the second half, but his contributions were limited. He totaled only 8 points and 3 rebounds, well below his averages for the series. As for Jordan, he did not have the best of games stat-wise. Yes, he did pour in 45 points, but he shot only 15 of 35 from the field. He did record 4 steals, but posted only 1 rebound and 1 assist.

As unfathomable as it seems right now, there will come a time when the world will be filled with basketball fans who never had a chance to experience Jordan's greatness firsthand. I would invite them to put in a videotape of the final 37 seconds of 1998's Game Six—Jordan's last game in a Bulls uniform. It will show them all they need to know.

With the Jazz ahead 86-83, Jordan spun around Russell and converted a layup over Carr, pulling the Bulls to within one.

On the other end of the court, the Jazz pounded it inside to Malone, who had 31 points in the contest, on the left block. Jordan trailed his man, Hornacek, past Malone and partway through the key. He then turned, snuck around, and stripped Malone from behind with under 20 seconds to play.

After running the clock down, Jordan converted his infamous game-winning jumper with 5.2 to play.

Bulls 87, Jazz 86.

But he still wasn't done.

Knowing Utah would turn to Stockton, Jordan hounded the Jazz point guard into a hurried 3-pointer that rimmed out at the buzzer—not a very good shot considering the time remaining and the score.

There were four big plays down the stretch of Game Six—and Jordan made every one of them.

He was, as he explained later, in the moment.

"My thoughts are very positive," he said. "And the crowd gets quiet. The moment starts to become the moment for me. And that's what we've been—that's part of the Zen Buddhism stuff. Once you get in the moment, you know you're there. Things start to move slowly, you start to see the court very well. You start reading what the defense is trying to do. And I saw that. I saw the moment. When I saw that Russell reached, I took advantage of that moment and I never doubted myself."

Looking back on that moment, it occurs to me that the NBA may never be the same after Jordan's shot as it was before it. It was a magical moment by a most magical player in a magical era of popularity for the league.

The NBA had lost a good deal of that magic that off-season with a huge labor impasse. The owners locked the players out the following

preseason and for the first time the NBA lost regular season games—
32 per team to be exact—to labor strife.

The San Antonio Spurs claimed the last championship of the decade, downing the New York Knicks 4-1 in the 1999 Finals. It was all
a rather anticlimactic ending to a most exciting decade.

I still wonder if the NBA will ever regain the level of popularity
and mystique it enjoyed on the day its greatest player experienced his
greatest moment.

I doubt it.

> Ten years from now, 20 years from now, what I hear people say-
> ing I would want people to say, and it's simple . . . that if Michael
> Jordan were still playing the game of basketball, he would dom-
> inate.

> Michael Jordan.[2]

NOTES

1. As assistant sports editor for *The Daily Herald* in Provo, Utah, Doug Fox covered the Utah Jazz from 1994 to 1999. He attended all twelve games between the
Utah Jazz and Chicago Bulls in the 1997 and 1998 NBA Finals. Most of the
thoughts, facts, quotes, and game highlights detailed in this chapter are the result of
his game, practice, and press conference and personal interview coverage during
that time for *The Daily Herald*. Some additional facts were verified through "The
Official NBA Encyclopedia," Doubleday, Third Edition, 2000.

2. "Michael Jordan: To The Max," presented by MVP.com, NBA Entertainment,
2000.

Chapter 16

King James: LeBron James, Hype, Hope, and the Future of the NBA

Bob Batchelor

And like most great players, the game seems like it's in slow motion when they play. They seem to visualize something before it happens. They *feel* it as much as play it, just as a virtuoso musician *feels* the notes without even glancing at the score in front of him.

Terry Pluto

A handful of years ago, on the playgrounds in and around Cleveland, whispers circulated about a young kid down in Akron who had mind-boggling basketball skills. He combined these traits with a kind of otherworldly athletic ability that cannot be taught: size, speed, vision, and a natural feel for the game. The budding superstar's name was LeBron James.

That anyone even paid attention to the rise of a player in Akron was news in itself—the gulf between the two cities, despite a distance of only forty miles, is like that of warring nations. Cleveland always captured the limelight in Northeast Ohio, particularly when the Indians were winning and the Browns returned from football purgatory. Akron, on the other hand, played the role of the region's lesser stepsister.

On the west side of Cleveland, where schoolboy legends (and future pros) Sam Clancy (USC/Philadelphia 76ers) and Steve Logan (Cincinnati/Golden State Warriors) ruled, there was too much excitement over the prospects of a state championship for traditional sports powerhouse St. Edwards High School to really pay attention to the

young superstar from the small school with the funny name, St. Vincent-St. Mary or, more commonly, SVSM.

But this kid was special. When sketchy rumors turned into hard
facts, the story seemed too typically rags-to-riches to be true, like the
creation of the perfect athlete by some shoe company for marketing
purposes. He hit 6'4" as a freshman and helped lead his team to the
state championship, despite a tumultuous home life and being raised
by a single mother in Akron's toughest ghetto.

With the state championship in hand and skills that seemed beyond
compare, sports enthusiasts in Ohio could no longer ignore what
seemed to be inevitable. James was a special athlete—the kind that
comes along maybe once in a lifetime. New whispers surfaced and almost always included the phrase, "the next Michael Jordan."

THE NATIONAL SPOTLIGHT
AND THE RISE OF "KING" JAMES

Two events changed LeBron James's young life forever: appearing
on the cover of *Sports Illustrated* in early 2002 (when only a junior in
high school) christened "The Chosen One," and then seven months
later having a game against perennial high school champions Oak
Hill Academy nationally televised on ESPN2.

The *SI* magazine article and flurry of copycat stories that followed
put him on the national radar screen. The hype machine included another cover story, this time for *ESPN The Magazine,* revealing a much
different James dealing with his newfound fame and the subsequent
avalanche of publicity. As Ohio's largest newspaper, Cleveland's *The
Plain Dealer* took over the James watch, virtually covering his every
move, including "The James Journal," a compendium of all things
LeBron.

The attention of the print media placed James on a pedestal. Before
the rise of the Internet and countless new media outlets (from talk radio shows to cable television programming), this degree of buildup
would have been reserved for a mere handful of proven superstars.
However, in the twenty-first century, when many celebrities are famous for little more than being famous, a high school superstar can
grab the interest of the world. And yet, despite all the hype, relatively
few people had actually seen James play basketball. Many people
could recite his statistics, they could relay what they had heard col-

lege and NBA officials say about him, and they knew his teams won, but they simply had never seen it for themselves.

That all changed, however, in late 2002 when ESPN2 televised the SVSM matchup with Oak Hill Academy. The network then followed the first broadcast with an early 2003 game against Mater Dei High School at the famed Pauley Pavilion on UCLA's campus, a basketball temple in the heart of La-La land. Befitting a legend in the making, James responded to the limelight in both games, thus cementing his position as the next big thing in the sports world.

Against Oak Hill, a crowd of more than 11,500 spectators packed Cleveland State University's Convocation Center, some paying more than $100 for courtside seats. Also in the mix were dozens of NBA scouts and officials and even a couple of players from the Cleveland Browns, all out to judge the skills of the seventeen-year-old high school phenomenon. More important, for the television network, the game drew a 1.97 rating, which equates to 1.67 million homes tuning into the high school basketball contest. James' star power made the telecast ESPN2's highest-rated program in the two years since its coverage of the death of NASCAR legend Dale Earnhardt.

James and SVSM started out slowly against Oak Hill. The young star nervously began his national television debut by missing his first three jump shots, but made up for it with several astonishing no-look passes. Rather than force the action, James attempted to get his teammates involved in the game by hitting them for wide-open baskets. As a matter of fact, in the early going, James looked more like Magic Johnson than Jordan.

Once James settled down, he took over the game as a force on offense. His most spectacular play occurred when he slipped behind the Oak Hill defense and rose up for a vicious right-handed tomahawk dunk. As James left the ground, it looked as if he was taking an elevator to the top floor, rising higher than seemed possible. Whenever he powered it through the hoop, his eyes looked at rim level. Replayed over and over on ESPN, and even leaving sideline commentators Dick Vitale and Bill Walton a bit breathless, the dunk solidified James' reputation and provided fans with a signature play by which to remember the youngster.

Years of whispered rumors were suddenly reality—the man-child had hops and could throw down. Obviously, James was a full-fledged NBA superstar trapped in the body of a teenager. Those who knew the game could sense the electricity in his play. This was no ordinary prep star, but the next coming of the NBA.

The final box score revealed SVSM's utter dominance over the former number-one high school basketball team in America, 65-45. James lit it up for 31 points, 13 rebounds, and 6 assists in his television debut. Dr. Jack Ramsay, a Hall of Fame coach and NBA analyst, gave James high praise after his performance, concluding, "I see something of Michael Jordan in his complete game, a little Kobe Bryant when he slashes to the hoop and a bit of Magic Johnson when he fires a no-look pass to an open teammate under the hoop." Ramsay, who won an NBA championship with the Portland Trailblazers in 1977, wrote that James "has NBA level skills now" and would be the first player picked in the 2003 draft.[1]

After the Oak Hill game, LeBron James would no longer be an urban legend, like playground heroes from yesteryear. His national debut and astounding success against one of the country's best high school teams turned skeptics into believers. The James hype machine went into overdrive.

Now that the world knew James's game was on another level, the stories about his friendships with NBA greats, including Shaquille O'Neal and Jordan, among others, seemed routine. Like his hoop idols, constantly on the road touring the nation each year as professionals, James and his SVSM crew embarked on a nationwide journey during the 2002-2003 season.

Like a barnstorming brigade from another era, the SVSM squad from Akron crisscrossed the country, from Philadelphia to Los Angeles and points in between, showcasing the nation's top high school player and the nation's (mythical) number-one team. For tiny SVSM, with a total student population of less than 600, James's star power enabled it to charge large appearance fees—allegedly ranging from $10,000 to $15,000 a game—and book first-class hotel accommodations, including, at one stop, a 30-foot-long stretch sports utility vehicle, to pick up and deliver the players.

STREET CRED

Many of today's heroes have an edge. They appear a little dangerous, often just half a step away from a good brawl or jail cell. This hardcore image appeals to the MTV generation. Teenagers always seem to fall for the kind of corporate-sponsored rebellion MTV peddles, whether it is the latest rap single providing a glimpse of street life, the "bling-bling" lifestyle, or violence-filled videogames and movies. As a matter of fact, many young people would rather sit around playing videogames than actually play a particular game itself, so the videogame companies fill their wares with action and graphics that are cartoonlike. Basketball games feature crazy dunks, high-flying acrobatics, and little, if any, fundamentals. Why shoot a 15-foot jump shot when a dunk could be had?

What may make LeBron James the perfect NBA idol for the twenty-first century is that he combines the style and grace of Michael Jordan with a healthy dose of urban culture, personified by young rappers and sports stars such as Nelly, Jay-Z, Ludacris, Allen Iverson, and the late Tupac Shakur. James has that big smile and natural good looks, which appeals to consumer product marketers, while at the same time possessing the skills and toughness that draws in the free-spending teenage demographic.

While a combination of talent and personality fueled Jordan's rise to icon status, James differs in that he is from the ghetto, thus naturally possessing more "street cred." James also more readily identifies with black urban culture. Unlike Jordan, who lived a middle-class lifestyle growing up in Wilmington, North Carolina, James has risen from the ghettoes of Akron—a rough town in the aging Rustbelt struggling to stay vibrant as the manufacturing-based economy vanished, leaving high unemployment rates and many people struggling to survive.

James and his mother (who gave birth to him when she was only sixteen years old) jumped from apartment to apartment when he was little, always searching for a little better way of life but unable to escape the vicious cycle of poverty. Similar to many young black men across the nation, James has never met his biological father.

His surrogate dad, Eddie Jackson, spent three years in jail in the early 1990s for trafficking cocaine. Jackson has been a part of James's inner circle since leaving prison, but has led a somewhat checkered path, often finding himself in trouble with the law. He recently served a three-year prison sentence for mortgage fraud, but still weighed in on James's decision-making process while behind bars.

Unlike some athletes who embellish the tough times of their youths to gain respect among their peers, James does not have to exaggerate about his experiences in the roughest sections of town. He told *Sports Illustrated,* "I saw drugs, guns, killings; it was crazy. But my mom kept food in my mouth and clothes on my back."[2]

On the court, James personifies the popular culture influences that shape today's teenagers. He wears it on his skin, in the form of multiple tattoos (which he had to cover with white athletic tape while in high school according to SVSM school rules) and the dress code teens follow—the ever-present headband, armband, droopy shorts, and oversized jersey. In the videogame and cable show world of spectacular dunks and highlight reel plays, James excels at symbolizing his generation, even though his individual game is about so much more than freewheeling acrobatics. For corporations looking for a fresh face, the youngster will appeal with his good looks and bright smile.

Some observers estimated (conservatively) that James generated $1.5 million in merchandise and revenue for a variety of companies his senior year, at a time when he could not collect a single penny from any of these outlets. With "rookie" James cards selling on on-line auction Web site eBay for up to $2,500 and autographed basketballs and jerseys going for hundreds of dollars, the $1.5 million figure could have easily been doubled, tripled, or more. While still an amateur, James was a budding industry, already outstripping most current NBA superstars as a merchandiser.

Given the notoriety of the SVSM team and James's own fame, he endured a great deal of scrutiny during high school, including some harm he brought on himself. A decade ago or more, a high school player, even of James's caliber, may not have recovered from the suspension handed down by the Ohio High School Athletic Association when the youngster accepted merchandise from a local sports apparel store. James, however, is no ordinary player and the fact that today's society revolves around lawsuits and threats of litigation helped him regain his place on the team.

Given the large amount of money James has already generated for everyone but himself, it is ironic that he was briefly suspended in early 2003 for accepting two vintage sports jerseys (a Gale Sayers replica and one of hoops great Wes Unseld). It is even more of a joke that the jerseys (valued at $845) will be considered worth little more than pocket change when the Akron player is an NBA rookie and marquee corporate spokesman.

The late-season encounter with the Ohio state athletic governing body actually did little more than feed the James frenzy. The spotlight intensified as the young star successfully played the role of victim against the state authority. James's lawyers and handlers turned the suspension into an attack on a mere high school student's desire to play basketball. For critics, however, James's defense rang hollow, principally because James was only tangentially an amateur player and his senior year was essentially one long rock-and-roll tour under the guise of high school basketball season.

James's brush with suspension may have also increased his credibility with young fans. His supporters certainly did not turn him into a villain for merely accepting a couple of shirts from a fan, a seemingly minor infraction when other athletes in the pro and college ranks are routinely arrested for everything from drug trafficking to assault and murder. The ordeal turned into something of a positive for James: many fans either viewed him as an underdog against "the man," or believed that the notoriety increased his cool factor. And, by the time he signed his big, nine-figure Nike shoe and apparel deal and landed atop the NBA draft, few even remembered the hiccup caused by the jersey fiasco.

On the streets, and particularly in the African-American community, respect is a key tenet of an individual's social mind-set. The idea of respect among young black males has been portrayed in numerous popular culture vehicles, from the Fox Network's high school drama, "Boston Public," to the lyrics of slain rapper Biggie "Notorious B.I.G." Smalls. James shows his respect for those who have given him guidance and support by publicly thanking God and showing his reverence for his mother. In return, James asks for the community to respect him for turning raw ability into brilliance.

In his first game back after the brief suspension, James put on a basketball clinic, scoring a career-high 52 points on a variety of long jumpers, slicing moves to the basket, alley-oops, and breathtaking dunks. James was so dominant that when he left the game in the fourth quarter, he had outscored the entire Westchester of Los Angeles high school team, which mustered a mere 43 points. In a nod to the respect he feels he and his team are owed, James told sports journalists after the game, "I worked hard. I made me famous." But at the same time, he thanked God and his teammates for moving one step closer to the mythical high school national championship.[3]

A few weeks later, on the night his jersey was retired from SVSM, James was similarly respectful, thanking his teammates, who have all lived through the media circus surrounding the team. "It's not just me, it's my teammates," James told the crowd in a postgame ceremony. "On the other side of the jersey from where it says 'James,' it should say, 'Teammates,' too. I couldn't have done it without them."[4]

Open displays of respect—giving people their "props"—are important signals in the African-American community and in the nation's locker rooms, where interviews are rife with talk of opponents not respecting the abilities of a certain player or team. Taunting, an attempt to demand the respect of an opposing athlete by demeaning his ability, has become such a pervasive part of sports that both the NBA and NFL had to institute antitaunting penalties to curb the outbursts.

James is not immune to the chest pounding, trash-talking style that pervades basketball, whether on the blacktop behind the local high school or in NBA arenas around the country. After dunking on an opposing player, James ferociously yells, "King James," or "You sorry," reports a writer who has covered James.[5] At one time this kind of behavior would have been punished or scorned, but now popular culture glorifies displays of individual self-importance that give athletes a kind of signature gesture that kids can mimic. Showing up an opponent not only ensures an athlete "gets his," but can make him more famous (or infamous). Several years ago, the symbolic knife across the throat had to be outlawed in many sports venues because people feared that it would lead to increased aggressiveness and violence off the playing field.

In the NBA, coaches have little or no control over the way the players conduct themselves on the court. Arrogant games of showmanship occur after so many plays that the game often devolves into successive incidences of chest thumping, muscle flexing, loud yells, and gesturing for the courtside cameras. Can anyone remember a play in which a guy scored and got fouled, then quietly went to the line to shoot the free throw without wildly mimicking or gesturing to the player he scored on?

The most ludicrous displays are when two teams are playing that are the doormats of the league, but the players are still out there talking trash, yelling into the stands, and trying to show up each other. These may be two teams who can't even sniff the play-off race and routinely get blown out by 20 points each night, but it is easy to see that the players are more concerned about their perceived status than winning games. In the NBA and NFL, players constantly celebrate individual plays, regardless of the larger context of the game. A high-light reel dunk or sack is rejoiced, even if the player's team is losing by 25 points or four touchdowns.

KING JAMES AND THE NBA

There are many similarities between James and Michael Jordan (circa the early 1980s) in addition to the familiar number 23. On the court, both have tremendous quickness and jumping ability. When the game ends, they each flash a similar multimillion-dollar smile and display an innate, natural charisma. Also, like the youthful Jordan before him, James is even criticized for having a weak jump shot—about the only Achilles' heel that can be found in his game.

Because he is routinely compared with Jordan and seemingly destined for NBA superstardom, James faces incredible pressure every single day of his life. These demands will only intensify with his status as the first pick in the 2003 NBA draft. He is supposed to single-handedly resurrect the hometown Cleveland Cavaliers, despite the franchise's history of underperformance and disappointment.

In fact, it is this level of anticipation and expectation that separates Jordan and James. Over the past several years, James has already experienced Michael Jordan-level attention. Every move he makes on and off the court is up for public consumption and scrutiny. Jordan, on the other hand, did not face this pressure as a rookie because the NBA was a different place then. Jordan certainly did not have much of a grace period, but there was a time when he still had some measure of privacy. Of course, as the team's number-one draft pick, Jordan was expected to help the club right away. No one, however, expected the scrawny kid out of the University of North Carolina to become the Michael Jordan that he developed into.

In contrast to the way James's star has risen, there is almost an innocence to Jordan's ascent to global icon status, even though he became a star in his freshman year at the University of North Carolina after hitting the game-winning jump shot against Georgetown in the NCAA Championship game. Observers who watched Jordan realized that he had the potential to be a special player, but no one thought he would develop into the greatest player to ever live. The general public gradually recognized Jordan's immense talent, hand in hand with seeing his face on television in Nike ads.

In his rookie year, James will be given little room for error and be watched with an intensity Jordan did not have to confront right away. James is expected to be the next Jordan on the court, even though he will be competing for the first time against athletes who can match his size and skill. *The Plain Dealer* ran a daily watch on James when he was in high school; imagine the focus he will receive playing for the home team as a professional. Maybe the paper will dedicate the whole sports page to him.

One NBA Western Conference scouting director explained how James would have to push himself to achieve the level of Kobe Bryant, Tracy McGrady, and the handful of top pro stars. "He's able to get by on his physical ability right now," the scout told sportswriter Marc Stein. "The question is, what happens when he can't just get by on physical ability alone? The mental side, the emotional side, those are unknowns. In high school, the only thing we're seeing is the physical ability."[6]

Interestingly, no one wants to go on record saying that James may not measure up to the bar Jordan set. All the scouts and personnel execs who question his future request anonymity from the writers quoting them. In Jordan's heyday, he would turn the slightest criticism into a personal attack and made the opposition pay for the remark. No one wants to be bulletin board fodder for James, even in his rookie year.

James is already considered the game's next great marketing hope. Experts estimate that his first shoe contract—signed with Nike after a years-long battle with Adidas—approached or exceeded $20 million over five years. Although he waited until after the draft to sign the Nike deal, college was never really an option for the youngster. He had been marketed too long to be put on the shelf while competing for any major college program.

Jordan has taken a liking to James, inviting him to Chicago to hoop it up together and giving the youngster his top-secret cell phone number. It is a role Jordan has taken with other young, African-American superstars, such as his close friendship with golf sensation Tiger Woods. Critics, however, view the James-Jordan relationship with a grain of skepticism, thinking that the move was intended to get James on the Nike payroll, like his basketball idol.

What James needs during his rookie year in the NBA isn't a gigantic shoe contract or the estimated $11 million guaranteed over three years he will earn as the first pick in the draft. James needs a mentor. He must find someone who will guide him through the maturation process.

As James's on-the-court exploits continue to electrify and his jumper has started dropping on a regular basis for the Cavs, thus muting the one criticism of his game, the only issue that concerns basketball experts is how the young man will deal with the fanfare. An NBA Eastern Conference scout explained the way a high school player affects a team, stating, "The problem with taking on a high school player is that, for the coach, you're dealing with a lot of things you don't normally deal with. And it takes up a lot of time." Summing up the challenge of easing a teenager into the game, the scout explained, "These kids don't even know how to keep a checkbook when they get to the NBA."[7]

Thus far, James has showed some important signs of maturity in handling all the hype surrounding his fabled career. Like other high school students, he liked spending time with friends playing videogames. He worked hard in school and earned good grades. His mother, Gloria, says that the two are best friends, "I brought him up to be his own man, to make good decisions," she explains. "He hasn't let me down."[8] One day, James carried a bag of shoes into the lunchroom at SVSM and put on a mini-auction, giving away the sneakers to students who could answer basketball trivia correctly. Know the birthday of high school teammate Sian Cotton, win a pair of authentic James tennis shoes.[9]

Yet, despite his mother's faith, the simple fact is that James's maturation process is steamrolled by skipping college, not to mention listening to years of hype about his place in the basketball pantheon. Given the several high-profile miscues his senior year, the Cavs would be wise to invest in one or several advisers to help the young man circumvent the numerous pitfalls that could impede his future success. Whether this is a veteran player who relates to the youngster or a father figure to guide James, the budding superstar needs to navigate through the murky NBA lifestyle.

When *ESPN The Magazine* featured James on the cover as its "next" athlete, writer Tom Friend questioned James's inner circle, explaining, "An ex-con is handling his business affairs. Another ex-con wants to tell him he's his biological father. Even his own mother, Gloria, has been seen trading Adidas gear to gain entry into local bingo games."[10] In addition, Gloria is notorious for confronting anyone she thinks is mistreating James, particularly opposing coaches, referees, and fans. At games, she is easily spotted in the crowd, always decked out in a jersey that reads "LeBron's Mom" or "James" on the back.

Showing a considerable lack of tact, Gloria, of all people, incited the first national discussion of James's blunders by buying him a $50,000 Hummer H2 for his birthday. Clearly, when a kid from the ghetto starts driving a sports utility vehicle favored by professional athletes the state athletic commission is going to investigate. Although ultimately cleared by the state body, the whole issue raised questions about James that he would not have faced otherwise, including the motivations of the people in his inner circle. If Gloria would have waited until after the basketball season to buy the Hummer, the entire spectacle and all the resulting criticism could have been avoided.

"On the court," explains sports journalist Tom Withers, "the kid compared to a young Michael Jordan is in complete control. Off it, others direct his every move." As outlined by Withers, James's life is already out of his control. "Gloria James makes most of her son's major decisions," he says. "There's a bodyguard and security staff. Attorney Fred Nance handles the family's legal affairs and there's a public relations executive for the media."[11] Gloria has been known to taunt opposing fans and saunter around various gyms waving her son's picture to the crowd.

Considering all the expectation heaped on James, from the anticipation that he will turn around the ailing Cleveland franchise that drafted him to the off-court demands of Nike (as well as the boatload of other endorsements he is expected to collect) James is facing a world in which his life will no longer be his own. There is only one person in the NBA who has lived this life, and his name is Michael.

The amazing thing about Jordan is that he somehow endures the throngs of fans constantly inching closer and closer to catch a glimpse or merely touch him. Granted, these are the people who pay his salary and buy the products he endorses, but is it a fair trade?

James's NBA career may very well be defined by the approach he takes in interacting with the hordes of people watching his every step, while still finding a way to focus on basketball. How will the young man carry himself in public? How will he interact with teammates on the court? The NBA is filled with talented athletes who are selfish and place their own interests above the team. Will James—a teenager—acquire the wisdom necessary to live up to the athletic potential he posseses?

HYPE, HOPE, AND THE FUTURE

LeBron James is an amazing basketball talent. He has the potential to become the next Michael Jordan. Along that yellow brick road, however, are going to be several bumps, a few detours, and maybe even some unpaved highway.

Or, James could be the next great flameout—a has-been before he turns thirty years old with no education and few future prospects.

How many other players have tried to inherit the Jordan mantle and never lived up to the burden that title carries? Remember Harold Miner? How about a more prominent star, like Grant Hill? After a couple of wonderful years in the league, ankle injuries have kept Hill out of action for nearly three years. Although he is still popular among the fans and an incredibly wealthy young man, after signing a $93 million contract with the Orlando Magic, he may never be the player he once was (if he's even able to return to the court) and certainly will not achieve the Jordanesque heights observers predicted for him. James is only a blown-out knee, Achilles' tendon rupture, or torn-up ankle away from obscurity—another body in "the next Jordan" dustbin.

The pressure on James is immense. You see, the simple fact of the matter is that no one has ever entered the NBA with as much buildup as this young man from Akron, Ohio. Not only is he physically gifted, in terms of basketball ability, but he also possesses a mix of charm and toughness at the same time—a star quality that must be natural to pass muster with fans. Equally important, he joins the professional ranks at a time when the league itself is searching for a post-Jordan identity. If David Stern and his minions have learned anything from MJ's several retirements it is that without him the NBA just isn't the same—attendance declines, ratings fall, and merchandise sales plummet.

Now that Jordan is retiring for good, the NBA needs a new talent that can get people energized about the pro game. For all their greatness, players such as Kobe, Shaq, McGrady, and Iverson simply don't resonate with the general public that tuned in to Bulls and Wizards games, whether they considered themselves fans or not, then bought the products Jordan plugged. The NBA needs LeBron James to live up to the hype and the hope. The future does not necessarily hang in the balance, but finding another Jordan to showcase could revitalize the game for another generation.

NOTES

1. Jack Ramsay, "LeBron's Best Individual Quality: Team Play," <espn.go.com/nba/columns/ramsay_drjack/1476123.html>, December 19, 2002.

2. Grant Wahl, "Ahead of His Class," *Sports Illustrated,* February 18, 2002, pp. 62-68.

3. Terry Pluto, "LeBron Back in Style," *The Beacon Journal* (Akron), February 9, 2003, p. A1.

4. Mike Peticca, "Joyce Pours it on on LeBron's Night," *The Plain Dealer* (Cleveland), February 25, 2003, p. D8.

5. Tom Friend, "Next: LeBron James," *ESPN The Magazine,* <espn.go.com/magazine/vo/5no26next.html>December 23, 2002.

6. Marc Stein, "Breaking Down LeBron James' Game," <espn.go.com/nba/columns/stein_marc/1475781.html>, December 12, 2002.

7. Ibid.

8. Sal Ruibal, "At 17, LeBron James Is the Hottest Hoopster," *USA Today,* December 10, 2002, p. A1.

9. Tom Friend, "LeBron's World," *ESPN The Magazine,* <espn.go.com/magazine/friend_20021118.html> November 18, 2002.

10. Friend, "Next."

11. Tom Withers, "Innocence Lost," <cincinnati.com/preps/2003/02/09/wwwprep4c9.html>, February 9, 2003.

Chapter 17

Conclusion: Basketball *Is* America

Bob Batchelor

We cannot direct the wind, but we can adjust the sails.

Anonymous

The love of the game begins in vastly different ways. For some, it is the youthful elation felt the first time the ball is thrown up with two hands, watching it bounce around and then drop through the hoop. Others try to emulate the older kids they see playing the game at the local playground. Some get hooked after they tune in to a game on television, mesmerized by its blurring quickness and grace. Thus begins a lifelong love affair with basketball.

I clearly remember my "love at first sight" moment—watching Dr. J bank in an 18-foot jump shot from the right wing on television. For some unknown reason, the novelty of that jumper set off fireworks in my mind. I immediately went to a friend's house in an attempt to emulate Dr. J. He was the only kid in our rural neighborhood that had a basketball hoop. We tentatively dribbled on his gravel drive—the ball careening off the uneven surface—tossing up shot after shot.

In the ensuing years, basketball became my favorite sport, even though baseball and football ruled the little Western Pennsylvania towns where I grew up. Pursuing our mania for the game, my friends and I snuck into college gyms through unlocked locker room doors, shoveled snow off driveways and cut holes in our gloves so we could play. Once, we even lifted off a manhole cover and walked below the college streets looking for a secret passageway into the gym. We put up Nerf hoops in our bedrooms and relentlessly talked, dreamed, and absorbed the game. We imagined every piece of paper or pop can thrown into the garbage as a last-second shot to win the NBA championship.

At the same time, though, basketball did not just grant us the skills to throw a rubber ball through a steel hoop. Basketball taught us about life. From basketball, I learned about commitment, pursuing perfection, and building individual skills, and then molding them into the team effort, dedication, discipline, and friendship.

One could argue that these principles are the same ones a person develops in any sport, but basketball has the unique advantage of being played year-round—often completely alone. These necessary hours of isolation give players time to work on the game and reflect on life. No other sport can duplicate the feeling of practicing jump shots or free throws for hours on a scorching blacktop, alone with nothing more than one's dreams and aspirations.

Looking at the lessons learned from the game of basketball, I am convinced that basketball reflects what it is to be an American. This idea becomes even clearer when examining these traits as they have developed in the past several decades.

Since the 1970s, basketball and its stars have moved from the periphery to the center of American popular culture. In today's world, basketball dictates dress styles for millions of people, influences movies, music, and art, and pumps billions of dollars into the economy. The sport has also been at the center of socioeconomic issues, such as race, poverty, drug culture, and class.

Of all the professional sports, basketball may be the one that most directly confronts the issue of race. On the positive side, the popularity of players such as Jordan, Magic Johnson, and Charles Barkley certainly makes the general public more comfortable with black athletes and heroes. For most of the twentieth century, the idea that white teens would emulate players such as Allen Iverson, Tracy McGrady, or Jordan would have been considered absurd. Now, these athletes are the most popular (outside British soccer phenom David Beckham) on the planet.

Jim Griswold, the advertising executive behind the Spike Lee/Nike commercials that catapulted Michael Jordan into the stratosphere, thought the spots featuring Lee's Mars Blackmon character worked because of the emphasis on athletic artistry, not Jordan's color. They figured that as more people saw the charming Jordan playing straight man to Lee, race would be less an issue. Even Jordan recognized the power of the commercials, "What Phil and Nike have done is turn me into a dream."[1]

Unfortunately, however, as African Americans have come to dominate the NBA and college basketball, new stereotypes have emerged. The negative image is centered on the lifestyle choices of the league's young, rich black men. Every drug arrest, assault case, or other brush with the law seems to fuel racist debate. In addition, charges of preferential treatment for college stars are rampant on every college campus, whether it is a Division I powerhouse or tiny National Association of Intercollegiate Athletics (NAIA) school that doesn't even offer scholarships. Since blacks make up the majority of players on most college teams, the criticism has a racial component.

Even the discussion regarding the lack of fundamentals in the pro and college game is usually little more than thinly veiled racism. Words such as "athletic," when applied to a black player, most often suggest that he or she relies on jumping and quickness rather than intelligence, a good jump shot, and other basic skills. In contrast, the familiar adage, "white men can't jump," leads white players to develop guard skills, particularly point guard, where they can use their "superior intelligence" to run the offense. Racial stereotypes such as these are detrimental to progressing realistic notions about society.

Despite the stereotypes, basketball provides the conditions for an honest appraisal of race in sports and America in general. Of all the major professional sports, basketball was the first to have a black head coach (Bill Russell) and owner (Robert Johnson).

POPULAR CULTURE

At best, driving in Chicago is a nightmare. The Kennedy Expressway into downtown is a never-ending stream of clogged lanes, a jumble of vehicles jostling for position, and constant hurrying up to slow down—gas, break, gas, break—for miles into the city.

In the early spring of 1996, as I traveled between Washington, DC, and the Windy City, the brutal logjams intensified. Thousands of rubbernecking drivers made the drive even more hazardous by continually slowing down on the highway. The mass gawk led to countless fender benders and added anywhere from half an hour to an hour to the rush-hour commute. It wasn't long before the reason for the slowdown came into view.

Staring out from my vantage point in the backseat of a Chicago cab, the faces were instantly recognizable. Rounding the bend, there was a 37-foot tall billboard of Bulls rebounding sensation Dennis Rodman with orange hair and smirking, right next to an image of the always-dapper Michael Jordan (ironically, looking away from the Rodman picture). The giant Rodman was part of a mural painted for legendary Chicago clothiers Bigsby & Kruthers, who used the wall of a building to publicize Chicago's favorite sons. Rodman's head protruded above the brick wall, making it look like the player was about to stand up, while his suit had the arms ripped off, exposing his flamboyant tattoos.

The next question is obvious. Why would harried adults on a busy highway slow down or even pull over to take pictures of a billboard showing two basketball players, even ones as famous as Jordan and Rodman? For those who don't understand or follow basketball, it must have seemed idiotic at best. Over a two-week period, however, the hoopla built up to the point that the company had to paint over the Rodman portrait so the commute could return to normal.

The answer is that basketball has become such an important part of popular culture that anything related to its big stars becomes a huge event. Even today, years after Jordan retired, people flock to Chicago Stadium to take pictures of his statue outside the arena. Jordan, in particular, has had a tremendous impact on our culture, from the shoes people wear (on and off the court) to the way youngsters dress. Scholar and social critic Eric Michael Dyson explained, "Michael Jordan has helped the business world seize upon black cultural notions of cool, hip, and chic, which have undeniably influenced the look and sound of America."[2]

LeBron James's arrival in the NBA is sparking a new wave of interest unmatched since Jordan's rise. In addition to a $90-million shoe and clothing deal with Nike, James also inked a six-year contract reported to be worth $12 million to promote Coca-Cola's Powerade sports drink and Sprite. The drink deal is one of the largest ever signed in the beverage industry, on par with the contracts of NASCAR drivers Jeff Gordon (Pepsi) and Dale Earnhardt Jr. (Budweiser). James is also expected to resurrect the flailing Cleveland Cavaliers franchise, much the way the young Jordan did for Chicago.

Basketball's influence on popular culture also intensifies when the news is controversial. In the summer of 2003, basketball dominated the news. In a Colorado ski village, Los Angeles Laker star Kobe Bryant faced allegations that he sexually assaulted a local teenager who worked at the resort where Bryant stayed. Elsewhere, in Waco, Texas, the disappearance of Baylor player Patrick Dennehy set off a nationwide manhunt, which eventually uncovered that he had been murdered by a teammate.

After Bryant's arrest, Coca-Cola stopped running the many ads featuring the young Lakers star. The company did not cancel its contract with Bryant, however, who is signed through 2005. The charges against Bryant are expected to cost him millions of dollars in endorsements. The case itself will probably turn into the biggest media frenzy since the O.J. Simpson murder trial.

Basketball does more than shape the public's thoughts on celebrity culture. The game influences the way people dress, talk, and represent themselves to the larger world. Who would have thought that Jordan's baggy shorts (so he could wear his lucky North Carolina shorts underneath) would impact generations of athletes and non-athletes? Today, even casual-wear khaki shorts are cut long and baggy, a modified version of those seen on the court. Tight shorts are now synonymous with old-school NBA days.

Nike's involvement in basketball has turned sneakers into a fashion statement. People buy shoes as an image enhancer, whether or not those kicks will ever see the hardwood. Jerseys have also crossed-over into day-to-day clothing choices. Teens wear baggy NBA jerseys to school over T-shirts and adults are routinely spotted in them as well. The look has become so universal that unless one intentionally tries to notice it, the impact is transparent.

RACE

Over the course of a fourteen-year career in which he averaged 25.7 points per game, Oscar Robertson was a consummate winner and nearly single-handedly redefined all-around greatness. By all accounts, Robertson played the game with style and grace, backed by extraordinary fundamental skills. Long before the triple-double statistic measured individual success, Robertson was a scoring, rebounding, and passing fiend. Topping his career, in 1971, with the help of a young Kareem Abdul-Jabbar, "The Big O" won an NBA Championship.

Despite his solid reputation off the court and impeccable skills, Robertson was not offered a single major product endorsement. His lone endorsement came after his fourth year in the league, when he was approached to endorse a basketball, which was a kind of perfunctory move to appease the black youngsters playing the game. Robertson's plight was typical in the pre-Jordan NBA, even for someone of The Big O's standing. In the 1970s, according to historian Walter LaFeber, "An unwritten, but acknowledged rule among advertisers had it that black players' endorsements did not sell products."[3]

Although the arrival of Larry Bird and Magic Johnson reinvigorated the NBA, the situation for most black players did not improve dramatically. In the 1980s, blacks dominated the college and professional games, which set off a national debate (some would say backlash) about why this had occurred. In the NBA, African Americans made up 80 percent of the league's starters. "When Michael Jordan joined the Chicago Bulls, half of the NBA's players hailed from the twenty largest cities, usually inner-city neighborhoods where African-American families had replaced the Jewish, German, and Irish," LaFeber explains.[4]

The discussion of racism magnified when observers looked at the disparity between African Americans on the court and those in management. While players made up the majority of the professional teams, coaching staffs and front-office personnel were overwhelmingly white. Clearly, racial overtones prevented white owners from trusting blacks with control of their teams, an issue that has dogged the sport for decades.

The greatest tragedy in American history is that we champion so many principles and are willing to die for them, but we have yet to solve the crisis of racism. Almost every significant problem in our society has a racial component, whether it is a question of economics, education, health care, or the countless other challenges that pull at the fabric of society. And yet, despite its place at the center of these issues, meaningful discussions of race are infrequent and, in some respects, almost completely unmentionable.

Frank talk concerning race and racism is even suppressed when it comes to popular culture topics, such as sports, the media, motion pictures, and music—though films and music are two areas more open to debate due to the rise of rap and hip-hop music and predominantly black movies. In late 2003, Chicago Cubs manager Dusty Baker (an African American) was criticized for stating that black and Latin athletes liked to play in the heat more than whites. Baker hypothesized that slaves were brought to America to work in the fields and could handle it better because of their skin color. Baker's critics and supporters had a field day arguing the point and whether the statement was racist.

In his groundbreaking and controversial book, *Taboo: Why Black Athletes Dominate Sports and Why We're Afraid to Talk About It,* journalist Jon Entine tackled the racially charged topic of black superiority in sports. The notion that one athlete has a natural advantage because of race carries such inherent controversy that Entine spent hundreds of pages simply leading up to why the topic needed to be examined and carefully outlining the history of the topic.

Entine contends that the reason society does not address the topic openly is that it is charged by the preconceived notions that people have developed regarding race. The controversy is in the psychological and sociological way people interpret the information. For example, whites equating athletic superiority with low intelligence or beastlike qualities that they want to assume in blacks. Even "hard" science is suspect when issues of race are involved.

Entine contends that science is bringing the truth to light, saying, "The evidence speaks for itself. Humans are different. No amount of rhetoric, however well-motivated, can undermine the intriguing kaleidoscope of humanity. It's time to acknowledge and even celebrate the obvious: It's neither racist nor a myth to say that 'white men can't jump.'" In the end, he explains, "The scientific evidence for black athletic superiority is overwhelming."[5]

Race issues in basketball extend well beyond the physical differences between blacks and whites. Socioeconomic aspects also open the dialogue. For former players such as Charles Barkley, the way the current generation acts accentuates the stereotypes of them. "Today's players are like what you see on TV," he explains. "It's gangs, kids killing kids. If they didn't play basketball, some of these guys would be in gangs that killed somebody."[6]

Even Jordan, who has the black community to thank for his incredible wealth, has grown frustrated with the way players act and how that is replicated by younger generations. Jordan, according to Dyson,

"Has become the supreme symbol of black cultural creativity in a society that is showing less and less tolerance for black youth whose support sustained his career."[7]

Jordan himself has been the target of backlash over the past decade, from representing a nearly unattainable goal for youngsters, to not speaking out on political and economic issues that affect the black community. John Hoberman, author of *Darwin's Athletes: How Sport Has Damaged Black America and Preserved the Myth of Race* (1997), sees the cult of Jordan as a cop-out—a way for whites to make themselves feel good about race without actually confronting it in any real way. According to Hoberman,

> The reason for the absurd dimensions of the cult of Michael Jordan is directly related to the depth of the racial crisis in the United States. The way we look at Michael Jordan constitutes pseudo-race relations, a way to accept black men into a society extremely concerned about their behavior. It doesn't involve the complexities of dealing with a black colleague, teacher, policeman or neighbor. It is "virtual integration."[8]

Clearly, race is a difficult issue because of people's perceptions, preconceived notions, and the difficulty of proving any inclination scientifically. Sports, however, as a part of society that has (at least on the field) been integrated, may hold the secret for the rest of society. Basketball has made greater advances in hiring African Americans in the coaching and front-office areas than other sports; thus it should provide the model in other areas.

"Maybe I am an idealist," explained former player and executive Wayne Embry, "but the NBA has done a lot of good for men of all races. It shows how blacks and whites can work together for a common goal." When the NBA promotes the violence and trash talking, according to Embry, "We are missing a chance to be a model that promotes the right kind of values, the values we saw in many of our teams and players in the 1980s."[9]

TRANSITION

The transition in professional basketball (from an era dominated by Jordan, Barkley, Patrick Ewing, John Stockton, and Karl Malone to one led by Iverson, McGrady, Jason Kidd, and Tim Duncan) has been rocky. If the NBA marketers had their way, the jump would probably be directly from the Jordan era to the James era.

Many of today's younger players seem to understand and accept the burden of carrying the game into the future. "We've been a league in transition, but we've had the golden era of basketball and now we're moving completely to a new generation," said Bryant. "It's up to us now to carry on the legacy."[10]

Jordan and others have their doubts. "Today they try to market the player before that player has grown into the image they are marketing," Jordan says. "You can't fool the public."[11] Prophetically, in his 1998 autobiography, Jordan wondered about the younger generation maturing as athletes at the same time they are growing into adults. "Can Kobe Bryant become a great player? Sure," Jordan said. "But it's going to take a lot more effort to refine his skills at the same time he's trying to survive."[12]

Jordan explains,

> Young players also need to know what makes them happy off the floor. I don't think a lot of players ever gain that knowledge about themselves. They think they know. They think watching videos, going out to clubs, or hanging out with a different woman every night is the answer. If that's what you think makes you truly happy, then you're going to get burned, because it's fleeting.[13]

The model for future NBA players—molding "old school" fundamentals with extraordinary skills—is two-time MVP Tim Duncan of the San Antonio Spurs. Since joining the Texas team as the first overall pick of the 1997 draft, Duncan has led the Spurs to two NBA Championships and put up amazing numbers. Like Jordan, Bird, and other former greats, Duncan's success is the result of an emphasis on fundamentals—excelling in passing, shooting, rebounding, and defense. There is no area of his game that is flashy by today's streetball standards, but he consistently wins.

Seattle Times columnist Steve Kelley writes,

> There is nothing flashy about Duncan. He doesn't pose after one of his smooth jump hooks. He's the NBA's quiet superstar. You don't see Duncan on "Access Hollywood." He doesn't travel

with a posse. He's the player you want as your teammate. He's
the man you want as your friend. The kid you'd like to have as a
son.[14]

Unfortunately, although every team would like to have a player of
Duncan's caliber, his brilliance is difficult to market to today's video-
game-influenced, hip-hop youngsters. Hence, although the league already has Jordan's successor in its midst, the hope of the NBA rests
on LeBron James's young shoulders—a Herculean responsibility for
an eighteen-year-old.

Legendary Coach Chuck Daly puts the dilemma more succinctly,
"It's the MTV generation. Kids want the $150 shoes. They want the
commercials. They want the dunks and the flash."[15]

BEYOND THE GAME

Just after the terrorist attacks on September 11, social critics assumed that the nation would undergo significant psychological
changes—becoming both a more serious and reflective society. In the
immediate aftermath, sports played a therapeutic role for a grieving
nation.

In the four years since the assaults on New York City and Washington, DC, took place, however, the country has basically returned to
status quo in most areas. The major long-term differences seem to be
a heightened sense of security issues and a deeper suspicion of those
perceived as outsiders. Sporting events give spectators a place to
show their collective patriotism, but any deeper meaning is dubious.
Whatever chance we had to address fundamental flaws in American
society probably slipped away under the twin visages of war in Af-
ghanistan and Iraq and a prolonged economic recession. September
11 presented an opportunity for the country to reassess challenges
such as homelessness, poverty, race, and immigration, but the national mood turned militaristic and vengeful, rather than introspec-
tive.

In the case of basketball, the public may be too jaded from over-
marketing to address troubles that confront the sport. At every level,
the corporate money has cheapened the purity of the game. Often it
seems as if the game has degenerated into little more than a giant marketing scheme. From Reebok using Mark Walker, a three-year-old, to

sell shoes to Nike sponsoring AAU leagues for middle schoolers, money has saturated the game.

The shoe companies and big-time college coaches run their own summer camps, searching for the next NBA star. What teenager is going to turn down an invitation when Nike or Adidas comes calling, or the coach they've seen on television all season? For the minuscule number of players who play professionally, these camps are wonderful. The majority gets chewed up in the machine. The odds are stacked against even the best players, in spite of the whispers they hear from friends, coaches, and others with hidden agendas.

According to veteran sports columnist Terry Pluto, the unlimited money in the NBA has changed priorities among its stars. "For Larry Bird or Magic Johnson or Michael Jordan, the bottom line that mattered was measured in rings," he says. "For the new breed, it's solely in their paychecks."[16]

Perhaps this thinking is the reason why hoops critics love blue collar superstars such as Duncan and New Jersey Nets point guard Jason Kidd. They exude old-school attitude and dedication to fundamentals. Most important, like their predecessors, they measure success by championship rings.

Given the flash of today's NBA, trying to teach young kids about the importance of fundamentals is problematical. They would rather worry about when they'll be able to dunk than practice free throws or the proper way to pass into the post. The chest-thumping, sweatband-wearing, shiny-sneakered NBA filters directly into the star-filled eyes of twelve- and thirteen-year-olds. These young players are the real future of the game. They need to be taught to love the game for the right reasons.

NOTES

1. Quoted in David Halberstam, *Playing for Keeps: Michael Jordan and the World He Made* (New York: Random House, 1999), p. 183.

2. Michael Eric Dyson, *Between God and Gangsta Rap: Bearing Witness to Black Culture* (New York: Oxford University Press, 1996), p. 58.

3. Walter LaFeber, *Michael Jordan and the New Global Capitalism* (New York: Norton, 2002), p. 45.

4. Ibid., p. 42.

5. Jon Entine, *Taboo: Why Black Athletes Dominate Sports and Why We're Afraid to Talk About It* (New York: PublicAffairs, 2000), p. 341.

6. Terry Pluto, *Falling from Grace: Can Pro Basketball Be Saved?* (New York: Simon & Schuster, 1995), pp. 106-107.

7. Dyson, p. 58.

8. Quoted in Phil Hersh, "Should His Airness Be a Cultural Icon?" *Chicago Tribune,* March 24, 1995, p. 3.

9. Quoted in Pluto, p. 21.

10. Michael Wilbon, "The Last of the Dreamers," *The Washington Post,* February 10, 2003, p. D1.

11. Michael Jordan, *For the Love of the Game* (New York: Crown, 1998), p. 79.

12. Ibid., p. 140.

13. Ibid., p. 141.

14. Steve Kelley, "MVP Duncan Stays NBA's Quiet Superstar," *The Seattle Times,* June 8, 2003, p. C4.

15. Quoted in Pluto, p. 23.

16. Pluto, p. 31.

Appendix

Selected Timeline

1970	"Pistol" Pete Maravich is the first college basketball player to score 3,000 points.
	The New York Knicks win the NBA Championship 4-1 over the Milwaukee Bucks.
	Bob Cousy and Bob Petit inducted into the Basketball Hall of Fame.
1971	UCLA begins an eighty-eight game win streak.
	Ruling enables underclassmen to enter the NBA before their college classes graduated.
1972	Wayne Embry becomes the first African-American General Manager (Milwaukee Bucks).
	Shaquille O'Neal born in Newark, New Jersey.
1973	Steals and blocked shots became official statistics in the 1973-1974 season.
1974	UCLA's eighty-eight game winning streak ends with a 71-70 loss to Notre Dame at South Bend, Indiana.
	Famed broadcaster Bob Costas gets his job as a radio announcer with the ABA Spirits of St. Louis for $11,000 a year.
	Oscar Robertson retires with career averages of 25.7 points per game, 7.5 rebounds, and 9.5 assists.
1975	UCLA wins its tenth NCAA title under legendary coach John Wooden.
	Kareem Abdul-Jabbar is traded from the Milwaukee Bucks to the Los Angeles Lakers in a six-player deal.
	Philadelphia 76ers star Allen Iverson born in Hampton, Virginia.
1976	College basketball allows the dunk shot in the 1976-1977 season.
	The American Basketball Association (ABA) folds with four teams joining the NBA and its remaining players taken in a draft.
	Minnesota Timberwolves star Kevin Garnett is born in Maudlin, South Carolina.

Nancy Lieberman is the youngest basketball player to win an Olympic medal, helping the U.S. women's team to a silver at the Montreal Olympics.

Two-time MVP Tim Duncan of the San Antonio Spurs is born in St. Croix, U.S. Virgin Islands.

1977 Center Bill Walton averages 18.9 points per game and 14.4 rebounds to lead the Portland Trailblazers to their first NBA Championship.

Toronto Raptors star Vince Carter is born in Daytona Beach, Florida.

1978 Carol "The Blaze" Blazejowski (Monclair State) is the first winner of the Wade Trophy as the Women's Basketball Player of the Year.

Dallas Mavericks sharp-shooting forward Dirk Nowitski is born in Wurzbug, Germany.

1979 Former Princeton and New York Knicks star Bill Bradley elected to the U.S. Senate from New Jersey.

Magic Johnson (Michigan State) and Larry Bird (Indiana State) meet in the NCAA championship game, won 75-64 by Michigan State.

The three-point shot is introduced to the NBA.

1980 Bill Russell is named the Greatest Player in the History of the NBA by the Professional Basketball Writers Association of America.

1981 Houston Rockets guard Calvin Murphy sets the NBA record for free throw percentage at .958 by making 206 of 215 attempts.

1982 Women's star Cheryl Miller scores 105 points in a high school game.

North Carolina wins the NCAA Tournament final over Georgetown when Michael Jordan hits the game-winning shot.

Pat Riley leads the Los Angeles Lakers to the NBA title after taking over the head coaching position the previous year.

1983 The Philadelphia 76ers win the NBA Championship 4-1 over the Milwaukee Bucks to give Julius "Dr. J" Erving his only NBA title, after winning two in the ABA.

1984 David Stern becomes NBA commissioner.

Larry Nance of the Phoenix Suns wins the first NBA Slam Dunk Contest held during All-Star weekend.

1985 The NCAA institutes a 45-second shot clock in the 1985-1986 season.

Lynnette Woodard becomes the first female member of the Harlem Globetrotters.

1986 NCAA adopts the three-point shot at 19 feet, 9 inches.

Standing only 5'7", Spud Webb (Atlanta Hawks), wins NBA Slam Dunk contest.

Based on the true story of a small-town Indiana team that made the state finals in 1954, *Hoosiers,* starring Gene Hackman, is a box office hit.

1987	Julius "Dr. J" Erving retires from the Philadelphia 76ers.
1988	Michael Jordan wins his first regular season Most Valuable Player (MVP) award and is named Defensive Player of the Year.
1989	The Spike Lee film, *Do the Right Thing,* introduces the character Mars Blackmon, who later stars with Michael Jordan in a number of popular Nike commercials.
	Kareem Abdul-Jabbar retires after twenty years in the NBA as the league's all-time leading scorer.
1990	The first regular season NBA game played outside North America takes place in Japan's Tokyo Metropolitan Gymnasium as the Phoenix Suns beat the Utah Jazz 119-96.
1991	Magic Johnson announces his retirement from the NBA after testing positive for the HIV virus.
1992	The film, *White Men Can't Jump,* starring Woody Harrelson and Wesley Snipes, is about streetball hustlers on the courts at Venice Beach and other locales around Los Angeles.
	Shaquille O'Neal is taken by the Orlando Magic with the first pick in the NBA Draft.
	The American "Dream Team" wins the gold medal at the 1992 Summer Olympics in Barcelona.
1993	The NCAA shot clock is reduced to 35 seconds.
	Michael Jordan shocks the world by retiring to pursue a career in baseball after leading the Bulls to three consecutive titles.
1994	The documentary *Hoop Dreams* follows two inner-city Chicago boys for five years as they pursue their basketball dreams of college and the NBA.
	Wayne Embry becomes the first African-American team president (Cleveland Cavaliers).
	Hakeem Olajuwon leads the Houston Rockets to the NBA Championship and is named MVP.
1995	Michael Jordan announces that he is returning to the Chicago Bulls with a simple faxed statement, "I'm back."
1996	*Slam,* by Walter Dean Myers, is a coming-of-age novel about a black teenager who must balance his bleak surroundings and personal uneasiness off the court with his phenomenal skills on the hardwood.
	Michael Jordan stars as himself in *Space Jam,* a movie that mixes live action with Looney Toons animated characters, and helps Bugs Bunny and friends defeat evil aliens who want to enslave them.
	Rebecca Lobo and Sheryl Swoopes are the first two players to sign with the Women's National Basketball Association (WNBA).
	On June 6, the NBA celebrates its fiftieth anniversary.

Magic Johnson briefly returns to the NBA, then retires again after the season.

1997   A. C. Green (Dallas Mavericks) plays in his 907th consecutive game, breaking Randy Smith's NBA record.

Robert Parish finishes his career with the Chicago Bulls after twenty-one seasons, breaking Kareem Abdul-Jabbar's record for most seasons.

1998   University of Tennessee coach Pat Summitt is the first female coach to appear on the cover of *Sports Illustrated.*

University of North Carolina Coach Dean Smith retires.

The Chicago Bulls win their sixth NBA title of the decade over the Utah Jazz.

One of the two women's basketball leagues, the American Basketball League (ABL) suspends operations and files for Chapter 11 bankruptcy protection.

1999   NBA season begins three months late because of the owners lockout.

San Antonio Spurs win their first NBA title over the New York Knicks in five games.

Wilt Chamberlain dies of a heart attack on October 12.

Duke University is the first college to have four players taken in the first round of the NBA draft.

2000   Bobby Knight's twenty-nine-year career at Indiana ends when he is fired on September 10 for the last in a series of altercations with university officials and students.

The Los Angeles Lakers win their twelfth NBA championship by beating the Indiana Pacers in six games.

2001   Michael Jordan announces that he is returning to the NBA to play for the Washington Wizards.

2002   The film *Like Mike* stars young rapper Lil' Bow Wow as an orphan who becomes an NBA superstar after finding sneakers with the faded initials "M.J." inside.

2003   Michael Jordan retires from the NBA after a two-year stint with the Washington Wizards.

A 52-48 loss to Villanova in the final of the Big East conference tournament ends the University of Connecticut women's basketball team's NCAA Division I women's record seventy-game winning streak.

Bibliography

Alexie, Sherman. *Smoke Signals: A Screenplay.* New York: Hyperion, 1998.

Axthelm, Pete. *The City Game.* New York: Harper's Magazine Press, 1970.

Banet-Weiser, Sarah. "Hoop Dreams: Professional Basketball and the Politics of Race and Gender." *Journal of Sport and Social Issues,* 23:4 (November 1999): 403-420.

Beckham, Barry. *Double Dunk.* Los Angeles: Beckham House, 1980.

Bergen, Ronald. *Sports in the Movies.* New York: Proteus Books, 1982.

Bird, Larry, with Bob Ryan. *Drive: The Story of My Life.* New York: Doubleday, 1989.

Bjarkman, Peter C. *The Biographical History of Pro Basketball.* Lincolnwood, IL: Masters Press, 2000.

_____. *The Encyclopedia of Pro Basketball Team Histories.* New York: Graf Publishers, Inc., 1994.

Boyd, Todd, and Kenneth L. Shropshire, eds. *Basketball Jones: America, Above the Rim.* New York: New York University Press, 2000.

Brill, Marlene Targ. *Sport Success: Winning Women in Basketball.* New York: Barron's, 2000.

Cahn, Susan K. *Coming on Strong: Gender and Sexualilty in Twentieth-Century Women's Sport.* Cambridge: Harvard University Press, 1994.

Cohen, Stanley. *The Game They Played.* New York: Farrar, Strauss and Giroux, 1977.

Corbett, Sara. *Venus to the Hoop: A Gold-Medal Year in Women's Basketball.* New York: Doubleday, 1997.

Creedon, Pamela J., ed. *Women, Media and Sport: Challenging Gender Values.* London: Sage Publications, 1994.

Ennis, Lisa. "Leslie, Lisa DeShaun." In *Scribner's Encyclopedia of American Lives: Sport Figures,* Arnold Markoe, ed. New York: Charles Scribner's Sons, 2002, pp. 37-38.

Feinstein, John. *The Last Amateurs: Playing for Glory and Honor in Division I College Basketball.* Boston: Little, Brown, 2000.

_____. *A March to Madness: The View from the Floor in the Atlantic Coast Conference.* Boston: Little, Brown, 1997.

_____. *The Punch: One Night, Two Lives, and the Fight That Changed Basketball Forever.* Boston: Little, Brown, 2002.

Festle, Mary Jo. *Playing Nice: Politics and Apologies in Women's Sports.* New York: Columbia University Press, 1996.

Ford, Linda. *Lady Hoopsters: A History of Women's Basketball in America.* Northampton, MA: Half Moon Books, 1999.

Gogol, Sara. *Playing in a New League: The Women of the American Basketball League's First Season.* Indianapolis, IN: Masters Press, 1998.

Grace, Kevin. *An Annotated Checklist of Basketball Films.* Wyoming, OH: Pargoud Press, 2003.

_____. *Bearcats! The Story of Basketball at the University of Cincinnati.* Louisville: Harmony House Publishing, 1998.

Halberstam, David. *Playing for Keeps: Michael Jordan and the World He Made.* New York: Random House, 1998.

_____. *The Breaks of the Game.* New York: Ballantine Books, 1983.

Hult, Joan S. and Marianna Trekell. *A Century of Women's Basketball: From Frailty to Final Four.* Reston, VA: National Association for Girls and Women in Sport, 1991.

Isaacs, Neil David. *All the Moves: A History of College Basketball.* Philadelphia: Lippincott, 1975.

Jabbar, Kareem Abdul. *Kareem.* New York: Random House, 1990.

Johnson, Earvin "Magic," with William Novak. *My Life.* New York: Random House, 1992.

Jones, Ryan. *King James: Believe the Hype: The LeBron James Story.* New York: Griffin, 2003.

Joravsky, Ben. *Hoop Dreams: A True Story of Hardship and Triumph.* Atlanta: Turner Publishing, 1995.

Kelley, Brent. *Women Who Win: Lisa Leslie.* Philadelphia: Chelsea House Publishers, 2001.

Krzyzewski, Mike. *Leading with the Heart: Coach K's Successful Strategies for Basketball, Business, and Life.* New York: Warner, 2000.

LaFeber, Walter. *Michael Jordan and the New Global Capitalism.* New York: Norton, 1999.

Lazenby, Roland. *The NBA Finals: A Fifty-Year Celebration.* Indianapolis: Masters Press, 1996.

Lee, Spike, with Ralph Wiley. *The Best Seat in the House: A Basketball Memoir.* New York: Crown, 1997.

McKissack, Frederick Jr. *Black Hoops: The History of African Americans in Basketball.* New York: Scholastic Press, 1999.

Neft, David S., and Richard M. Cohen. *The Sports Encyclopedia: Pro Basketball,* Second edition. New York: St. Martin's Press, 1989.

Pluto, Terry. *Falling from Grace: Can Pro Basketball Be Saved?* New York: Simon and Schuster, 1999.

_____. *Loose Balls: The Short, Wild Life of the American Basketball Association.* New York: Simon and Schuster, 1990.

Riess, Steven. *City Games: The Evolution of American Urban Society and the Rise of Sports.* Urbana: University of Illinois Press, 1989.

Rodman, Dennis. *Bad As I Wanna Be.* New York: Delacorte, 1996.

Shropshire, Kenneth L. *In Black and White: Race and Sports in America.* New York: New York University Press, 1996.

Smith, Sam. *The Jordan Rules.* New York: Simon and Schuster, 1992.

Telander, Rick. *Heaven Is a Playground.* Lincoln: The University of Nebraska Press, 1976.

Tudor, Deborah V. *Hollywood's Vision of Team Sports: Heroes, Race, and Gender.* New York: Garland Publishing, 1997.

Whiteside, Kelly. *WNBA: A Celebration—Commemorating the Birth of a League.* New York: Harper Horizon, 1998.

Wolf, David. *Foul! The Connie Hawkins Story.* New York: Warner, 1972.

Wooden, John, with Steve Jamison. *Wooden: A Lifetime of Observations and Reflections On and Off the Court.* Lincolnwood, IL: Contemporary, 1997.

Zucker, Harvey Marc, and Lawrence J. Babich. *Sports Films: A Complete Reference.* Jefferson, NC: McFarland and Co., 1987.

Index

Order a copy of this book with this form or online at:
http://www.haworthpress.com/store/product.asp?sku=5287

BASKETBALL IN AMERICA
From the Playgrounds to Jordan's Game and Beyond

_____in hardbound at $44.95 (ISBN-13: 978-07890-1612-6; ISBN-10: 0-7890-1612-5)

_____in softbound at $29.95 (ISBN-13: 978-0-7890-1613-3; ISBN-10: 0-7890-1613-3)

Or order online and use special offer code HEC25 in the shopping cart.

COST OF BOOKS_____

POSTAGE & HANDLING_____
(US: $4.00 for first book & $1.50
for each additional book)
(Outside US: $5.00 for first book
& $2.00 for each additional book)

SUBTOTAL_____

IN CANADA: ADD 7% GST_____

STATE TAX_____
(NJ, NY, OH, MN, CA, IL, IN, & SD residents,
add appropriate local sales tax)

FINAL TOTAL_____
(If paying in Canadian funds,
convert using the current
exchange rate, UNESCO
coupons welcome)

☐ **BILL ME LATER:** (Bill-me option is good on
US/Canada/Mexico orders only; not good to
jobbers, wholesalers, or subscription agencies.)
☐ Check here if billing address is different from
shipping address and attach purchase order and
billing address information.

Signature_____

☐ **PAYMENT ENCLOSED: $**_____

☐ **PLEASE CHARGE TO MY CREDIT CARD.**

☐ Visa ☐ MasterCard ☐ AmEx ☐ Discover
☐ Diner's Club ☐ Eurocard ☐ JCB

Account # _____

Exp. Date_____

Signature_____

Prices in US dollars and subject to change without notice.

NAME_____

INSTITUTION_____

ADDRESS_____

CITY_____

STATE/ZIP_____

COUNTRY_____ COUNTY (NY residents only)_____

TEL_____ FAX_____

E-MAIL_____

May we use your e-mail address for confirmations and other types of information? ☐ Yes ☐ No
We appreciate receiving your e-mail address and fax number. Haworth would like to e-mail or fax special
discount offers to you, as a preferred customer. **We will never share, rent, or exchange your e-mail address
or fax number.** We regard such actions as an invasion of your privacy.

Order From Your Local Bookstore or Directly From
The Haworth Press, Inc.
10 Alice Street, Binghamton, New York 13904-1580 • USA
TELEPHONE: 1-800-HAWORTH (1-800-429-6784) / Outside US/Canada: (607) 722-5857
FAX: 1-800-895-0582 / Outside US/Canada: (607) 771-0012
E-mailto: orders@haworthpress.com

For orders outside US and Canada, you may wish to order through your local
sales representative, distributor, or bookseller.
For information, see http://haworthpress.com/distributors

(Discounts are available for individual orders in US and Canada only, not booksellers/distributors.)
PLEASE PHOTOCOPY THIS FORM FOR YOUR PERSONAL USE.
http://www.HaworthPress.com   BOF04